THE JAZZ TEXT

THE JAZZ TEXT

Charles Nanry

with Edward Berger

VAN NOSTRAND REINHOLD COMPANY

NEW YORK   CINCINNATI   TORONTO   LONDON   MELBOURNE

This work is
dedicated to
Victoria Elizabeth and
Abigail Suzanne

Copyright © 1979 by Litton Educational Publishing, Inc.
Library of Congress Catalog Card Number 78-11822
ISBN 0-442-25904-2

Printed in the United States of America

Published in 1979 by Van Nostrand Reinhold Company
A division of Litton Educational Publishing, Inc.
135 West 50th Street, New York, NY 10020, U.S.A.

Van Nostrand Reinhold Limited
1410 Birchmount Road
Scarborough, Ontario M1P 2E7, Canada

Van Nostrand Reinhold Australia Pty. Ltd.
17 Queen Street
Mitcham, Victoria 3132, Australia

Van Nostrand Reinhold Company Limited
Molly Millars Lane
Wokingham, Berkshire, England

16 15 14 13 12 11 10 9 8 7 6 5 4 3 2 1

Library of Congress Cataloging in Publication Data

Nanry, Charles.
    The jazz text.

    Bibliography: p.
    1. Jazz music.   I. Title.
ML3561.J3N37   785.4'2'0973   78-11822
ISBN 0-442-25904-2

Acknowledgments

Acknowledgment is made to the following publishers and individuals for permission to reprint material:

Walter C. Allen. *Hendersonia: The Music of Fletcher Henderson and his Musicians. A Bio-Discography.* Published by Walter C. Allen, 1973.

Whitney Balliett. *The Sound of Surprise.* Copyright © 1959 by Whitney Balliett. Reprinted by permission of the publishers, E. P. Dutton.

Daniel Bell. *The End of Ideology.* Macmillan Publishing Co., Inc., 1961.

Rudi Blesh and Harriet Janis. *They All Played Ragtime.* Copyright © 1950, 1959, 1966, 1971 by Rudi Blesh and Estate of Harriet Janis. Reprinted by permission of Oak Publications, New York. All rights reserved.

Joseph Blum. "Problems of Salsa Research," in *Ethnomusicology, 1978.*

Margaret Just Butcher. *The Negro in American Culture.* Based on materials left by Alain Locke. Alfred A. Knopf, Inc., 1956.

Gilbert Chase. *America's Music.* Copyright © 1966. Used with permission of McGraw-Hill Book Company.

Stephen Couch. "Class, Politics, and Symphony Orchestras," in *Society,* 1976.

Emile Durkheim. *The Elementary Forms of Religious Life.* Macmillan Publishing Company, Inc., 1954.

Edward Kennedy Ellington. *Music is my Mistress.* Copyright © 1973 by Duke Ellington, Inc. Used by permission of Doubleday & Company, Inc.

Kai T. Erikson. *Wayward Puritans.* Published by John Wiley & Sons, 1966.

H. H. Gerth and C. Wright Mills. *From Max Weber. Essays in Sociology.* Published by Oxford University Press, 1946.

Charlie Gillett. *The Sound of the City.* Copyright © 1970 by Charlie Gillett. By permission of the publisher, E. P. Dutton.

Ira Gitler. *Jazz Masters of the Forties.* Reprinted with permission of Macmillan Publishing Co., Inc. Copyright © 1966 by Ira Gitler.

Richard Hadlock. *Jazz Masters of the Twenties.* Reprinted with permission of Macmillan Publishing Co., Inc. Copyright © 1965 by Richard Hadlock.

W. C. Handy. *Father of the Blues.* Reprinted with permission of Macmillan Publishing Co., Inc. Copyright 1941 by W. C. Handy, renewed 1969 by Irma L. Handy, W. C. Handy, Jr., Katherine Handy Lewis, and Wyer Owens Handy.

Thomas Hennessey. *From Jazz to Swing.* 1973.

Nat Hentoff. *Jazz Is.* Published by Random House, Inc., 1976.

Nat Hentoff. *The Jazz Life.* Published by Dial Press, 1961. Reprinted with permission of International Creative Management.

LeRoi Jones. *Blues People.* Published by William Morrow, 1963.

Ekkehard Jost. *Free Jazz.* Copyright © 1975 by Universal Edition A.G., Wein. Used by permission of European American Music Distributors Corp., sole representative for the U.S.A. and Canada.

Charles Keil. *Urban Blues.* Copyright © 1966. University of Chicago Press.

John Lovell, Jr. "The Social Implications of the Negro Spiritual," in *The Journal of Negro Education.* 1939.

Wilfred Mellers. *Music in a New Found Land: Themes and Developments in the History of American Music.* Copyright © 1967. Alfred A. Knopf, Inc.

Milton Mezzrow and Bernard Wolfe. *Really the Blues.* 1946.

Leroy Ostransky. *Understanding Jazz.* Copyright © 1977. Prentice-Hall, Inc., Engelwood Cliffs, New Jersey.

Henry Pleasants. *The Agony of Modern Music.* Simon and Schuster, Inc., 1955.

Fredrick Ramsey, Jr.,and Charles Edward Smith. *Jazzmen.* Harcourt Brace Jovanovich, Inc., 1939.

Hildred Roach. *Black American Music, Past and Present.* Crescendo/ Taplinger Publishing Co., Inc., 1973.

Ross Russell. *Bird Lives. The High Life and Hard Times of Charlie (Yardbird) Parker.* Copyright © 1973. Reprinted by permission of the publisher, David McKay Company, Inc.

Brian Rust. *Jazz Records A–Z, 1897–1942.* Storyville Publications and Company, 63 Orford Road, London, E17, 9NJ, 1970.

Carl Sandburg. *Chicago Poems.* Copyright 1916 by Holt, Rinehart and Winston, Inc.; copyright 1944 by Carl Sandburg. Reprinted by permission of Harcourt Brace Jovanovich, Inc.

William J. Schafer and Johannes Riedel. *The Art of Ragtime.* Louisiana University Press, 1973.

Gunther Schuller. *Early Jazz. Its Roots and Musical Development.* Oxford University Press, 1968.

George Simon. *The Big Bands.* Reprinted with permission of Macmillan Publishing Co., Inc. Copyright © 1967 by George Simon.

Willie Smith and George Hoefer. *Music on My Mind.* Copyright © 1964 by Willie Smith and George Hoefer. Used by permission of Doubleday & Co., Inc.

Marshall Stearns. *The Story of Jazz.* Oxford University Press, 1956.

Max Weber. *The Rational and Social Foundations of Music.* Translated by Martindale, Riedel and Neuwirth. Southern Illinois University Press, 1958.

Martin Williams, Editor. *Jazz Panorama.* Reprinted with permission of Macmillan Publishing Co., Inc. Copyright 1941 by W. C. Handy, renewed 1969 by Irma L. Handy, W. C. Handy, Jr., Katherine Handy Lewis, and Wyer Owens Handy.

Martin Williams. *Where's The Melody? A Listener's Introduction to Jazz.* Copyright 1967. Published by Pantheon Books, a division of Random House.

FOREWORD

This is a book that needed to be done, and Charles Nanry was the man to do the job. Though there has been an unprecedented proliferation of jazz books in recent times, no doubt in response to the equally unprecedented growth of jazz courses in our colleges and universities, few of these have addressed themselves to the needs of the beginning student of jazz, and none as cogently and directly as THE JAZZ TEXT.

Nanry combines the expository skills and know-how of the experienced teacher with a sincere and deeply rooted love and understanding for his subject. He is not an academic who has belatedly jumped on the jazz bandwagon, but a man with a lifelong, central interest in the music. While still a student, he was a founder of Jazz Interactions, one of the first and most durable jazz service organizations. He was the first curator of the Institute of Jazz Studies when it came to Rutgers University and, later on, with David Cayer, founded and co-edited *The Journal of Jazz Studies,* the first and only English-language scholarly periodical devoted to jazz.

Beyond that, and his previous extensive writings on jazz, Nanry has formed close and lasting relationships with many prominent jazz artists and remains a dedicated follower and listener. Thus, he comes to jazz not as an outsider, but with the special insights that enable him to shed light on his subject and bring it to life for the reader.

If I seem to dwell on this point, it is because jazz is, its proven capacity for survival against many handicaps notwithstanding, a tender and easily bruised subject. Theoretical knowledge is not enough, as those who have tried to fit jazz into preconceived intellectual molds have discovered. While it has become a bona fide academic field of study, true knowledge of it has to be gleaned outside the groves of academe, without benefit of grants and stipends, in a labor of love such as Nanry has performed.

In these pages, Nanry places the extraordinary American phenomenon called jazz in a social framework, illuminating the complex and often contradictory forces that helped to shape it and sometimes nearly pulled it out of shape. He is, happily, not afraid to explain. His aim is to instruct the novice, not to dazzle the expert. Furthermore, the student and teacher will find here the tools and guidelines for further study in clear and helpful form.

The story of the music called jazz is a unique and fascinating one, and Charles Nanry has done well by it. With the help of this book, the newcomer to the music will be well launched on the road to a lifetime of discovery and enjoyment of one of America's key contributions to world culture.

Dan Morgenstern
Director
Institute of Jazz Studies
Rutgers University

PREFACE

THE JAZZ TEXT is a general introduction to jazz. It is aimed at students of the music and its performers. It also encourages serious listening and study. I hope that those interested in jazz will find in it a sense of joy and a sense of seriousness in America's most important art form.

THE JAZZ TEXT is divided into three parts. The first, "An Introduction to Jazz," which includes Chapters 1 and 2, defines terms and presents some background on the origins and development of early jazz. The second, "The Emergence and Development of Jazz," includes Chapters 3 through 6 and covers the places and styles of jazz development. The third section, "Jazz Research," includes Chapters 7 and 8 and gives the reader a glimpse into jazz research techniques and possibilities.

A major weakness of many publications on jazz has been a preoccupation with the cult of jazz, that is, an emphasis on particular musicians. Since jazz is a performer's idiom, that emphasis is quite natural. But jazz, like other social phenomena, is also a product of its times. A total emphasis on individuals can lead to distortion.

In THE JAZZ TEXT individual performers are presented in the social context that influenced and shaped their art. Chapters 4, 5, and 6 include a special section called "The Personal Dimension," which presents carefully selected biographical and discographical references. The figures selected for the Personal Dimensions are intended to be representative of the periods or styles of jazz under study. They do not attempt to cover all or even most of the major figures of jazz. Using the research strategies suggested in Chapter 7 and THE JAZZ TEXT's bibliography, the inquiring student can pursue other figures and historical and musical issues in considerable detail.

A large number of people deserve special thanks in the long process of my general education and formal preparation of this book. Jazz musicians Benny Powell, Joe Newman, Jerome Richardson, Tony Scott, Chris White, Eubie Blake, and Dizzy Gillespie, among others, spent many hours over the years teaching me about the jazz culture. The late Willie "The Lion" Smith and I became very close near the end of his life, and I am very proud that he called me one of his cubs. His influence is critical. Al Pepper, Stan Snadowsky, Bob Menges, and Ray Ross remain close friends, and our activities in the early days of Jazz Interactions gave me insights into jazz that have proved to be invaluable. Rudi Blesh, Nat Hentoff, Fred Ramsey, the late Walter C. Allen, and the late George Hoefer were always generous with their time and knowledge.

Irving Louis Horowitz has been a major influence in my intellectual development and an endless source of insight into jazz. Harry C. Bredemeier, Richard Stephenson, Earl Rubington, Bernard Goldstein, Matilda White Riley, Morroe Berger, and Howard S. Becker each made important indirect contributions to this work through their special encouragement to me as a student and colleague. Phil Hughes, with his encyclopedic knowledge of jazz and of sociology, and I have spent endless hours listening to jazz and talking about it. David Cayer, my co-editor for *The Journal of Jazz Studies,* William Weinberg, Floyd Sumner, William Walling, George Gonos, and Vincent Pelote offered valuable comments and criticisms of early drafts of THE JAZZ TEXT.

A very special note of appreciation is due Dean Nathaniel Pallone, of University College, Rutgers, for his support during the writing of the manuscript and for generously granting me released time. Associate Deans Jacqueline Lewis and James Coe offered help and encouragement as well. The members of the Sociology Department at University College and students in my jazz-related seminars at both the undergraduate and graduate levels made many valuable contributions.

Dan Morgenstern, Director of the Rutgers Institute of Jazz Studies, read and commented in great detail on THE JAZZ TEXT manuscript. Many of the strengths of this book are a direct result of his worthwhile remarks. Edward Berger, Curator of the Institute of Jazz Studies, worked very closely with me and drafted sections of THE JAZZ TEXT. His assistance and contribution to this work are inestimable. Mary Ann Szymanski typed, edited, and made suggestions on endless early versions of THE JAZZ TEXT. She also prepared the bibliography and index with great efficiency and intelligence.

I would like to thank Professor George Eason of West Texas State University and Professor Ron Caviani of Northern Michigan University for their helpful suggestions throughout the development of the manuscript.

D. Van Nostrand Company may very well be the ideal publishing house. Judith Joseph, who helped conceive the project, kept the faith in those dark hours that every author faces. My gratitude to her is without bounds. Harriet Serenkin is a superb editor who quietly solved every sort of difficulty. She and Ethel Cunningham are truly "author's editors." The whole D. Van Nostrand team, in short, has been an author's dream to work with.

My parents, Ambrose and Frances Nanry, loved the big bands, loved to dance, and instilled in me an early love of good music. My beloved wife, Jacqueline, has encouraged, supported, and critically evaluated my efforts. My children, Vicki and Abby, are a constant source of inspiration through their dedication to improvisation on the theme of life.

CONTENTS

THE
JAZZ
TEXT

PART 1
An Introduction

to Jazz

The Bettmann Archive, Inc.

chapter 1

Head Arrangement

In the great slurry of sound that pours from the mass media, only a small proportion is real jazz. Yet, much modern music—from some of Stravinsky's music to many of the TV commercials we see—is jazz influenced. Jazz influence, however, is rarely properly assessed. Among jazz players and listeners, great controversy swirls around the sorting out of real jazz, jazz influence, near-jazz, and nonjazz. Questions of taste (aesthetics) and historical development are commingled with social issues, especially race, in any serious discussion of the music.

Until very recently, jazz has been a marginal art form. Jazz is marginal in the special sociological sense that it has always been on the cusp where serious and popular music intersect. The marginality of jazz is also rooted in the Afro-American origins of the music. Moreover, the marginality of jazz stemming from racial issues generates a paradox. David Cayer describes it: "So it is a central paradox of jazz that an enslaved and debased minority produced a major art form and powerfully shaped the majority's culture" (Cayer, 1974, p. 39). Jazz—the considerable contributions of whites to the art notwithstanding—is primarily the creation of black Americans, and this fact must be dealt with plainly and directly.

Jazz is a performer's music. The centrality of improvisation to the art of jazz makes the actual musical performance the key to understanding it. With considerable emphasis on formal composition, a major tendency in Western music has been to force it to translate an aural phenomenon into a visual one. The written score—the sheet music—takes on the characteristics of other written work and is often judged accordingly. The vocabulary of serious music criticism is typically the same vocabulary as that of literary criticism. While formal written composition has an important place in jazz and while its written legacy stands up well when it is addressed in literary terms, the essence of jazz remains aural. The real history of this Afro-American musical genre called jazz is contained in phonographic recordings of jazz and not in books about jazz.

Writing a book about jazz immediately puts the author into a double bind. One is not only writing about an aural phenomenon, but one is also

4

writing about an aural phenomenon that has resisted the transformation to formal composition. A chronic complaint by jazz musicians and jazz scholars alike, for example, has been the difficulty of using written notation to capture jazz performance. This complaint reaches the very heart of the matter: written-down jazz follows rather than precedes the essential act of jazz.

The major implication of the preceding paragraphs is clear. You must *listen* to jazz in order to understand it. Throughout this book there will be many references to recorded jazz. Take them seriously and listen to the music. I have restricted references to easily available jazz recordings on the assumption that nothing is more frustrating to the initiate than hard-to-find sources. I have also tried to write a book that reflects my own interests and my professional training as a sociologist. Words are the medium for someone writing a book, and so lots of words follow. At the outset, our contract must include, however, the agreement to listen to jazz. Without that agreement, the words simply turn about each other in a grotesque caricature of the essence of the music itself.

As a starting point, I would invite you to listen to any jazz performance—recorded or live. Certain key musical elements are likely to be present: **(1)** polyrhythm, **(2)** syncopation, **(3)** swing, **(4)** improvisation, **(5)** the use of "blue" notes, and **(6)** the employment of a theme-and-variation form. Some excellent jazz may not include one or more of these elements; much nonjazz may have one or more of these elements present. I would argue that these elements, however, give us a "model" of jazz and that adding or subtracting other musical elements represents modification of this typical jazz model. Later in this chapter I shall discuss the issue of the elements of jazz more fully and define the jazz model in some detail.

Melody, Rhythm, and Harmony

If someone asked you to describe Beethoven's Fifth Symphony in less than a minute, it is a safe bet that you would hum the opening motive, "bum-bum-bum-baaa,"

rather than indicating overall harmonic or rhythmic structures. Melody is the means by which most people identify music. And in most formal, traditional music, the notes are set down by the composer and followed by performers. Jazz alters melody without destroying melodic appeal, which is critically important in capturing the attention of most listeners. New melodies (or tunes) are created on the spot as a jazz performance unfolds. Jazz musicians also alter rhythm and harmony.* In another work, Irving Louis Horowitz and I have argued, however, that melody provides a bridge for most Americans to "get to" jazz (Horowitz and Nanry, 1975). In *Where's the Melody?* Martin Williams makes a similar point.

> Thus a great deal of jazz variation is recognizably made on a fa-
> miliar melody, and there are players from all styles and schools who
> use this approach. They may elaborate the melody, they may deco-
> rate it, or they may reduce it and simplify it (basically, these are what
> a classicist would call kinds of "melodic variation"), and they may
> re-harmonize it. But it is always there somewhere. The art lies in
> how well they transmute it, in how good a paraphrase they come up
> with while transforming what is written (p. 7).

For most of us, then, melodic invention is the easiest place to begin our understanding of jazz because we are culturally conditioned to listen for melody. For the serious student, however, the melodic beachhead must be broadened to include other relevant factors. Jazz is Afro-American, Euro-American, and American. In order to comprehend where jazz came from, we must understand something about the fusion of all these sources. In order to understand what jazz is, we must know something about the characteristics of jazz rhythm, harmony, and melody.† Williams has put it rather well:

> Thus there are three kinds of variations—those that involve
> rhythm, which are intrinsic in jazz performances, as we have seen;
> those that involve embellishing or paraphrasing a written melody, ei-
> ther decorating it or subtracting from it or both; and those that in-
> volve the invention of new melodies within a harmonic outline. They
> are all found, alone or more often in combination, in all styles and
> schools of jazz except the most recent (Williams, 1967, p. 9).

* Most jazz scholars would agree that the rhythmic origins of jazz are African and its harmonic origins European. The question of origins is important, but the issue here is really about audience acceptance.

† Most music scholars agree that these three characteristics, rhythm, harmony, and melody, are the key building blocks of music. Defining them beyond an intuitive common sense level is too complicated and even unnecessary here. Musicologists are, of course, not unanimous in emphasizing only these three characteristics; some add dynamics to the list (Lomax, 1970). It should be clear that the choice of these three characteristics is not meant to indicate that they define the parameters of musicology.

Rhythm, harmony, and melody can be analytically separated. We can also separate the lives of jazz musicians from the formal development of the music. Yet there is what social scientists call an interaction effect. Although we shall discuss various elements separately throughout this book, the interaction effect must be understood. Jazz is synthetic insofar as the perception of what jazz is, the lives of those producing it, and the perceptions of those enjoying it all merge in the jazz experience.

What jazz is and where it comes from are two major questions that must be interwoven in any attempt to understand it. Sometimes one question or the other will be stressed. It should be clear that I consider both to be important, but since I am a social scientist, those issues that revolve around the social history of jazz will be emphasized more than those demanding musical analysis. (For those interested in pursuing the purely musical side, references in the bibliography will aid the reader.) I will provide, however, some discussion of the music as music to give the reader a sense of what I think is important to listen for in jazz. One way to enjoy jazz is simply to "dig" it, to let it just soak in. It is more satisfying, however, to react to a broader range of elements in this complex musical genre. For the serious student of jazz, a cognitive approach is absolutely necessary and, in fact, will enhance the emotional reaction. Earlier I mentioned several key elements common to most jazz: polyrhythm, syncopation, swing, improvisation, the use of blue notes, and the use of a theme-and-variation form. These are structural characteristics. They are, if you will, the syntax of the jazz language. Jazz as language, that is, as a symbol system, shares certain characteristics with language as conventionally understood.

JAZZ AS LANGUAGE

All of us recall the difficulties involved in learning correct English. Rules of grammar, punctuation, and spelling had to be learned. Much of this process, of course, involved mere codification. The hardest part of learning the language came when we were infants. Somehow we picked it up, and by the time we went to school, we could express ourselves pretty effectively. Just how we pick up language is, interestingly enough, still a subject of great debate and controversy among scientists interested in linguistics. On one side are those who argue that it is primarily a process of conditioning (Skinner, 1957); on the other, some argue that we are born with an innate capacity for language—"deep linguistic structures" (Chomsky, 1968).

How we develop an ear for music in general and jazz in particular evokes a similar debate. There are those who come very close to arguing that jazz is an expression of blacks whose inner meaning can never be penetrated by white folks (Jones, 1963). Others approach jazz as a discipline to be learned much as any other (Tanner and Gerow, 1973). While my position is closer to the latter than to the former, it is necessary to have a feeling for music in general and a feeling for American popular music in particular to understand jazz.

Albert Einstein is reputed to have said that he spent a major portion of his adult life unlearning what he had been taught. The serious student of jazz must spend some time listening for things deemed less important in other music.

The musical language we have grown up with in modern industrial society is polyglot, that is, composed of many diverse elements. In America that which is "proper" is usually taught, however, by those trained in the Western (European) classical tradition. Ever since we started school, we have been asked to go back to Greece, Rome, and the British Isles to find our intellectual and cultural roots. To understand jazz (and its stepchild rock music), we must also go back to West Africa. In the European tradition, musical elements such as harmony and melody are emphasized, sometimes at the expense of rhythm. West African music, on the other hand, tends to emphasize rhythm (Herskovits, 1941). What would happen if, somehow or other, both these musical languages came together? Jazz provides an exciting answer.

The story of jazz is the story of black American slaves (and, later, blacks "freed" into a racist society) maintaining some elements of their ancestral musical language in the face of a white European cultural hegemony.

Jazz has its roots in the expression of an oppressed people. It began in the field chants of black slaves so constricted by their cruel environment that only a primal cry could be their emotional outlet. Slaves from many distinctive African cultures, often speaking in tongues foreign to each other as well as to their oppressors, were forced to reach deep within themselves in order to find common modes of association, shaped always by the repressive social structure which channeled, restricted and directed the breadth if not the depth of their expression.

Those field chants, coupled later with work songs, spirituals and the blues, created an amalgam within the American black social world that interacted with forms already present in the larger society. Jazz was born. This lusty offspring of cross-cultural fertilization, this slave child of the arts, was to achieve heights rarely paralleled in the history of music. Born in America at the turn of the century, in something less than the biblical four score and ten years, jazz has grown to maturity. It has produced offspring, most notably rock. One can hardly understand musical America without knowing its biography (Nanry, 1972, p. 5).

The most profound and primary lesson taught to us by social science is that of cultural relativity. Unlike the genetic consequences of biological inheritance, cultural products such as language are accessible to "outsiders" through learning. Nothing is detracted from the pride that black people can and should feel about their origins and contributions to jazz when we recognize that nonblack listeners and musicians participate and have participated in the jazz experience. The jazz story is not simply the story of the survival of an alien musical language in a hostile environment. It is the story of a fantastic combination. A new music, happily experimental, developed a robust new cultural product unfettered by the deadening conventions of tribal (or folk) tradition or the bureaucratic rationalizations of industrial society.

Jazz can be learned as a second musical language by those outside the jazz milieu; its worldwide acceptance is ample evidence for that. But anyone who has attempted to learn a second language knows the problems in such an endeavor. For example, nonnative speakers usually have a difficult time with accent and with nuance. Even among those who share a common language, different idioms arise. Winston Churchill's classic remark that the British and American peoples are separated by a common language illustrates this notion. Students of language speak of language and language groups and the incredible differentiations that may occur within and between them. Some languages have common origins—for example, the Indo-European—and therefore have cognates. Knowing Spanish will help in learning Italian, but not in learning Chinese.

Fortunately, jazz as a musical language shares some cognate characteristics with both African and European music. Unlike language, where few, if any, cognates exist between English and African tribal languages, certain factors in the music of the two cultures (for instance, melody and some aspects of harmony), provide a bridge between the two. The fusion between European and African music in American jazz did not occur easily and without resistance (Leonard, 1962). Nor did the fusion occur randomly in the American population. Rather, it grew out of the folk music of black America and especially among those blacks who, for one reason or another, had retained an African connection while absorbing something of the European musical ambience.*

---

*I shall discuss this African connection later. The important point here is that slaves continued to be imported into the United States in large numbers until the Civil War. When jazz first emerged, many blacks were only one generation away from Africa.

Dictionaries, grammar books, and anthologies of famous writers are among the devices used as exemplars in language courses for those learning written language. In the Western tradition, musical scores serve the same function for those who would learn music. But formal written composition in jazz has always been subordinate to improvised performance. The folk roots of jazz are evidence of this, even though jazz is an urban rather than a rural music. While its roots may be folk and rural, it developed in the sophisticated context of urban heterogeneity. Thus jazz presents an enigma because of another aspect of its marginality, that is, its mixture of contradictory rural-urban influences.

Jazz, based on an aural tradition, is thought of by some as more "primitive" than music based on formal written composition. As the social psychologist Georg Simmel long ago pointed out, city dwellers (and "moderns" in general) have learned to depend more and more on their eyes and less and less on their ears (Simmel, 1950, pp. 409—24). Even when jazz is formally composed and arranged, it often consists of "head arrangements," that is, partial ensemble structure through several written bars with much open space for soloists and for thematic elaboration. Jazz defies the stereotyped notion of folk art because of its complexity; yet it does not fit into the equally stereotyped notion of "high" art as formalistic. It defies the "astronomy" implied by the Western rational tradition and labeled by Marshall McLuhan as the "Gutenberg Galaxy" (McLuhan, 1964). However, under the pressure of modern heterogeneity—the mixing of peoples and cultural influences—even formal written language eventually breaks the bonds of conventional vocabulary and syntax, as the works of James Joyce and ee cummings in contemporary English literature have shown.

Dictionaries and epic poems contain archaic words. Grammar books still warn us that prepositions are bad things to end a sentence with. Idiomatic usage tends to reshape conventional language. When such usage becomes widespread, it leads to changes in the rules of grammar and the inclusion of new vocabulary in dictionaries. The pioneering work of Whorf and Sapir, symbolic interactionists (a branch of social psychology), has emphasized the idea that language structures thought (Stone and Farberman, 1970, p. 80). Language is an active rather than a passive element in the development of mind, self, and society. Thus linguistic constructions are "plans of action" for social actors.

Authenticity and Originality

A musical idiom such as jazz is made up of various plans of action for the organization of sound. Yet music as a plan of action is not idiosyncratic. It is collective in nature. Whether implied or explicit, there are agreed-upon rules that have arisen through interaction. Every jazz performance (live or recorded) represents an event shaped by the understanding of each participant involved in it. For listeners it represents their understanding of it. There must be enough common understanding, however, for the music to make sense to participants. Without that, it is just so much noise. Alternatively, if only a very few understand, jazz language runs the risk of becoming esoteric. The melodic bridge once again provides the key.

> Jazz tends to be more successful the closer it adheres to conventional and recognizable melodic lines. True, such melodies, whether derived from Tin Pan Alley or more orthodox musical sources, may provide only an introduction to rich innovation and embellishment, but the music must stay close to a strong melodic sense if a reasonable hope to capture an audience is to remain. . . . Hence, the jazz musician is in the odd position of either doing battle with the "corruption of tastes" (a more likely activity of ideologists in search of social change) or adopting the popular tastes and bending them to jazz inventions. For the most part, the latter course of action has been pursued (Horowitz and Nanry, 1975, p. 33).

Good jazz performance, therefore, is a high-risk enterprise where the performer tries to extend the musical form to the perimeter of tradition without breaking faith with those who are trying to comprehend the meaning of the very act of performance.

Jazz as a musical language and as an idiom has elements of both stability (convention) and change. Furthermore, the areas in which change is likely to occur are not random; they follow the internal logic of the musical form as that logic has been shaped by the historical factors impinging upon it. This is so because of the shared (collective) nature of the phenomenon. Without some convention, one jazz player would not be able to comprehend, or even recognize, the principles of organization of sound being employed by another. But convention goes even further than that: the performance of music usually implies that there is an audience which also comprehends the interactive and symbolic language employed by the performers. Jazz, indeed, represents a delicate balance between authenticity and originality, between convention and creation.

> The double-edged problem in any creative process is the interchange between originality and authenticity. It is an issue which strikes with particular force to the heart of jazz performers; since historically the most devastating criticism that can be leveled at them is

imitativeness, insincerity or inauthenticity. Of course the accolades of being original and authentic . . . mean a great deal as well.

. . . The important recurrent theme is that originality and authenticity are directly linked to past performances and performers. Jazz musicians and arrangers have the peculiar and unique task of appearing to be in the mainstream of jazz tradition with identifiable sounds, and yet distinctive enough and different enough not to be subject to the accusation of imitation or derivation (Horowitz, 1973, pp. 58—59).

JAZZ AS "SOCIAL FACT"

If you think of something as real (as a fact, as "there") and behave as though it is real, it might as well be, *for you* (Thomas, 1923, pp. 41—50). If others also believe that something is real, that something is a social fact. If others do not believe it is real, you are in danger of being labeled odd, crazy, or even dangerous. Jazz is a social fact. It involves a symbol system (just as language involves a symbol system) that is real to some people. Social facts have two major characteristics, according to Emile Durkheim: **(1)** no single individual possesses a social fact, although all members of a group embody the consciousness of the group as a group; **(2)** social facts limit the behavior of individuals because they need, or value, or are entrapped in a group (Durkheim, 1950, p. 2). Since the time of Durkheim, sociologists have considered social facts to be those things that are the possession of some group. They may be outside the existence of any single individual, but are part of *every* individual who is included in the group. (No one *is* the English language, but many share and shape the English language.) Social facts have what philosophers would call "quiddity" or "thingness," although they may not have physical reality. They have only the manifestation of reality in the physical world, since they cause patterns of behavior.

Jazz as a social fact poses a problem for jazz players and listeners. Certain established conventions may be broken, but they must be understood if breaking them is to make any sense. Breaking a rule that no one recognizes as a rule is simply crazy, inchoate behavior, not protest—and certainly not social protest. One of the rules of jazz is that the jazz player must improvise. Thus a dynamic tension is created when one of the rules involves rule breaking. As I have already hinted, however, there are "metarules" in jazz for the conditions under which some of the rules are broken.*

* In an interesting way, jazz becomes a metaphor for science in modern industrial society. One of the rules (or norms) of science is innovation. Yet the innovative

Thinking about jazz as language or as a social fact raises some questions that allow a return to the issues broached earlier in this chapter about the characteristics of jazz. What are the usual rules that guide jazz performances? How did jazz come to be a social fact for those who play it and listen to it? What rules of Western classical and popular music does jazz usually break? How do innovations (originality) in jazz become conventions (authentic)? For example, when something new is attempted, what determines whether it establishes a new style or school or simply becomes an experiment that fails? The answer involves an interaction effect involving *who* plays *what for whom* in what *context*.

Let us start with a series of tentative definitions, simply put, of some of the key musical elements in a typical jazz performance. If we keep these characteristics in mind, it will become possible to extend the discussion to nonmusical (historical and sociological) considerations and to modify and refine our key-elements list in the light of the newly unfolded knowledge.

JAZZ AS MUSIC

Jazz is, among other things, polyrhythmic improvised music that swings, is syncopated, employs blue notes, and often uses the theme-and-variation format. I shall now tentatively define each of these terms. This will provide a tentative vocabulary within which we can continue our discussion.

Polyrhythm

Rhythm refers to the sense of time or propulsion in any piece of music. Clap your hands. Look at the second hand on your watch, wait three seconds, and then clap your hands again. Repeat a few times. Now take your watch off and place it in front of you. Clap your hands every time a second ticks off. Tap your foot as you clap your hands. Now try clapping your hands every one and one-half seconds while you tap your foot every second. You have set up two rhythms* that are synchronized and have a regular relationship. As long as you are tied to the regular ticking of your watch, all the rhythmic variations that you might try will be tied to one-second intervals. Suppose, however, that you have a watch

scientist runs into the difficult problem of having his or her work accepted if it is outside the bounds of conventional institutionalized science (Kuhn, 1970).

*Technically, regular pulses are usually called meter. In popular music and jazz, the term "rhythm" is broadly defined as everything pertaining to the duration of music. The jazz usage is followed here.

whose second hand can be slowed down or speeded up. Musicians have such an instrument; it's called a metronome. By adjusting it, one can establish a fast or slow (but steady) tempo.

Let us now suppose that you have or have developed a strong metronome sense—an automatic feeling for what the pulse ought to be in some musical piece. Let us further suppose that you are in the company of others who also have the same sense. A lot of possibilities open up. You can clap slightly ahead of the beat (on top of the beat) or slightly behind it. You know that this will not confuse your fellow musicians or that they will think you are just mixed up. You all know just where the beat is supposed to be. Retarding or rushing the beat is a technique that adds excitement to the rather boring and mechanical work of the metronome. You can also liven things up by thinking of a rhythmic structure based on a different but complementary setting of the metronome. Instead of dividing the equal beats into fast sets of four, for example, you might divide them into slow sets of three. Then, you might put these two actions together. The whole process demands a development of the dexterity children use in learning to pat their heads with one hand while rubbing their other hand in a circle on their stomachs.

A kind of game develops whereby you and your musician colleagues can figure out ways to play different rhythms so that you come together on the same beat in predetermined places or even by accident. What you have done is to add an interesting vertical dimension while the forward or horizontal function of rhythm is being carried out.

Polyrhythm is the technique of combining various competing rhythmic structures in the same musical frame. It is the superimposition of various metronome speeds and tempos upon one another. In jazz the origins of this polyrhythmic propulsion is clearly African. Rhythm, for Africans, is such a central element in their musical culture that understanding polyrhythm in the kind of linear Western way I have just described is not necessary for them (Kofsky, 1977). Every piece of music has built into it a rich sense of varied pulse that is explored by the native West African musician.

Early jazz recordings reveal that this polyrhythmic sense evolved rather slowly in the United States. It is there, but most early jazz sticks fairly closely to a four-beats-to-the-measure format. The drummers and bass, tuba, or banjo players often contented themselves with providing a metronome reference while other instrumentalists and singers "fooled around" with the rhythmic structure, constantly orienting themselves to the clearly stated central rhythm. Toward the end of the big band era (most of these bands were primarily dance bands, and dancers looked for a steady beat above all) in the early 1940s, the potential for more polyrhythmic exploration became a reality in the smaller combos of the bop period.

Syncopation

A key characteristic of Western "classical" music through the end of the nineteenth century was its use of regular meters. It is astonishing to realize how little attention was devoted in classical music to subtle and complex rhythmic variation. Black folk music, however, was in some ways immune to this neglect. As performers of music based on folk origins, many black pianists and instrumentalists used altered meters to great advantage.

During the "Gay Nineties," many American homes had pianos in their parlors. Sheet music, much of it "hacked out" by Tin Pan Alley tunesmiths, sold well. In the mid-nineties a new form of piano music— ragtime—burst on the popular music scene. Based on the experimental use of rhythmic variation found among black piano players, the heart of ragtime was (and is) its use of syncopation. No better definition of both syncopation and ragtime exists than that given by Blesh and Janis in their book *They All Played Ragtime.*

> Ragtime is mainly distinguished from most other music by its use of the rhythm loosely called syncopation. The really unique thing about ragtime when it appeared was the way the pianist opposed syncopations (or accents on the weak and normally unaccented second and third beats of the measure) in his right hand against a precise and regularly accented bass. Syncopation in its simple form—that is, uncombined with regular rhythm—is a familiar device used a few measures at a time with fair frequency in European music. It is disturbing in a context of regular meter; its upsetting of the normal pace led to the Italian term for syncopation, *alla zoppa,* meaning lame or limping. Continued syncopation, however, far from limping, builds up greater and greater momentum, hence the old English term for syncopated notes: "driving notes." Continued syncopation is deeply stimulating and exciting, and European masters seem always to have been wary of it. So the thorough use of these delayed and misplaced accents (misplaced, that is, in the sense of our regular meters) and their employment with regular meters to set up complex multiple rhythms, or polyrhythms, were never seriously explored in our music. The use of this driving, exciting propulsiveness in the most complexly developed ways is, on the other hand, a commonplace in the Negro music of Africa and the

Americas. Retained for over three centuries in this country, it is used by the Afro-American to transform all of our music (p. 7).

Syncopation is important to jazz because it helps to explain at least one powerful source of polyrhythm in American popular music. Although much of the so-called ragtime music that poured out of Tin Pan Alley was very mechanical in its employment of syncopation and although some so-called ragtime was not even syncopated (for example, "Alexander's Ragtime Band" is not a true rag at all, although it is syncopated), the way was prepared for broader use of unexpected accents in popular music. In general, the usual ragtime accent on notes two and three has been transformed into the expectation of off-beat accents in contemporary jazz. It is usual, in other words, for jazz pieces to be counted one-TWO-three-FOUR rather than ONE-two-THREE-four. "Remember to pop your fingers on two and four" is a common farewell among jazz devotees. Accenting or extending the value of a normally weak beat is a common device used to stimulate polyrhythm in all jazz playing.

Swing

The term "swing" in jazz has two (at least) very different meanings. Swing is sometimes used to refer to a particular era in jazz that roughly coincided with the decade of the 1930s. It was that period in American music when big name bands and their vocalists were most popular (Simon, 1974). The second meaning of swing is a bit more elusive. It refers to that easy quality of rhythmic propulsion that flows from both relaxation and coordination of tempi within a jazz group. Perhaps the easiest way to think of it is to think once again about metronome sense. Swing was a felt quality of the best of the big name bands.

If more than one person is playing music, there has to be a "common sense" among the various players about how to keep together. In the Western tradition, this common sense is often provided by a written score with a straightforward and simple rhythmic structure. The introduction of a sense of syncopation and polyrhythm complicates interpretation. It is as though a monorhythmic implied understructure that everyone understands and may even depart from is present. Each accent of the music provides a fulcrum point around which each player is free to pivot as long as the point itself is kept somewhere either in the conscious or unconscious mind. Usually the tempo (the pace of the music) will remain steady during this process. The tempo may shift, and, if the players are in touch with one another, the shift will be smooth. Afterward, everyone will still feel the point of the fulcrum even though it may have been shifted ahead or behind.

Both syncopation and swing are aspects of polyrhythm commonly used in jazz. There are others. Some advanced modern groups depart from any sense of monorhythm. Some critics then argue that they have also departed from jazz. That discussion, however, must await further elaboration. The point here is that you now have some idea of what usually happens in jazz playing.

Improvisation

Improvisation in music means pretty much the same thing it means in other areas of life. It is a synonym for spontaneous creativity, for solving a problem that has not been solved before when working with existing materials. In jazz playing, improvisation usually refers to melodic invention that is created out of conventional melody. Improvising new melodies on old ones has been a part of the Western musical heritage since the time of the early Greeks. The great European baroque and classical composers were all improvisers, including Bach, Mozart, and Beethoven. In fact, improvisation of rhythmic, harmonic, or melodic elements is a part of all except the most stilted formal music. What makes jazz different is the *institutionalization* of creating new melodies on the spot. Every time a jazz player plays a solo, he or she is expected to develop a new melody that refers to some standard melody (tune), keeping within the bounds of the harmonic structure of the standard.*

The difference between a good musician and a good jazz musician is the ability to improvise. It is a dizzying feat. A great deal of technical information must be kept in mind. If we think of a melody as a series of notes having some established relationship on a horizontal plane, improvisation involves thinking about the vertical dimension of each note as well, understanding that each note has some known relationship to an infinite series of other single notes. Some of these notes when played together are pleasing to the ear; others are not. The jazz player is enjoined to select some pleasing note or notes other than the one expected from a knowledge of the horizontal melody. (Once in a while, the expected note may be played, just to surprise.) The problem is to select the next note that has a relationship to the note just played as well as a relationship to the original melody. Carried on for a while, this process involves a geometric progression of things to be kept track of: the original melody, the new melody, and the various harmonic and rhythmic relationships between the two.

---

*Harmonic improvisation also occurs in jazz. Its consideration will come up later.

Harmony in this context means the mixture of pitches heard at some given moment in time. These are called chords. There is a mathematical quality to all of this. A thick string, stretched to proper tautness, will vibrate, say, thirty-two times per second when plucked. This note is called, in the Western system of notation (invented by the Greek philosopher Pythagoras), low C. Doubled at sixty-four vibrations per second, the pitch becomes C an octave higher. Divided by thirds each pitch produces G a fifth higher; in sixths, E a sixth higher than that, another G, B-flat, C, D, E, F-sharp, and so on. Every note implies other notes in harmony with it, that is, notes that have a complementary rate of vibration. Overtones are those notes in a harmonic series produced by the sounding and fading of a particular note, especially by a woodwind instrument. After bop (in the 1940s), sophisticated strategies of playing progressions based on complementary chords developed (even to the point of playfully limiting invention to unconventional intervals such as the ninth and even the thirteenth). Keeping in mind that certain "irrational" dissonances tend to occur where flats and sharps appear, it becomes clear that to be truly inventive in jazz means to have an extraordinary musical sense of what tones fit with what other tones.

In addition to individual improvisation, the demands of collective improvisation, coupled with the complexities of rhythmic structure, gives some indication of the level of understanding needed to play the music well.

Blue Notes

Blue notes, or blue tonality, refers to the penchant of most jazz players to play certain notes "flat." Since the earliest attempts at jazz scholarship, most analysts have noted that the tendency to "fool around" with pitch (the sounding of a note or notes) has not been random. Jazz players have tended to slide into and out of the central pitch of certain notes common to Western music since the establishment of the well-tempered scale. There are several competing hypotheses about why this has been the case.

On one extreme are those musicological theories that blame the problem on the "irrationality" or tonal perversity of certain areas of any scale. Max Weber suggests such a solution in his discussion of the "problem of thirds" in *The Rational and Social Foundations of Music* (1958b). Another explanation, more widely accepted in jazz circles, is the possible ambiguity created by the imposition of the pentatonic (five-note) scale, common in West African music, over the Western diatonic (seven-note) scale. In this case, two areas around the third and seventh notes of the

Western diatonic scale are problematic: the notes "left out" of the West African five-note scale. In the key of C, players remembering the pentatonic scale would slide somewhere between E-flat and E at the third interval and somewhere between B-flat and B at the seventh (Tanner and Gerow, 1973, pp. 30–31).

Later, especially in bop, fifths also tended to be flatted. In fact, most notes have been susceptible to "bending" in the jazz tradition. Whether this can be attributed to some elegant musical theory about the imposition of one scale over another, to irrationalities in music in general, or to the tendency in jazz for instrumentalists to attempt to imitate the human voice (with its nearly limitless potential for variability) is not important. What matters is that the listener realizes that "wrong" notes are not a mistake in jazz unless they fail to fit in with the jazz conception, that is, unless they add nothing to the excitement and fulfillment of the musical idea itself. Wrong notes do occur in jazz if the player loses the sense of structure.

Theme and Variation

A theme is a musical phrase or motif, usually established at the beginning of a composition. Variations consist of disassembling this motif into successive parts that have a relation to the motif but do not repeat it exactly. The variation may be rhythmic, harmonic, or melodic. In jazz the most common theme-and-variation structure involves the statement of a theme (a tune) well known to the audience, followed by variations on the melody that lead to the creation of whole new melodic structures. The new melodic statements may then lead to further variations ad infinitum.

From the beginning, jazz has emphasized personal expression by the individual jazz artist. To take a theme and creatively alter it has always been the essence of the jazz art. Many jazz melodies are based on the melodic structure of a few tunes. For example, Gershwin's "I've Got Rhythm" has led to countless jazz tunes (Patrick, 1975). For the listener, the key is to understand the tune being played. It helps if the original point of reference is known, but that is not necessary to enjoy the spontaneous creation of a new melody (Williams, 1967b). What is critical is the realization that what is being heard is not some random jumble of sound but rather the careful construction of music. This construction is based on an understanding shared by the musicians (if not the audience) of the common point of reference for the creative effort. The development of a consensus of what is and what is not jazz begins with the internal and external dynamics of jazz history.

JAZZ AS SOCIAL HISTORY

The social history of jazz involves two interrelated, yet analytically separable, phenomena. One is the external dynamic of the form, in which the development of jazz has been shaped and even contained by the larger world of entertainment. (The tendency toward discrimination in studio hiring practices is an example of containment.) In this sense, jazz is a music shaped and molded by the mass media, in particular the worlds of radio broadcasting and the phonograph recording studio. Most Americans first hear something called jazz on a record or over the radio. While it is true that what they hear is probably not "pure" jazz, it is a modified version of the real thing. Since the production of records and radio broadcasting is motivated by the desire for profit, the most widely disseminated jazz is closer to "easy listening" and to rock than to modern chamber music. This pattern of cultural diffusion is not an unusual one in mass societies; any form that seeks a wide audience must have recognizable elements in order to be accepted (Leonard, 1962; Kamin, 1975). This process sets up a tension between the best jazz and the most easily understood elements of jazz.

Jazz also has an internal dynamic. Jazz musicians, like everyone else, have to make a living. While they are doing that, however, they are expected to extend and re-create the form itself. But there is risk involved in attempting to create art in a popular context, the risk of losing one's audience if the music goes beyond what the audience understands. This sets up a tension between the acts of performance and the act of creation. This tension is nowhere more evident than in jazz, because it is a music where creation (formally, musical composition) usually occurs during performance. One of the key elements of jazz—improvisation—demands that new melodic, harmonic, and rhythmic patterns emerge in the context of performance. But limits have to be imposed both by audiences and by performers. Performing jazz is not a random process. The narrow line between authenticity and creativity must be perceived and manipulated by the good jazz player.

I do not wish to suggest that there is a rigid dichotomy between the internal and external factors affecting jazz. Rather, there are large-scale, global factors constraining the development of jazz as well as small-scale, internal constraints on the music and the musicians who play it. The jazz community is only one community existing side-by-side with other cultural communities in the social world of the arts. The external history of jazz starts with the broadest popular conception of how jazz came to be. This conception is then susceptible to refinement in the same way as other historical and sociohistorical phenomena. The internal dynamic of jazz implies, alternatively, an understanding of the people and of the social organization of the jazz community.

THE POPULAR CONCEPTION OF JAZZ HISTORY: THE EXTERNAL DYNAMIC

Jazz entered America's consciousness sometime after the turn of the century. In the teens and early twenties, it gradually spread throughout America and even Europe. New Orleans, the most cosmopolitan nineteenth-century American city, was the first jazz capital. But if jazz was born in New Orleans, it grew up in Chicago. The popular and over-simplified historical conception is that jazz "went up the Mississippi" from New Orleans to St. Louis, Kansas City and, most important, to Chicago. In Chicago black jazz met white jazz, and a new fusion, which laid the foundation for the swing era of the thirties took place.

In Chicago the big white dance bands began to adopt "hot" jazzisms in their playing. This musical integration, however, went no further; musicians remained formally segregated. Because the bands that achieved widespread popularity were white, much of white America accepted jazz as a white phenomenon. Most black jazzmen played for black audiences, a few "hip" white musicians, and even fewer white people who were not musicians. This was the era of "race record" labels.* Formal segregation existed in almost every aspect of the music industry. Many well-known black bands did play for white audiences. They were excluded, for the most part, from the mass media and therefore did not reap the benefits of the wider exposure often given to inferior white groups.

Because of opportunities in radio and in the music-recording and publishing industry, jazz musicians migrated to New York City in the 1920s and 1930s, where a big band jazz tradition had been flourishing for some time. The swing era was born, and the big white bands became immensely popular. Jazz (as popularly conceived) had become a national craze in the twenties; it also became, under the name of swing, *the* popular music of the thirties. Paul Whiteman became the most popular of the commercial dance band leaders in the twenties, and Benny Goodman (a Chicagoan) was crowned the "King of Swing" in the mid-thirties.

Whiteman and Goodman were white. Many younger black musicians became frustrated and bitter about what had happened to their

---

*Later, we shall discuss race records at some length. They were specialized records produced for black buyers and featured material, especially blues recordings, that would have shocked many whites.

music and in the early forties began to do something about it. The bop revolution of the early forties was a conscious attempt on the part of many black musicians to develop a music that would be too difficult for whites to copy. The center of the revolt was in New York City's Harlem. After-hours clubs in Harlem became the headquarters for the revolution. The new music was difficult and complex, and, because of its complexity, it did not become a popular music in the same sense that Dixieland and swing music had become popular. The revolution, however, was only partially successful. White players did, in fact, learn the new music, and jazz became an art music—music for listening and appreciating rather than for dancing. In the process of developing a new style, the bop innovators lost a large proportion of the black audience, which preferred simpler, more folk-oriented rhythm and blues.

In the fifties jazz developed other styles of its own—cool jazz, third stream (a fusion of jazz and European classical forms), and others. A new popular music, rock and roll, developed. Rock evolved out of rock and roll in the sixties as a more sophisticated musical genre. The sixties were a period of transition with a jazz avant garde music or "New Thing" music developing as a reaction against the excessively chordal structure of bop. A great deal of musical interaction between the best rock musicians and the best jazz musicians led to a new form, jazz-rock. These groups tend to combine a strong, even overpowering, beat with a jazz sense of improvised solo work.

So far, the 1970s have seen a period of retrenchment for jazz. There is much interest in older forms of jazz, especially among students. A substantial number of jazz musicians and scholars have established courses and programs in jazz at major colleges (Scott, 1973). Jazz has gained considerable recognition as America's classical music. Discrimination against the use of jazz-oriented musicians (especially black musicians) in radio, recording, and television has declined sharply. Nonetheless, because of its complexity and multiplicity of forms, jazz will probably never become America's popular music. Jazz hits will emerge from time to time, and the jazz influence will continue to be felt in most broadly popular music. But it is too early to tell what will happen in the 1980s.

Jazz and the Media

The basis for the interpretation of popular jazz history as outlined above is its diffusion through the mass media. The word "jazz" came to the attention of America with the release of a record by The Original Dixieland Jass Band* in 1917, which sold a million copies. The ODJB was a

* In the early days, jazz was often spelled jass.

group of white New Orleans musicians who had traveled north to appear in New York City in 1917. Their performances during an extended stay generated much excitement; the new music they played was widely perceived as a fresh sound that went beyond conventional dance music.

Given the success of the ODJB recordings, it is not surprising that other records began to appear with the word "jazz" on the label.* Yet the jazz records that sold well were not always the most authentic examples of the genre but rather those the mass audience could easily assimilate. Often the most authentic jazz records in the twenties and thirties were those produced for the black market, the so-called race records. In American mass musical culture, jazz has always tended to be an influence rather than the essence of popular music. Subject to the vicissitudes of fad and fashion, jazz has become central to popular music only once, during the 1930s, when one type of jazz, swing, became popular primarily because it was dance (and therefore functional) music.

From an external point of view, jazz is a subgenre of popular music. It therefore tends to emerge strongly in popular consciousness only on those occasions when it has some impact on the popular music market. From this perspective, jazz is a musical commodity, competing on the popular music market with many other types of music.

The recording industry, like other large industries in the United States, follows the model of monopolistic capitalism (Denisoff, 1975; Peterson and Berger, 1975; Hirsch, 1964). At first there is diversified competition from a variety of producers for consumers. This was the case for jazz recordings in the 1920s. Consumers respond in the aggregate, giving the edge to certain producers who are giving the people what they want, or, through advertising, persuading people to want what they are getting. Finally, through financial control and control of raw materials (musical talent in this case), one or more producers corner the market and drive out competition. This happened in popular music in the United States in the 1930s. The giants, such as CBS (Columbia Records) and NBC (RCA) in

---

*The origins of the word itself are obscure, as, indeed, are the origins of jazz music. The word "jazz" may be a corruption of the Elizabethan "jas," or the Creole "jass" (both words have sexual connotations). A favorite candidate for another hypothesis is Charles "Buddy" Bolden, the first New Orleans "jazz king." Charles was often shortened to Chas, with the soft French *ch* sound becoming a *j* in English. By the late twenties it was all called jazz, and the alternative spellings disappeared. Looking backward, it is clear that jazz is rooted in a combination of New World African cultural survivals, in Puritan psalmody, in European concert and salon music, in black folk music, in nineteenth-century American popular music such as ragtime and martial airs, and in a host of other forms. The search for individual and etymological origins is rather fruitless (Schafer, 1974).

recording and broadcasting, can then control the tastes of their consumers by limiting output.

While powerful producers under monopolistic capitalism do everything they can to keep their consumers under control, innovation does occur, usually through small independent producers. Ironically, even this may aid the giants, since the smaller producers take the highest risks and can often be bought out relatively cheaply, should their product catch on. Rock and roll in the 1950s provides an example of this latter process (Gillet, 1970). Sometimes, however, the innovation may even occur within the oligopoly, especially by those who are diversified or who are losing their share of the market. In short, if the outsiders cut far enough into the marginal profits of the inside giants, the insiders either co-opt the innovation by incorporating it into their own production or they squeeze out the innovative competitor.

When this model is applied to, say, the American automobile industry, the process is clear. When, however, cultural production becomes the matter at hand, certain cautions are in order. In the first place, consumer investment may be quite small—the purchase of a single record. Also, the product is not created in quite the same way. While some recording stars may be "manufactured" by the recording industry à la the Hollywood star system, very often the raw material of the recording industry comes out of various specialized and demographically specific sectors of the population, such as the "Nashville Sound." This means that those who control the mass music market carefully watch trends from special markets. The jazz audience, of course, makes up one of those special markets.

For the creators of specialized music, however, the choice of making it in the mass market may mean selling out, risking one's integrity insofar as the demand is for a commodity that is standardized for the broadest possible distribution. The selling-out process may be even more subtle, of course, as the jazz artist becomes a craftsman, playing nonjazz music in the studio under the direction of commercially oriented producers (Nanry, 1970).

INNOVATION AND CONVENTIONALIZATION: THE INTERNAL DYNAMIC OF JAZZ

Jazz in America is like a deep underground spring. From time to time and in different places, it surges up to the surface, sparkling, surging, challenging. To understand the development of jazz, it is necessary to go underground to penetrate its inner history. There is a jazz community based on communication, rather than territoriality, which shapes the music whether or not it comes to the attention of a mass audience. This community is made up of musicians, dedicated fans, some critics, and those who provide the ambience in which real jazz is played and appreciated.

The jazz community, though, is far from monolithic. There are as many jazz communities as there are coteries of players, fans, critics, and promoters. While the tendency toward diversity is blocked by the leveling influence of the mass media, diversity still persists in jazz. Groups of young jazz players do get together and play. There are audiences for Dixieland revival groups who play a style of jazz rooted in the 1920s. Although jazz is played in communities throughout the United States, New York City is still the mecca of jazz. While success for a young jazz player still means making it in New York (the Big Apple), even in New York there are many different jazz subcommunities with various characteristics of style, age, and race (Nanry, 1970). Yet there is a jazz elite—players who are recognized as powerful because they control access to jobs, recording studios, and record dates.

While elite jazz players control jazz internally, they do not control the music industry. In fact, they often act as "gatekeepers" in transmitting, by such means as hiring practices (Nanry, 1972), the pressures for making it to those coming up through the ranks. The attrition rate for aspiring jazz players is cruelly high. Most will not make it in jazz; many will not make it in music.

Young players perform in "kid" bands. Some older players are content to establish themselves in a local bar, dance hall, or nightclub and stay there for years, supported by a faithful audience. There are many jazz players who do not get into the rat race. Making it today, however, means exposure through the mass media, records, radio, and television. This was not always the case, certainly not during the early days of jazz before the mass media brought to large numbers of people a conception of jazz. Once any discipline is given a mass outlet, its subtle qualities tend to be lost. The popular conception of jazz history is, therefore, a media conception.

Regional Variations

Long before there was a popular conception of jazz, however, there was jazzlike music flourishing in many American locales. At the turn of the century, this jazzlike music was nearly the exclusive property of black Americans. Some of the excitement of this music was captured in the work of "serious" composers such as Louis Moreau Gottschalk, who employed Afro-Caribbean rhythms and melodies, and in American popular music like ragtime. Ragtime, however, soon became extraordinarily conventionalized, and Gottschalk never enjoyed more than a passing popularity.

I do not want to give the impression by emphasizing the pluralistic origins of jazz that those playing and singing jazzlike music never came in contact with one another prior to the phonograph. Nothing could be further from the truth. But America in the nineteenth century was close to the model described by C. Wright Mills as the "self-balancing society." Transportation and communication had not developed to the degree they did later. It was possible to be born, grow up, and pursue a career without a great deal of contact beyond one's own part of the country. The global village was still far in the future.

The distribution networks for musical and other entertainment in nineteenth- and early twentieth-century America involved a series of overlapping circuits. Thomas Hennessey has argued that by 1924 there were four major jazz circuits in America (called territories) and that until well into the 1930s musicians found employment within one or another of them (Hennessey, 1972). The fact that most entertainment was live meant that there was a demand for it, especially for dancing. Hennessey maintains that the territories were arranged into a loose status hierarchy, with Chicago and New York at the top. Many of the best musicians from other territories would move up into the Chicago and New York circuits. Like baseball's minor leagues, the other circuits provided a training ground for major jazz players. At the same time, players moving into the major circuits would bring with them regional specialties that often became incorporated into the major-league style. The hegemony of New York and Chicago was confirmed by the centering of the mass media and especially the recording industry in those two cities.

The internal dynamic of jazz, then, involves an understanding of the regional variations in jazz playing up until the mid-thirties, and the external dynamic is the structure of the record industry from the mid-twenties on. It involves an understanding of how different elements from various sources contributed to the essence of jazz.

A facile conception of the New Orleans-Chicago-New York jazz axis does not wholly account for the history of jazz in the United States. It is necessary to go back a bit further: to African survivals in various parts of black America; to the socialization process as it affected the shift from folk to professional and specialized jazz playing; to the conventionalization of musical form in an industrial milieu.

Jazzman Jackie McLean is reputed to have once said that he studied at the University of Miles Davis and that his textbooks were Davis's records. In order to understand the development and perpetuation of jazz as a cultural phenomenon, it is necessary to recognize two factors: the teaching function of the jam session, where musicians get together and play informally; and the role of formal music instruction in the lives of most successful jazz players who have extensive knowledge of music theory and practice.

Jazz is a cultural phenomenon that follows the same rules as other cultural phenomena. It is learned and transmitted to each succeeding generation through a process of socialization. When this is understood, it is possible to see jazz music and musicians as part of a larger context.

Coda

The title of this chapter, "Head Arrangement," is an allusion to the widely used technique in jazz of lining out major themes that call for development. Several themes have been sounded in this chapter. Jazz is not only music but also the history of those who make jazz music. Jazz has an internal as well as an external dynamic. All these themes demand further elaboration. These motifs and others will be discussed, expanded, and developed in subsequent chapters.

Six musical elements have been described as key elements in most jazz performances: polyrhythm, snycopation, swing, improvisation, blue notes, and the theme-and-variation format. Each must be understood in the context of jazz performances.

I have stated that external factors have shaped the development of jazz, especially the movement of American popular entertainment into the mass media. I have also described the jazz community made up of jazz players, fans, critics, and promoters who all play a part in influencing the authentic versus the creative dialectic of jazz. Each of these themes will be analyzed in order to convey a holistic sense of the phenomenon called jazz.

Listening and Reading

Among the various record sets available for students of jazz, I believe the best is the one produced by Martin Williams and the Smithsonian Institution. (*The Smithsonian Collection of Classic Jazz,* Smithsonian P6 11891, 1973, available from Smithsonian Customer Service, P.O. Box 10230, Des Moines, Iowa 50336.) You should listen frequently to various selections at random, giving your full attention to the music.

There are many other excellent collections and single records that are also helpful. For a full discussion of the merits and disadvantages of various widely available materials, consult John Hasse, "The Smithsonian Collection of Classic Jazz: A Review Essay," *Journal of Jazz Studies,* Vol. 3, No. 1 (Fall, 1975). The *Journal of Jazz Studies* is published by the Rutgers Institute of Jazz Studies and Transaction Periodicals Consortium, Transaction, Inc., Rutgers University, New Brunswick, New Jersey, 08903.

If you live in an area that has a radio station which broadcasts jazz, try to listen regularly. The Public Broadcasting System also has jazz programs from time to time on television and radio; you should keep a sharp eye out for these special programs. Jazz Interactions, Inc., in New York City, disseminates information on jazz in the mass media, and you might ask them for information.

For written material, DaCapo Press (227 West 17th Street, New York, New York 10011) has a fine assortment of books in its "Roots of Jazz" series.

chapter 2

Themes and Variations in Early American Musical Life

"I hear America singing, the varied carols I hear." Long before and long after Walt Whitman penned these famous lines, the diversity of American music has confounded those who have tried to capture its essence. It is perhaps fitting that only one musical form—jazz—expresses that diversity. America is a mixture of African and European elements. Just as a column of air is shaped by the wind instrument through which it is blown, jazz has been shaped within the American context from European and African music.

The first white settlers in the New World encountered a native American (Indian) musical culture that they virtually ignored. Instead, they brought their own musical traditions with them. Settlers from Spain and Portugal brought an Iberian musical influence to western and southwestern North America, South America, and the Caribbean. French settlers in the North but also in the Midwest formed a thin crescent of trade from Canada to New Orleans. The Dutch held a toehold on the Eastern seaboard around what is now New York City, but left little lasting musical influence. It was the English, radiating inland from hard-won colonies all along the East Coast, who eventually established the frontier tone of early American music. Even the large number of German immigrants who came early to these shores usually came under the carapace of the antiestablishment religious sects (mostly Puritan) of England.

African musical influence came to the New World in chains. From the seventeenth century onward, black slaves with a variety of tribal traditions were brought to America. The slaves were from specific areas in Africa and in no way represented either the bottom of tribal social status or the entire African continent.

29

It is becoming clear, for example, that the various stages in the development of the slave trade had a decisive influence on what part of Africa the slaves came from, as well as where they were taken in the New World. It was once thought that the slaves came from all over Africa and that only weak and "inferior" Africans were captured and sold into slavery. Under such conditions, African customs would have a poor chance of survival. But the majority of slaves came from the West coast of Africa—especially Senegal, the Guinea coast, the Niger delta, and the Congo—as anthropologist Melville J. Herskovits has shown, while inter-tribal raids and dynastic wars in West Africa led to the selling of kings and priests into slavery, people who were specialists in their own tribal music and rituals (Stearns, 1956, p. 20).

During the period of the slave trade, slavers moved down the African coast and inland in search of human chattel. The Portuguese, who dominated the early phase of the slave trade, captured Senegalese and transported them to Brazil. The Spanish took Yorubans, and Spanish planters in Cuba came to prefer Yorubans. In Haiti, French slavers brought people from Dahomey to the planters there, and the British slavetraders brought the Ashanti to Jamaica in large numbers. While there were major exceptions to this pattern, slave importation was not random, and the full implication of the interaction of certain ethnic European and ethnic African groups in the New World should provide ethnomusicologists (those who study folk music) years of work. Certainly Melville Herskovits and Marshall Stearns have been trailblazers in this regard.

The importance of New Orleans in the development of jazz is a result of the mix of various European and African ethnic influences—an importance that will become clear in the next chapter. But the emergence of jazz occurred in the late nineteenth and early twentieth centuries. In the seventeenth and eighteenth centuries, the control of America was a contest among the major European powers. Culturally, the English won. They won because of superior numbers and because they established hegemony on the Eastern seaboard, sweeping westward from there. Spain was too intent on garnering quick riches from the New World. France claimed a vast underpopulated territory. England focused on trade and commerce; Virginia, for example, was established as a business venture—a joint stock company.

The sociologist Max Weber has argued that certain types of religion have an "elective affinity" with certain types of economic enterprise. Specifically, he said that "aesthetic Protestantism" (Puritanism in

America, for example) went hand in hand with the development of capitalism (Weber, 1958a). While the establishment of capitalism is incidental to our discussion at this point, the Puritan influence on music is not. And the struggles of Puritan divines for "pure" music defined the terms of musical taste.

Not all the British colonists, however, were Puritan. In the southern colonies, the Pilgrims maintained closer ties to the Crown than in the North, where the settlers tended to be religious separatists. Based at first on tobacco and later on cotton, the plantation economy of the South led to a demand for agricultural labor not found on the same scale in the North. That peculiar institution, slavery, flourished in both North and South in the beginning. (In the eighteenth century, it must be remembered, Newport, Rhode Island, was the major port of entry for slaves.) As industrialism began to take hold in the Puritan North, however, so did the abolition movement. Although outlawed in the United States after 1808, an illegal slave trade, focused in the South, continued until the end of the Civil War. The great failure of the American Revolution to resolve the slavery issue and the rift between the abolitionist North and the slaveholding South were deeply imprinted on the character of America.

WHITE ROOTS

Singing musical versions of the psalms was a strong tradition among all Protestants after the Reformation, with the exception of the Lutheran chorale among the Germans. Psalm singing went hand in hand with ballad singing, and although Pilgrims and Puritans were moralistic about music (spiritual leaders recoiled at the use of music for bawdy purposes), Gilbert Chase has demonstrated that a strong secular music tradition existed among even the sternest elements of colonial American society (Chase, 1966). Although there were periods of repression, the historical records of the Salem witch trials, for example, have tended to bias our view of the entire colonial period, especially in New England. Supporting Chase's diversity hypothesis, sociologist Kai Erikson in *Wayward Puritans* has suggested that the persecution of deviance (including, one presumes, musical deviance) was a means of defining community boundries (we become more sure of who *we* are by defining more precisely who *they* are). Erikson has also presented evidence that the extent of deviance in Puritan New England was remarkably stable, outside of three "crime wave" periods.

During the first six decades of settlement in Massachusetts, three serious "crime waves" occurred which affected the young colony in decisive ways. Each of these waves became an object of wide public concern and each of them drew large numbers of deviant offenders.

. . . [This study] will try to argue that the Antinomian controversy of 1636, the Quaker persecutions of the late 1650's, and the witchcraft hysteria of 1692 were three different attempts by the people of the Bay to clarify their position in the world as a whole, to redefine the boundries which set New England apart as a new experiment in living (p. 67).

"Proper" Music v. "Corrupt" Music

Within socially prescribed limits, there existed from the very beginnings of American musical life a certain tension between "official," proper music and the music of those outside strict control. Sometimes this dialectic operated between sacred music and folk music, and sometimes it operated within the context of sacred music. Chase provides us with an example of the latter conflict, which began in England after Queen Elizabeth approved the English Psalter* in 1559. Sternhold and Hopkins completed their "official" psalter in 1562. But the psalter brought to the New World by the Plymouth Colony was the "liberal" one compiled by Henry Ainsworth in 1612, not the psalter of Sternhold and Hopkins. The Ainsworth psalter contained thirty-nine tunes, many of which were based upon popular folk motifs of the period, including the French secular *chanson* (Chase, 1966, pp. 16–17). In the Massachusetts Bay Colony, Sternhold and Hopkins was used until 1640, when a group of New England divines published the *Bay Psalm Book* because they felt that Sternhold and Hopkins was too liberal. In 1692, after their merger with the Bay Colony, the Plymouth group adopted the *Bay Psalm Book* as well. By the ninth edition of the *Bay Psalm Book* in 1698, the psalter had been greatly expanded and, unlike earlier editions, music was included. Thirteen tunes (in common meter), less than half the number contained in Ainsworth, were proscribed in the *Bay Psalm Book*. This important book became the standard against which later "corruptions" were compared. In the southern colonies, a variety of psalters were in use, but there was a tendency toward the most conservative ones.

While this official constriction was occurring, the common folk developed their own traditions of psalm and hymn singing. This style was improvisational and based on a small core of stock folk tunes from Scotland and England. This practice, as Chase acknowledges, was a dramatic

* A psalter is a book of psalms.

foreshadowing of the theme-and-variation structure of improvisational jazz.

> Summarizing the characteristics of the Early New England Folk Style as described by contemporary writers: the singing is very slow; many grace notes, passing notes, turns, flourishes and other ornaments are used; pitch and time values are arbitrarily altered; there is a lack of synchronization among the voices; everyone sings as best pleases himself.
>
> . . . In England, in Scotland, in America, the same pattern prevails. This small inherited repertory of tunes (five to eight) provided a firm foundation for the improvisations and embellishments of the folk style. There was a core of unity with scope for endless variety (Chase, 1966, pp. 30–31).

Lining-out

Another practice adopted in the colonies was "lining-out." Lining-out was an ancient Gaelic tradition in which the minister of a congregation would read a line from a psalm; the line would then be repeated by the entire congregation. The practice apparently developed because many, if not all, of the members of a congregation could not read. It also became customary for the minister to give the pitch for the singing of the psalm. This "call and response" pattern goes back, of course, to the very beginnings of a sung liturgy in the Christian church. It is a common feature of Gregorian chant. It also became a common feature in the singing and preaching of black American churches and anticipated "riffing" (repetition of a short musical phrase) in jazz bands. In fact, lining-out is common to many folk song traditions. It can be found in both African and European singing. A practice such as lining-out invites embellishment and improvisation.

The addition of grace notes, singing in parts, and alterations of melody seem a natural consequence of the variations made by participants in terms of pitch, ability, and training. But as embellished psalmody in seventeenth-century New England grew, it generated a "conservative" response from those who, as advocates of "Regular Singing," wished to preserve "correct" plain psalmody.

> The Plymouth colonists took up the practice of lining-out at about the same time that they abandoned the Ainsworth Psalter, around the year 1692. And lining-out, as we have seen, prepared the way for the growth of responsorial, embellished, and improvisational psalmody. Now, only a few years later, in 1699, the practice

of lining-out was abolished at the Brattle Square Church in Boston. In other words, the relatively backward and undeveloped colony at Plymouth was taking up a traditional practice which the relatively advanced and progressive city of Boston was on the point of abandoning. The sophisticated urban congregation was discarding a custom that already began to be associated with rural crudeness and backwardness. In the course of time, as urban culture tended to dominate the whole New England area, lining-out disappeared from that region and took refuge in the relatively undeveloped frontier sections (Chase, 1966, p. 39).

Singing Schools

The response of zealous divines to musical deviance was the establishment of Singing Schools. The purpose of these schools was to instruct Puritans, wayward and otherwise, in the proper singing of psalms. "Regular Singing" (as the movement came to be called) promoted singing by note and, as an unintended consequence, became an important social institution. Sacred music publishing flourished, providing instruction and singing books for the schools. In the cities, Singing Schools became the basis for the establishment of choirs and choral societies; the famous Handel and Haydn Society of Boston had its origin in such a school. In the South and Midwest, the schools led to the development of communal singing, revival spirituals, and, finally, camp meeting songs. They became the base camps on the frontier for the emotional religious revival known as the "Great Awakening," which swept America in the eighteenth century.

The process discussed above may be outlined: **(1)** Singing by note is followed by **(2)** the practice of lining-out where the tempo of the music is slowed dramatically, leaving musical "space"; **(3)** florid styles or "filling-in" is invited, which leads to a reaction from purists; **(4)** Singing Schools are established. At this point a new element is introduced: emotionalism.

Emotional Singing

In 1735 Governor Oglethorpe of Georgia brought John and Charles Wesley to America to preach. The Wesleys had been influenced by the evangelical hymnody (not just psalmody) of the nonconformist English divine, Isaac Watts (1674–1748). On the crossing to America the Wesleys encountered Moravian missionaries. Also called the United Brethren, the Moravians were and are a German Pietistic sect well known for vocal and instrumental music composition. Converted to the Moravian style of hymn singing, John Wesley integrated their emotional fervor into the spirituals, which became an important part of revival meetings, the heart of the "Great Awakening." However, even John Wesley himself eventually became concerned with the excesses of "vain repetitions" in congregational singing and the florid style that flowed from the movement he had begun. The model outlined above for the development of Puritan music repeated itself once more.

> In opposing the popular trend toward florid singing of hymns, John Wesley, paradoxically, allied himself with the conservative and "respectable" elements who advocated a decorous and dignified type of congregational singing and would not tolerate any liberties taken with the tunes.
> . . . Thus, in Wesleyan hymnody, as in New England psalmody, we witness what is essentially another manifestation of the perennial conflict between "conservative" and "liberal" elements. John Wesley, at first considered "radical" because of his leaning toward evangelical hymnody of the German Pietist type, becomes the upholder, within his own Methodist movement, of an "authorized" body of hymnody and an "authorized" style of singing which he seeks to impose upon his followers but which is rejected or freely altered by the more radical or less conventional proponents of personal salvation and revivalism (Chase, 1966, p. 50).

A Variety of Traditions

Many other groups brought their own particular religious musical traditions with them. For some, music was peripheral, but for other groups, such as the Shakers, music and dance were the very essence of their religious fervor. The music of the Catholic church was present in both the English colonies and in the Spanish colonies. In fact, in California and in the Southwest, missionaries established schools and traditions that long outlasted the formal control of Spain. Thus the music of Europe was woven and rewoven into the fabric of American culture, often leading to interesting and unusual combinations. In almost every tradition, "liberal" and "conservative" positions were taken with regard to the proper form of religious music.

A helix of conformity and deviance asserted itself as antiestablishment musical sects formed and contested the establishment churches' dogmas concerning proper musical form. While we have looked at this phenomenon from the point of view of music, the ubiquitous process of sect formation itself had a profound impact on America.

If one looked more closely at the matter in the United States, one could easily see that the question of religious affiliation was almost always posed in social life and in business life which depended on permanent and credit relations.

. . . It is crucial that sect membership meant a certificate of moral qualification and especially of business morals for the individual. This stands in contrast to membership in a "church" into which one is "born" and which lets grace shine over the righteous and unrighteous alike. Indeed, a church is a corporation which organizes grace and administers religious gifts of grace, like an endowed foundation. Affiliation with the church is, in principle, obligatory and hence proves nothing with regard to the member's qualities. A sect, however, is a voluntary association of only those who, according to the principle, are religiously and morally qualified. If one finds voluntary reception of his membership, by virtue of religious probation, he joins the sect voluntarily.

. . . Competition among sects is strong, among other things, through the kind of material and spiritual offerings at evening teas of the congregations. Among genteel churches also, musical presentations contribute to this competition. . . . Despite this sharp competition, the sects often maintained fairly good mutual relations (Weber, 1946, pp. 305–7).

This quotation from Max Weber provides a bridge to another important point that must be made here. Although the discussion above has focused on religious music (a proper focus in discussing American music until late in the eighteenth century), nonreligious music also evidenced divisions parallel to the church *v.* sect process. By the late eighteenth century, a musical elite had formed in American secular music; it focused on the "proper" cultural productions of Paris and London and disdained crude American folk styles.

In *America's Music,* Gilbert Chase argues that the musical taste of the American elite at the time of the Revolution was a great deal more sophisticated than is usually thought (Chase, 1966, pp. 84–105). Key revolutionary figures such as Jefferson, Franklin (inventor of the glass 'armonica, guitar teacher, and formidable music critic), and Francis Hopkinson were accomplished amateur musicians and patrons. One evidence of this attitude was the establishment in 1762 of the St. Cecilia Society in Charleston, South Carolina, which brought professional musicians from London and Paris to play in America. After the Revolution, New York, Boston, and Philadelphia also became centers of European-based musical life. Especially in Philadelphia, art music flourished. This penchant for the music of the European masters set a pattern that persists even to the present day. In times past, the dichotomy this preference created was between the music of the aristocracy and the folk music of the masses. For half the existence of the Republic, the contrast has been between art music and commercial or popular music. In either case, the dialectic between proper and "corrupting" music is the same: moral entrepreneurs make an aesthetic judgment about what is good and what is harmful to the soul or to educated taste.

What evolved was a four-way tug-of-war among "good" and "bad" religious music and "good" and "bad" secular music. In both cases, the argumentation was (and continues to be) couched in moralistic tones. The tone for the American debate on music and art, moreover, was set back in Puritan New England. The eighteenth century marked the beginning of the transition to a commercial/secular dichotomy. The form of the debate remained the same. By the nineteenth century, the debate became primarily secular.

> The development of art-music in the American cities was associated with the assimilation, and then perhaps with the imposition, of European models. Indeed, there had been a precedent for this way back in the eighteenth century, contemporary with the New England hymnodists: for the Moravian Brethren in Pennsylvania had attempted to transport their European music, along with their way of life, to their new home (Mellors, 1967, p. 17).

Shape-note Systems

An additional remark ought to be made here about the growth of shape-note systems following the development of Singing Schools. Shape notes were groupings of notes whose tonal quality and/or duration were designated by using various symbols such as squares, triangles, and so on—a kind of return to the simplicities of, for example, Gregorian chant notation.

> The more "civilization" encroached on New England, bringing with it professional teachers of polite music from Europe, the more the primitive American hymnody moved back into the wilderness. Now it was disseminated not only along the eastern seaboard, but also south and west, written in a curious notation called "shape-note," which was a compromise between normal staff notation and the empirical method of tonic solfa (Mellers, 1967, p. 15).

Shape notes were a reversion to pentatonicism (the five-note folk scale without sharps and flats). Uusually based on melodic rather than harmonic needs, this process resolved some of the difficulties of teaching tunes to large numbers of unlettered and untutored peoples.

> Many primitively rationalized scales content themselves with the addition of only one tonal distance. This is regularly one whole tone within the diazeutic fourth. It is the essence of pentatonic scaling.
> . . . Pentatonicism is frequently closely linked in a musical ethos to avoidance of the semitone step. It has been reasoned that this very avoidance constitutes its musical motive (Weber, 1958b, pp. 15–16).

Although it is highly speculative, one can hardly resist the temptation to point out the affinity of the five-note shape system for African-based pentatonic scales. Recalling the discussion in chapter 1 (pages 18–19) of blue notes and their importance to jazz, shape notes take on a new significance.

The florid hymnody of the Great Awakening eventually led to the institutionalization of revivalist sects, offshoots of Wesleyan Methodism. At the beginning of the nineteenth century, a second revival led to camp meetings, which drew thousands of participants. Often racially integrated (at least in the sense that blacks attended, though often restricted to a particular section of the meeting grounds), these meetings were the core of what has come to be called the "Second Awakening" of the late eighteenth and early nineteenth centuries (Southern, 1971, pp. 93–94). Musically, the development of "open" singing styles between the "Awakenings" is obvious.

> The shape-note tunes proliferated with remarkable rapidity, and the revivalist sects that flourished in every state took them up the more readily because they could appeal immediately to the illiterate. Shape note method encouraged the singers to make up their own versions of the tunes on the spur of the moment, so that a wild heterophony must often have resulted. This would have accorded, musically, with the physical excesses of revivalist fervour; and contemporary descriptions make clear that this was not far removed from the ritual exercise of voodoo-worship. In the South the shape-note tunes were the main "white" source for the Negro's spirituals; together, white and black Christians sought a refuge from Calvinistic fire and brimstone (Mellors, 1967, p. 17).

BLACK ROOTS

Africans came to the New World under a wholly different aegis than did Europeans. Africans did not come seeking adventure, riches, or freedom from religious persecution; they were brought in bondage as human tools. They became another commodity in a world of expanding commodity markets. The connection of slavery (an ancient human practice) with race in America created a scar on the very fabric of social life. It established a caste system that made a sham of the rhetoric that formed the basis of the new republic. The robust dream of a shining city on a hill became a nightmare of ugly division within the human family. While the trauma of the barracoons, the Middle Passage, and the human auction block still haunts us, the analysis of jazz provides some opportunity to think about a cultural product that transcended the very inhumanity which gave it life. And because jazz is a cultural product, all of us, no matter what our racial heritage, can share in its strength.

The uprooted Africans came from rich and varied cultures. An important part of those cultures was the musical traditions that were woven like a bright thread through every aspect of social, political, and religious life. There were songs and dances to lighten the burden of work, sung poems to ridicule political enemies and to celebrate every conceivable aspect of social life.

African Song

Song was, and is, a characteristic musical expression of African tribal life. The pattern of solo and chorus is ubiquitous. It must not be forgotten, however, that African musical culture was and is no more homogeneous than, say, European or Asian musical culture. For example, harmony was rare among the Dahomeans, common among the Ashanti. Yet African music does have commonalities (as does European music). *Portamento* (the sliding from one note into another using variable pitch) is found throughout Africa. And, of course, an emphasis on rhythmic complexity prevails everywhere. Although it is an admittedly Western way of looking at things, polyrhythm provides an analogous complexity for African music that harmony provides for European music.

In chapter 1, I suggested that harmony may be thought of as adding a vertical dimension to melody. That same verticality is provided in African music by polyrhythm—a kind of "rhythmic harmony." While an overall beat often exists (carried characteristically by the largest drum), a variety of alternative rhythms may be built into a typical African performance. These rhythms may seem contradictory to Western but not to African ears, for underlying the entire rhythmic structure is what Richard Waterman has labeled the "metronome sense" of African and Afro-American listeners and players (Waterman, 1948). Metronome sense provides the same kind of explicit or implied unity to a musical production that we experience when we "naturally" understand any theme-and-variation structure. We hear and feel a total musical construction in its parts. Even when it is only implied, we have the right feeling for musical structure.

Musical idioms reflect cultural and social structures. Musical thought-ways also channel the ways in which people characterize their own reality. Music as well as language structures thought.

A leader and a chorus part are normally implied in Negro African song, whether or not the performance is solo, for both elements are essential to African song structure. The song leader never performs for long without complex counterbalancing comment by the instrumental or vocal chorus. Furthermore, our research indicates that the length of the leader's part varies roughly with the importance of tribal chiefs over against the tribal council. In more or less acephalous (leaderless) African tribes, song leaders usually perform against a constant background of choral singing. Where chieftainship is paramount, vocal solos are longer and more prominent.

. . . This brief sketch of African song performance structure matches in a remarkable way the gross structure of most African Negro societies. An African normally belongs to several interlocked groups—to a tribe, then perhaps to a series of segmentary patrilineal kin groups, to one or more cult groups, to a work organization, to an age group, to a political faction, and so on. Each of these groups may have a different head, and in each of them an individual may achieve a varying degree of prominence in accordance with his talents and his status. Although the society is stratified, it is quite possible for a witty man with a highly developed sense of political maneuver to rise to the top of one or several of the organizations of which he is a member. If he is an hysteric, he may become a religious leader and prophet. This provides an exact analogy to the emergence of a talented individual in the African musical group. African music is full of spaces. The loose structure of this musical situation gives the individual dancer, drummer, or singer the leeway to exhibit his personality in a moment of virtuosic display. He will then be replaced, but later on he may pre-empt longer and more elaborate solo passages, thus establishing himself as a recognized and talented musical leader.

Since music is keyed to a group integration in a wide variety of African activities, a musical virtuoso may be or become a religious or political leader. Yet the very structure of African melodies stands in the way of the L/N [leader (L) and audience (N)] dominance pattern, for African melody is litany and responsorial, made up of more or less equal contributions from solo and chorus, with the chorus part dominant more often than not. Thus, in Negro Africa, musical performance structure and social structure mirror one another, reinforce one another, and establish the special quality of both African music and African society—whether in Africa or in the African enclaves in the New World.

The strong rhythmic bias of African music also represents this many-goaled, many-headed, group-oriented culture. African rhythm is usually anchored in a strongly accented two- or four-beat rhythm, but around and through this positive, thrusting rhythmic unity plays a variety of contrasting counterrhythms on numbers of instruments that give voice to the diverse groups and personalities bound together in tribal unity. At any moment, one of these tangential rhythms can seize the imagination of the group and become dominant, just as in a West African cult ceremony an individual may be mounted by his cult deity and rise from obscurity to total group dominance for a period (Lomax, 1970, pp. 67–69).

Early Plantation Life

It is difficult to learn about Afro-American music in the seventeenth and eighteenth centuries. The official historical record is usually written by rulers rather than the ruled, slaveholders rather than slaves. We know that Africanisms survived because of their strong emergence later, but much of the early evidence of African "survivals" can only be inferred indirectly. We have established that the Africans who came to the New World came from a wide variety of musical traditions, that they represented various strata in the groups from which they were taken, and that successive waves of Africans brought to these shores renewed the African connection. Since culture is transmitted through the socialization process, we can be certain that nonmaterial aspects of African tribal life were carried in the wretched holds of the slave ships. On the other hand, it is also likely that most material artifacts were stripped from the slaves before and after their arrival. Since they were from radically different traditions than the Europeans whom they came to serve and since they had different traditions and even languages among themselves, it became imperative for them to improvise with whatever they found at hand.

It must also be noted that slaves in America were treated very differently by different slaveholders and in different parts of the New World. In New England, for example, black slaves were sometimes treated in a manner similar to the white indentured servant and were freed (or allowed to purchase their freedom) after a period of servitude. Ethnocentric and conversion-minded slaveholders (and white society at large), on the other hand, often viewed black Africans as primitive, cultureless children or as barely domesticated beasts of burden. After the invention of the cotton gin and the establishment of the large-scale plantation economy in the South, these two views became more regionalized. Drums, for example, which were central to African music making were often outlawed in the South because slaveholders realized that they could be used for extramusical communication. Some slaveholders, however, encouraged their slaves to learn conventional European instruments because of their "natural ability" to make music in order to entertain.

The banjo is an African musical instrument. Basically, it is a transmogrified drum with strings stretched over the drumhead. Without the strings it becomes a tambourine. The banjo is mentioned as far back as Thomas Jefferson (Chase, 1966, p. 67). The banjo was assimilated in American culture, one presumes, because of its kinship with the familiar European guitar. Both instruments, by the way, were derived from a common Arab ancestor, an interesting example of cultural "survival."

Eileen Southern, in *The Music of Black Americans,* has uncovered an interesting cache of data regarding early black virtuosos by examining colonial newspaper ads for runaway slaves (Southern, 1971, pp. 27–29). These ads often mentioned that the runaway carried with him a violin or "he plays remarkably well on the violin." Southern also refers to diaries and journals kept by travelers about plantation life and the music of the slaves. From these and other sources, it becomes clear that this period represented the incubation of Afro-American music and that major cultural adaptations were occurring. We have glimpses of singing and dancing, of renowned black fiddlers playing for white dancers. Accounts of black holidays like Pinkster Day in New York and Lection Day in New England obviously kept the tribal spark alive. The latter holiday was especially interesting because amidst great celebrating a black king was elected who, like a remembered tribal chieftan, would adjudicate disputes and make decisions for his subjects (Southern, 1971, pp. 49–55). In the South, slaves were sometimes given days off, such as Christmas and Easter, and reports of great merrymaking have trickled down to us. We may presume that African traditions were kept alive even as European folkways were being absorbed and transformed by the Africans.

The Influence of Religion

Earlier in this chapter, I stressed the importance of religion and religious music in shaping both the form and content of colonial and revolutionary America. That emphasis reflects the importance of religious dissent as a motive for European immigration. For the African exiles, religion was not a reason for coming to America, nor was religious practice typically differentiated from the activities of everyday life. Social life for an upright Puritan conformed to formal religious dogma. For the Africans, religion was simply a reflection of the culture.

In the sense in which anthropologists use the term (nonperjoratively), African religions tended to be more "primitive" than the religions of Europe, where sharply honed institutional differences were the cause and the result of endless wars and dissensions. In his discussion of primitive religion, Emile Durkheim suggested this seamlessness of religion and other aspects of social structure.

> Religion is something eminently social. Religious representations are collective representations which express collective realities; the rites are a manner of acting which take rise in the midst of the assembled groups and which are destined to excite, maintain or recreate certain mental states in these groups (Durkheim, 1954, p. 22).

And collective representations are the result of social interaction, so that religion in primitive societies is a wellspring of the very categories of thought through which social life is processed. Religion in this sense is a synonym for one's conception of one's place in the scheme of things.

> Collective representations are the result of an immense cooperation, which stretches out not only into space but into time as well; to make them, a multitude of minds have associated, united and combined their ideas and sentiments; for them, long generations have accumulated their experience and their knowledge. A special intellectual activity is therefore concentrated in them which is infinitely richer and complexer than that of the individual (Durkheim, 1954, p. 29).

Although there was deep ambivalence and resistance to proselytizing, especially in the South, major efforts were made to convert slaves to Christianity. These efforts led to what both theologians and anthropologists call syncretism. Syncretism, the combination or reconciliation of differing religious beliefs, was more likely then a combination of political or other African institutional systems. Furthermore, African cultural survivals couched in religious terms had a greater chance to endure because they were perceived as less of a threat to white Americans. I have argued above that Africans wore their religions more comfortably than Protestant Europeans. Adaptation to changed conditions, under such a circumstance, would not involve the betrayal of one's church, just the natural adjustment to a new social order. Permitted religious expression (but not political expression), Afro-Americans channeled a wide variety of concerns into an ostensibly religious framework. In discussing the well-known Negro spiritual, "Michael Row the Boat Ashore," Gilbert Chase recognizes this infusion.

What is distinctive about the Negro song, besides the manner of singing, is the adaptation of the imagery and vocabulary of evangelical hymnody to concrete situations related to his own environment and experience. For instance, in the last verse the idea of the sinner saving his soul is fused with the necessity of performing a given task (rowing) and attaining a practical objective (the shore). The crossing over Jordan is identified with the immediate task of rowing across a body of water. The line "Michael boat a music boat" probably an improvised variant on the line "Michael boat a gospel boat," takes one by surprise; yet it leads naturally to the mention of Gabriel's trumpet in the next line. This in turn suggests the Last Judgment and the need to care for one's soul:

O you mind your boastin' talk.
Boastin' talk will sink your soul.

There the soul, like the boat, is in possible danger of *sinking*—a bold and appropriate metaphor. The danger incurred by the sinner is assimilated into the prospect of danger that could beset the boat in landing if overtaken by darkness and rising waters:

When de ribber overflo,
O poor sinner, how you land?
Ribber run and darkness comin'.
Sinner row to save your soul.

The more one lingers over this Negro spiritual, the more one becomes aware of how beautifully its seemingly disparate elements are bound together by an imaginative fusion of themes and images (Chase, 1966, p. 235).

The emergence of the secular blues in the twentieth century out of sacred spirituals may be explained through an extension of the same hypothesis: After emancipation, cultural expression was no longer limited to a religious vocabulary. Black Americans did not abandon religion in any sense; they just flowed with the shift in social organization that permitted a broader range of expression.

Latin America and the Caribbean

In our consideration of the white roots of jazz, emphasis was placed on the English tradition. Only passing attention was given Portuguese, Spanish, and French influences. The African connection, however, demands a broader consideration of all the Americas. Slaves were imported into South America and the Caribbean in large numbers. The Latin influence shaped (and still shapes) jazz music. It shaped jazz because, for example, New Orleans became a black melting pot for inter-American culture after the Civil War and because many areas south of the border permitted the survival of Africanisms to a greater extent than did the United States.

The question of slavery was discussed and debated in the Roman Catholic church from the time of St. Paul. The official position of the church on slavery was that it could be tolerated as a labor system yet not defended as a natural state of man. The slave codes developed in Latin Catholic countries insisted on two major conditions: that slavery was contractual, a result of historical accident, and that all slaves had to be given religious instruction and baptized within one year of their arrival in the New World. By law, any person, including all blacks, was free unless someone could prove ownership. All slaves, again by law, had the right to purchase freedom and had to be given specified amounts of "free" time to accumulate a fixed purchase price. While the condition of slavery was often just as cruel, and sometimes crueler, in the Latin countries, just as harsh, and sometimes harsher, the humanity of the slave was never at issue as it was in North America (Elkins, 1963, pp. 63–80).

The Moorish penetration of Iberia, the ancient intercourse between Africa and Europe around the Mediterranean, and other factors (such as the holding of white Christian slaves by black Moslems) could be cited as reasons for the very different conception of class and caste in Latin America and the Caribbean. Each island and every country in this area deserves full and elaborate discussion, although this is beyond the scope of this book. Instead, we must be content with some generalizations based on research in this area, which will be woven into the narrative of the next chapter.

Africanisms survived better outside the United States. In countries where Africans were not considered "alien creatures," central cultural features, such as drumming and dancing, were less likely to be suppressed. In *The Story of Jazz*, Marshall Stearns makes a very strong case, based on his own field work and the research of others, for the survival of "pure" African (Dahomeyan) drumming in Haiti, African (Bush-Negro) song styles in what was then Dutch Guiana, Spanish-African music in Cuba, and French-West African political satire in the calypso "put down" songs of Trinidad. Stearns and Stearns in *Jazz Dance* provide us with ample evidence of the African influence in Latin dance from the tango to the bossa nova and beyond.

Catholicism also encouraged religious syncretism. The hierarchy of the saints—missing in aesthetic Protestantism—offered parallels with specialized African dieties. St. Patrick, who was reputed to have driven the snakes out of Ireland, became identified with the Dahomeyan snake god Damballa, Ogun, the Yoruban god of war, with the sword-wielding St. Michael. The eventual result of these combinations was the development of voodoo, an important force in the early development of jazz—as we shall see.

Work Songs and Dance

The song tradition was strong among Afro-Americans. Slaves, stripped of their overt African cultures, improvised work songs based on acceptable religious themes. Deprived of conventional means of expressing themselves musically, they developed techniques of self-expression that were as unique as they were brilliant. One such technique was the "field holler." The field holler was a musical cry distinctive enough to identify its user. Often based on the "falsetto break" * common to much African song, this idea of a "musical signature" led, in apposition to the European classical tradition, to the notion that a musical performance must be the unique expression of individual performers. Shouts and hollers represented individual outlet to a people denied the visual and other arts because they were seen as dangerous.

The ring dance was yet another example of this process. In African communal dancing, the participants often formed a circle and moved in a counterclockwise direction (one could not present his or her right shoulder to the gods). Baptists defined dancing (which was proscribed) as

* Falsetto breaks are common to much "primitive" music. Akin to the stylized European yodel, they represent an upward octave shift used for dramatic effect. They also represent, sometimes symbolically, the shift from a male "voicing" to a female one.

the crossing of the feet. As long as the ring dance involved only shuffling and not the crossing of feet, even the Baptists could not object to it. Ring dancing survives to the present day (in its secular form as the conga line and the bunny hop), and the falsetto break in both jazz and rhythm and blues (à la Al Green) is a widely used device.

THE NINETEENTH CENTURY

There is no way to characterize adequately in a sentence or two what happened to America, and indeed a large portion of the world, in the nineteenth century. C. Wright Mills has described this period as one in which America moved from "a self-balancing society" to one in which all parts of society became interlocked (Mills, 1953). For Mills self-balancing meant the condition under which various groups, regions, and segments of society could maintain relative autonomy. The industrial revolution, invention, and the emergence of capitalism all led to a great "sifting and sorting" of populations (Wilensky and Lebeaux, 1958). Events such as the Civil War were symptoms of this global process. Peoples once separated by eons of time and vast distances of space were now thrown together in the name of enterprise. Industrialism itself, through the proliferation of the division of labor, created a world in which some workers made pinheads, others made shafts, and still others brought them together. The simple organic unity of the agrarian tribe was replaced by the willful unity of specialized function.

Yet this smashing of the social atom drove people to create wholeness out of diversity. Often cruel and inhuman, the new industrial order operated on a scale that demanded the discovery of purpose beyond narrow conceptions of local meaning. Max Weber saw the "Protestant ethic" as the force behind this purpose; Karl Marx saw it in the historical necessity of productive forces. In any case, technology (invention both social and nonsocial) became the cause and effect of the new "economy of scale." A new order, which changed everything, emerged.

Industrialization and Art

Industrialization and its concomitants—urbanization, technology, population density, and heterogeneity—also had an important impact on the development of art. A key characteristic of industrialization is the creation of large-scale markets. A key characteristic of capitalism is the pressure toward the transformation of virtually everything into commodities that can be bought and sold in the marketplace. (Music and art are not immune to this process.) And while the roots of this process go far back into the late medieval period in Europe, these commercial transactions were carried out on an immense scale in the nineteenth century. In American music the beginnings of what later became the music industry can be traced back to the publishing houses that produced song books and instruction books for eighteenth-century singing schools. The profit motive led these publishing firms to expand their offerings beyond psalm books and hymnals to the production of sheet music with broad popular appeal. In short, industrial capitalism provided the model.

Support for music came more and more to rely on public concerts. Though small in number at first, a cadre of professional musicians grew, depending on public rather than private patronage. This dependence in turn made those who produced music sensitive to the demands of a mass market rather than the tastes of a small elite. Popular culture—music and art produced as a commodity and altered to suit as broad an audience as possible—came of age in the nineteenth century. It borrowed shamelessly from both folk and elite sources in the hope of realizing profit. Money itself, intrinsically without value, but valued because of its capacity to command any and every product, became the anchor upon which the entire system rested. One dollar apiece from a million people without taste was equal to a million dollars from one exquisitely educated patron. Using Marxist terminology, Stephen Couch has described a historical process that applies not only to the symphony orchestra but to most art forms.

> Since the seventeenth century the orchestra has been appropriated by the bourgeoisie from the court-centered aristocrats. The connection of this appropriation to larger social forces seems obvious. It occurred during the period of rise and entrenchment of the bourgeois class, a time when bourgeois power became dominant in all fields. The appropriation of the orchestra, however, cannot be seen in terms of a simple class analysis, but is subtle enough to require more detailed examination. Another appropriation is the appropriation of the orchestra from the musicians themselves by the business and social elite. This process can be seen as a proletarianization of the performing orchestral musician during the past century, and therefore as part of a much more general social occurrence.
>
> The musician began this process as an independent businessman (in musical jargon, a free-lancer), and, in most cases, ended it assimilated into the working class, selling his or her labor to those people who had (or had access to) capital (Couch, 1976, p. 25).

Although C. Wright Mills was clearly talking about the limitations of transportation and communication networks when he introduced the concept of "self-balancing" to describe preindustrial America, the same idea applies to music and art. And when the idea is applied to music and art, cultural groupings become as important as the geographical. Certain divisions in American music, such as the racial, are obvious. Yet variation within both black and white music cannot be overlooked, nor can certain "crossover" influences. The channeling of African song into a religious context is one example. The influence of plantation life (often sentimentalized) on American popular song is another, especially in the work of composers such as Stephen Foster. Elements of chance, as well as predictable patterns of interaction, shaped the various combinations of musical form and content leading to the modern era. While we cannot hope to untangle all these elements, we can, with the help of hindsight, trace some of the most important. Indeed, that has been our task all along.

The Negro Spiritual

The Afro-American musical centerpiece of the nineteenth century was the Negro spiritual. An outgrowth of the florid hymnody of the "Great" and the "Second" Awakenings plus the integration of African singing practices, the spiritual, both because of its legitimacy in the larger society and because of its intrinsic power, made the Afro-American musical tradition available to significant strata—black and white—in the American population.

> The Negro slave was the largest homogenous group in a melting-pot America. He analyzed and synthesized his life in his songs and sayings. In hundreds of songs called spirituals, he produced an epic cycle; and, as in every such instance, he concealed there his deepest thoughts and ideas, his hard-finished plans and hopes and dreams. The exploration of these songs for their social truths presents a tremendous problem. It must be done, for, as in the kernel of the *Iliad* lies the genius of the Greeks, so in the kernel of the spiritual lies the genius of the American Negro (Lovell, 1939, pp. 642–43).

The "Second Awakening" provided an opportunity for the penetration of Afro-American religious interpretation into American religion. The epitomization of this emotional turn in folk religion was the camp meeting. The first camp meeting took place in Logan County, Kentucky, in July, 1800. Thousands of people gathered, tents were set up, and great camp fires were started. Preachers took turns whipping up the religious fervor of the assembled masses. The tradition, thus established, became a permanent fixture of American religious life. Though these gatherings are rather tame by comparison now, we can still observe some of the enthusiasm when we see on TV the Pope or Billy Graham or the Reverend Moon stir a capacity crowd at Yankee Stadium. While a Yankee Stadium spectacle is limited to a few hours, however, the original camp meeting typically went on for days. When conventional forms of worship and ritual were exhausted, the black participants would sustain the fervor through the chanting of chorus "tag lines" to combined scriptural and everyday exhortations by a leader (lining-out). In this context the folk melodies and the oral tradition, strong among black participants, carried the meeting (Southern, 1971, pp. 93–99).

While camp-meeting spirituals provided an avenue of pentration for Afro-American style into the mainstream of American religious music, another development in the nineteenth century nurtured the independent growth of the Negro spiritual. That development was the establishment of independent black churches.

Although there is ample evidence that blacks held secret religious services throughout the period of slavery (Southern, 1971, pp. 158–63), the beginning of independent black churches dates from 1794 when Richard Allen established the Mother Bethel Church in Philadelphia. Reverend Allen, affronted by the indignities suffered by blacks in conventional white Methodist churches, founded the African Methodist Episcopal Church (A.M.E.) as a wholly independent black congregation not affiliated with any white denomination. Others soon followed suit, and the number of unaffiliated and affiliated black congregations grew substantially. In many of these churches, variations on conventional ritual fostered a strengthening of traditional Afro-American musical practices. The independent black congregation became an important institution both before and after the Civil War since there were few other institutions permitted *de facto* or *de jure* in black communities. It is, moreover, no accident that much leadership among black Americans, up to and including the recent civil rights movement, has come from the ministry.

In the latter part of the 1800s, the Negro spiritual came to national and international attention through the tours of groups such as the Fisk Jubilee Singers, who won great acclaim for their concert versions of spirituals. This troupe was launched in 1871 to raise money for the struggling Fisk College, established in the postwar period to educate blacks. A short time later, Hampton Institute also sent out a touring company for the same purpose. The Negro spiritual gained recognition as a distinctive and respected genre in American religious music. So many jazz musicians have said that they first acquired a feeling for jazz in church that it has become almost a cliché. Yet the cliché makes sense when one considers the commonalities underlying Afro-American music.

Black Secular Music

It is important here to reemphasize the fact that not all, or even most, black American music was church music. Since religious songs were the least threatening and provided a comforting uplift to most of the population, there probably is an overrepresentation of them in the written literature of early black music in the United States (Southern, 1971, p. 175). It must be remembered that there were large numbers of blacks working on American waterfront docks before and after the Civil War. Blacks were also employed in stores and factories both as slaves and as free persons throughout the antebellum period. After the Civil War, large numbers of black workers were employed in mines, in logging and turpentine camps, and as cowboys and railroad workers. In each case, the Afro-American musical influence was felt. One of the most famous railroad songs in our folklore is "John Henry." John Henry was, of course, black. His tragic struggle to defeat technology is told in the cadences of the classic black work song. "Michael Row the Boat Ashore" is a song that illustrates the black boatman tradition as well as the melding of religious and everyday themes.

The failure of Reconstruction resulted in the exchange of slavery for the wage slavery of sharecropping, the chains of slavery for the chains of prison. Chain-gang songs carried forward the work-song tradition into the era of emancipation. A treasury of prison songs and remote congregational singing has been preserved in the recordings of John and Alan Lomax for the Library of Congress. In these poignant recordings, we can get a glimpse of both the melancholy and the solace that these songs must have provided for those who could not "lay their burdens down." These recordings provide the only direct evidence of a song style that has had to rely on written records of persons trained in the Western tradition of musical notation. They also offer living evidence of the three-line "sorrow song" stanzas that shaped both the Negro spiritual and later the blues form.

It should also be noted that in certain areas (such as Philadelphia) a "black bourgeoisie" was developing even prior to the Civil War (Frazier, 1957). Music was important to this group, and formal musical training as well as recitals and the sponsorship of "proper," that is, European, musical production was encouraged. A few black concert artists gained widespread recognition in the nineteenth century (Southern, 1971, pp.

305—9), and their fame was certainly noted by black communities throughout America.

As far back as colonial times the black dance musician was an important figure on the American musical scene. Providing music for dancing was not considered a proper pursuit for middle-class white Americans. By default, from the days of the slave fiddler until well into the twentieth century, the occupation of dance musician had fallen to blacks and other déclassé troubadours in America. Black "musicianers" played for dance bands (with both black and white patrons), and were employed in circus and medicine-show bands as well as every kind of traveling road show before the pre-mass media era. While the American cultural elite looked to London and Paris for its musical entertainment, black musicians "did the job" of diverting the masses. In terms of popular nineteenth-century entertainment, however, one form stands out—the minstrel show.

Minstrelsy

Starting in the second decade of the nineteenth century, a new entertainment form began to take shape in America. At first it involved the popularization of plantation life in sentimental songs. Many performers incorporated these numbers, called "Ethiopian melodies," into their theatrical routines. Many of them depicted inaccurate and stereotyped scenes of Afro-American existence. Most of them revolved around two caricatures. The first was the shuffling, shiftless, and happy-go-lucky image of childlike rural Negroes, the Jim Crow stereotype. The other stereotype was that of the city Negro, the smartly dressed ladies' man or "Zip Coon." The popularity of the Ethiopian melodies and the staged characterization of slave existence, which ranged from naiveté at its best to ugly racism at its worst, led to the emergence of entire shows with the Ethiopian theme.

Borrowing the name given to traveling lyric poets, singers, and musicians of the Middle Ages, the American minstrel show achieved stability of form by mid-century. With an interlocutor in the center, the performers arranged themselves in a semicircle with a tambourine player on one end ("Tambo") and a bone castanet player on the other ("Bones"). Under the direction of the interlocutor, a routine of jokes, stories, and songs done in a parody of black dialect constituted the first half of the program. The second part, the "olio," was made up of variety acts and sometimes a short play or burlesque opera. The finale was called "the walk-around," a song-and-dance routine involving the entire cast. The walk-around owed its origin to the plantation cakewalks, dancing or strutting contests in which the slaveholder would award some prize, usually a cake, to the best dancer. Revivalist camp meetings also included the custom of the walk-around at the end of the final day of praying and preaching.

E. P. Christy is often given credit for developing the classic format of the minstrel show. Christy's Minstrels, the Virginia Minstrels with Dan Emmett (who, incidentally, wrote the song "Dixie" as an Ethiopian melody and bitterly decried its adoption by the Confederacy), and others assembled large touring minstrel troupes. But not all minstrel shows operated independently; truncated versions, for example, were often incorporated into circus performances. In fact, the classic clown makeup worn by, say, Emmett Kelley, which has its origins in the European Middle Ages, resembles the stylized makeup of the blackface minstrel. In a kind of parody of the white minstrels (themselves a parody of plantation life), black minstrel shows also flourished. Whether the performers were black or white, they all darkened their faces with burnt cork and painted on grotesque lips. Somehow the tragedy and the threat of black subjugation was mitigated behind the blackface mask.

Minstrelsy provides a metaphor of American race relations as revealed in popular music. Unable to deal with the real black experience, the mass audience can accept a "sweetened" version, which is an imitation or even a parody. Blacks may then reclaim the parody in some measure by adjusting to the stereotype. Hot jazz and the evolution of swing and the growth of rock 'n' roll out of rhythm and blues are twentieth-century manifestations of the white/black minstrel show. Yet even the Ethiopian business is not without redemptive characteristics. Some beautiful songs did emerge, for example, Stephen Foster's "Old Folks at Home," and minstrelsy did provide theatrical training for blacks who would later emerge as black faces rather than in blackface.

The Promoter

Between 1850 and 1900, the number of urban centers in America with a population greater than 8,000 grew sevenfold. Between 1880 and 1900, the urban population more than doubled, from 14 million to 30 million. The rural-to-urban shift and the waves of newcomers from Europe created masses of city dwellers who sought inexpensive entertainment to replace the folk culture from which they had been uprooted. In the latter half of the nineteenth century, a new figure—the promoter—appeared on the American scene. The promoter gave the masses what they wanted—spectacle. And the quintessential promoter was P. T. Barnum. He "sold" America on Jenny Lind, "the Swedish Nightingale,"

Jumbo the elephant, and the midget Tom Thumb. Combining noontime parades, ballyhoo, and the notion of a circuit of entertainment, Barnum transformed the circus into a gigantic spectacle that would have been the envy of any Roman emperor.

P. T. Barnum saw what was going on in America. He saw that a mass audience, rootless and yearning for diversion, was being created. He saw that steamboats and railroad trains could bring spectacle to masses of people who were so concentrated in single areas that huge profits could be realized. In short, he epitomized the concept of traveling entertainment on the grand scale. Barnum, of course, could not foresee that when the railroad was supplanted by the automobile, the Main Street parade would be crowded off the scene. Nor could he have foreseen that mechanical forms of entertainment, the piano roll and the phonograph, would bring entertainment into the parlor. But the Barnum spirit did invade the area of musical production itself. This spirit was manifest in the creation of Tin Pan Alley.

Tin Pan Alley

Looking backward, it is clear that Tin Pan Alley* was a necessary stage in the evolution of the modern music industry. Up until the last two decades of the nineteenth century, the emergence of a "hit" tune was pretty much a haphazard thing. Traveling entertainers would spark interest in a tune by performing it, and scattered music publishers would respond to demand without much analysis. Major music publishers rather grudgingly supplied popular sheet music. Since the time of the Singing Schools, the backbone of their business had been the production of hymn books and instruction books. For most, music publishing in general, and certainly popular-music publishing, was considered peripheral. In the 1850s Stephen Foster, for example, agreed to let E. P. Christy's name appear on the title page of "Old Folks at Home" as author and composer since he did not wish to be identified with the "Ethiopian business." Three brash young entrepreneurs stand out as founders of Tin Pan Alley and the "pop music industry"—Frank Harding, T. B. Harms, and Willis Woodward.

*Tin Pan Alley was named by the journalist/songwriter/public relations man, Monroe Rosenfeld, in a series of articles for the New York *Mirror* in 1903, when he referred to Harry von Tilzer's out-of-tune piano as the producer of "tin pan music" and the street—Twenty-eighth—where von Tilzer's music-publishing firm was located, as Tin Pan Alley. Later, von Tilzer claimed credit for the sobriquet. Irving Berlin began his career as a "song plugger" for von Tilzer. Berlin was part of an act, the Three Keatons, and Buster Keaton was the youngest member of this trio.

Frank Harding was the son of a New York publisher (we would call the elder Harding a "job shopper" today). In 1879 Frank took over his father's business and hit upon the idea of hiring songwriters, for a few dollars or a drink, to give him the publishing rights to sentimental ballads. Immortal ballads such as "My Sweetheart's the Man in the Moon," "Where Did You Get That Hat?" and "Throw Him Down McCloskey" earned a fortune for Harding. Tom Harms, together with his brother Alex, struck gold by publishing hit songs from successful Broadway musicals. They also discovered the technique of "placing" songs in successful shows. Into a rather pedestrian musical called *A Trip to Chinatown,* they interpolated three tunes, "The Bowery," "Reuben, Reuben," and "Push Dem Clouds Away." Each song became a hit in 1892. Willis Woodward captured the sentimental ballad market by publishing Banks Winter's "White Wings" in 1884. Introduced by the Thatcher, Primrose, and West Minstrels in Boston, "White Wings" became a phenomenal hit. Later, Paul Dresser (brother of the novelist Theodore Dreiser) wrote sentimental hit after hit for Woodward. Paul Dresser had achieved considerable fame as "Mr. Bones" with the Billy Rice Minstrels in 1885. Woodward also hit upon the idea of paying entertainers to sing songs published by him. It was the beginning of payola.

Another Tin Pan Alley denizen was Jay Witmark. Witmark pioneered the idea of composing and publishing songs *and* paying for the interpolation of his songs into theatrical productions. The king of composers *cum* publishers, however, was Charles K. Harris. Starting out in Milwaukee, Harris created a "monster" sentimental ballad, "After the Ball." Moving to New York, Harris built a successful publishing house around this single hit tune, the first multimillion seller (Ewen, 1964). But our purpose here is not to document the rise and fall of Tin Pan Alley; David Ewen has already done that in a lively manner. Tin Pan Alley is crucial to our narrative because it represents an important precursor to the model of monopolistic capitalism discussed in chapter 1. Tin Pan Alley brought about the concentration of music publishing in New York. It rationalized—through production with purpose—the popular-music industry. It created the idea of a standardized product in popular music through the sentimental ballad produced on cue. And, most important, Tin Pan Alley represented the control of popular taste, not from the point of view of some religious or elite set of standards but through the market mechanism.

Tin Pan Alley sweatshops produced some great music. Its composers, such as Irving Berlin, George Gershwin, and Jerome Kern, wrote popular music that approached greatness. New forms—musical comedy, the Broadway show—emerged. At their best, they yielded a musical literature to rival the musical literature of European operetta. The creative human spirit triumphed over the profit motive.

Students of industrialization often divide manufacturing into three major functions: production, distribution, and consumption. The production of goods and services essentially involves the application of technology (including the social, such as bureaucracy). Consumption is controlled by the amount of demand for some product or service; the economies of scale achieved after the Industrial Revolution came about only with the discovery that demand could be created. Distribution is the connection between producers and consumers. Song plugging, payola, and the post-Civil War boom in parlor pianos and pump organs created a demand for sheet music. This demand in turn stimulated Tin Pan Alley tunesmiths to crank out songs using the assembly line model. Not just a few, but hundreds of sentimental ballads would be turned out until the market was saturated.

Standardized products always lead to a rationalized (and therefore predictable) market. Distribution (selling) replaces production as the creative center of the industrial process. P. T. Barnum learned to sell anything from midgets to elephants. Tin Pan Alley publishers learned to sell genre tunes, as transportation and communication networks destroyed a self-balanced America. The father of vaudeville, which together with burlesque replaced the minstrel show as a favored mass entertainment, was B. F. Keith. B. F. Keith, who came to vaudeville promotion from the circus, used the idea of a nationwide circuit to generate a large-scale demand for popular variety entertainment.

The paradigm, first developed in the industrialization of textile production in England, was applied to popular entertainment. A mass audience was created through immigration into urban centers; a cheap standardized format developed, and the circulation of the product on a mass scale was fostered through the circuit. Stars became important not only because they could draw audiences but also because they could sell a product—the sheet music of the songs they sang. From this perspective, the mass media of radio, the record industry, and the movie business were dramtically foreshadowed in the minstrel show, the circus, vaudeville, and burlesque. That the mass media "killed" these earlier forms (and eventually Tin Pan Alley itself) was simply a further rationalization of the process. The identification of the movie star with his or her image on the screen, the association of the recording artist with recorded output, and the definition of radio (and later TV) as sponsor-controlled brings the threatening mystery of artistic creativity under the less threatening (to capitalists) mystery of the market.

Ragtime

Tin Pan Alley bowdlerized another Afro-American musical form after it had exhausted the sentimental ballad. In the 1890s Tin Pan Alley discovered ragtime,* a style that evolved out of an earlier dance tradition. Slaves were often forced to substitute stomping and hand or foot patting for the drums denied them by their slave masters. Complex rhythmic patterns were established for ring shouts and dances in this manner. (So-called "hambone" is a reflection of this process; it is the slapping and patting of the body to establish astonishing rhythmic patterns. Most of us have seen it on TV shows such as the "Amateur Hour.")

In most instrumental dance music, the melody was carried by either the fiddle or the banjo. A natural division was created by this process: complex rhythm apposed by conventional melody. A conventional popular trio of the nineteenth century consisting of fiddle, bass, and wind instrument could create this syncopated dance music. But dance hall owners, always looking for a way to cut overhead costs, substituted one musician (the piano player) for three. The result of this effort at conservation was the creation of the "jig piano." The jig piano (or dance piano) replaced the small dance ensemble with the piano keyboard. The left hand took over the task of stomping and patting out a rhythm, and the right hand produced the melody. With the functional separation of right and left hand came a different way to use the piano as a substitute for the whole band. A kind of wonderful schizophrenia developed, involving a contrapuntal sense of the bass and treble halves of the piano keyboard.

Thus the figure of the honky-tonk pianist became a part of American folklore. At its best, true ragtime became an important influence on jazz. Deeply rooted in Afro-American music, both as piano music and in larger orchestral works, ragtime music demonstrated that syncopation could be at the core rather than on the periphery of a musical form. In the hands of a master such as Scott Joplin (who, incidentally, had performed as a minstrel-show musician), rags elevated popular music to new heights. The verve, drive, and beauty of Joplin's "Maple Leaf Rag," published in 1899, is ample evidence of this. In the hands of the Tin Pan Alley tunesmiths, using a simplified bass figure and a lightly syncopated melody, it also became a form that lent itself to parlor piano cliché.

The ragtime influence was also evident in the music of syncopated dance bands and brass bands. At the turn of the century, America was caught up in a craze of march music. It was a period of chauvinism, and

---

*No one is sure about the origin of this name. The best guess is that the term refers to the "ragged," or syncopated, nature of the music.

the military march provided a patriotic outlet for this spirit. John Philip Sousa, a composer of great skill and an indefatigable organizer, flooded America's consciousness with well-crafted marches and fired the imagination with lavish military parades. March music provided an important bridge to early jazz, especially in New Orleans. With its steady four-four meter, the march makes "metronome sense" obvious and arouses a conscious recognition of the importance of rhythm. A syncopated march illustrates the possibility of adding complexity to a steady beat.

The late nineteenth century was a critical time in the cultural transition of American society to secularism. The industrial takeoff documented by Rostow, and cited in the opening paragraphs of this chapter, meant a shift of religious justification for the profit motive to an economic one. The exuberant nationalism of many of the Sousa marches manifested this optimistic self-sufficiency. The American eagle replaced the Christian cross as a symbol of the good. The case for ragtime as an important independent musical influence should not be understated. The "Maple Leaf Rag" had structure and formal discipline as well as the other characteristics I have emphasized.

Sousa did a lot to popularize the cakewalk (especially in Europe) and ragtime. So did Arthur Pryor and other famous brass band leaders. The impact of religious music has been emphasized in this chapter because it covers three centuries of American history. With the growth of transportation and communication networks toward the end of the nineteenth century, secularization simply overcame earlier conceptualizations of what was important. Writing the history of this period is a little like looking through a telescope at the wrong end. Ragtime, the march music craze, and the growth of Tin Pan Alley caught up earlier, less hectic musical developments into the whirlwind of the emerging music industry. In the next chapter the development of the music industry will be considered in some detail in order to reassess the influence of black America on the rural industrial crossover music called the blues.

The purpose of this chapter has been to lend support to the hypothesis that many of the elements that later emerged as jazz were deeply rooted in American musical culture. The patterns of settlement and the rich and varied musical heritages, both European and African, that came together in the early American period laid the foundation for the emergence of a new musical genre. Folk pentatonicism and the musical deviance manifested in the Singing Schools, together with the characteristics of African song styles and polyrhythm, gave American music, with its two divergent cultures, a base upon which to build a new music. The religious connection between these two cultures provided a common ground through camp meetings and the spiritual that permitted this syncretism to develop. Industrialization in the late nineteenth century and the need for mass entertainment fostered the growth of a unique popular music industry based on the urban industrial model. In the next section the focus will be on immediate precursors of jazz and the emergence of that music out of the welter of cross influences.

PART 2
The Emergence and

Development of Jazz

chapter 3

Am I Blue?

INTRODUCTION

Walt Whitman Rostow has suggested that the United States experienced an economic "takeoff into self-sustained growth" between 1843 and 1860 (Rostow, 1956). This takeoff led to phenomenal industrial development, especially in the decades following the Civil War. Cycles of economic boom and bust followed the takeoff of capital development. Waves of immigration from Europe and internal migration transformed the United States into an urban society. A spirit of restlessness and movement overtook the land.

A key social invention necessitated by large, heterogeneous, dislocated urban populations and an expanding frontier in the world of late nineteenth-century American entertainment was the circuit. Shows of every kind were put on the road to reach as large a proportion of the new mass audience as possible. Entertainment circuits would hardly have been possible without the development of the railroad as a major means of transporting people as well as goods and material throughout an expanding America. The circus wagon was replaced by the railroad car; the railroad station itself became as much a part of the folklore of minstrelsy, vaudeville, and burlesque as the asbestos curtain. Trains meant movement and became a symbol as well as a sign of the new industrial order. Trains, however, provide more than a metaphor for the most important wellspring of jazz—the blues.

> Railroads . . . have been a powerful symbol in Negro folklore since the *ante-bellum* years of slavery. Figuring prominently in spirituals and ballads, they have provided an unending stream of blues since the earliest noted examples. Though other subjects may have declined, blues about railroads still figure in the work of most singers. Symbolic of migration, power, escape, the locomotives have also served as an important sexual symbol (Charters, 1975, p. 21).

The key to the blues lies in understanding their sense of eternal melancholy. The blues are as crucial to jazz as steam power is to the locomotive; the power of the blues propels most authentic jazz just as surely as steam drove the early trains. It should be clear, however, that not all jazz is blues-based, but without the blues, the shape of jazz as we know it is inconceivable.

THE BLUES FORM

In chapter 1, I offered a tentative definition of jazz. I also made it clear that not all the elements discussed were present in all jazz. I shall offer here, in the same fashion, a tentative definition of the blues. As was the case with jazz, these extracted elements of the blues profit from hindsight. Most authorities would now accept a definition of the "standard" blues as a form consisting of four stanzas of three lines each, with each stanza sung or chanted to the instrumental accompaniment of twelve bars of music based on the common three-chord harmony of tonic, subdominant, and dominant notes or chords. Four bars on the tonic, two on the subdominant, two again on the tonic, two on the dominant, and two final bars on the tonic make up the typical blues progression. Typically pentatonic in conception, the blues generate tonal ambiguity around the third and seventh degrees of the diatonic scale.* Around these degrees, microtones—smaller than a halftone—become a possibility.

Very many blues, especially early blues, contained eight or sixteen bars or measures. (A bar or measure indicates the meter or "pulse" of a piece of music. Four-four time means that each unit of music is divided into four equal beats, each representing a quarter of the total time elapsed; three-four time divides the same time into three beats with one of the beats held over two of the quarters, and so on.) Not all blues stanzas

---

*These blue notes or tones are usually thought of as flat, but it is more accurate to think of them as off the expected pitch. Here again is an African influence, since that music is typically not constructed around tonal keys as in the Western tradition. The term "worried" best describes this phenomenon. Other tonal intervals, such as the fifth, also occasionally have this same characteristic in the blues. These notes are microtonal rather than flat. The blue notes suggest chromaticism.

Chromaticism is the introduction of half steps between the whole tones of the scale. By convention there are five such tones in Western music. They are represented by the black keys on the piano. Seven full steps plus five half steps yield a twelve-tone scale. The theoretical and aural implications of twelve tones versus seven or five are enormous, and even today in most popular music, semitones are used sparingly—except for jazz-related music.

follow the three-line format. All blues, however, tend toward the common three-chord harmonic resolution of much Western music.*

As Southern amply demonstrates (1971, p. 192), early slave "sorrow" songs often used the three-line stanza. Stearns (1956, p. 104) also suggests that this poetic format is African in origin. The problem is then to square the three-stanza (often in iambic pentameter) poem with the usual bar structure of Western music. The answer, musically, is to allow instrumental improvisation to fill out bars three and four of each line. In jazz this instrumental fill-in is called a "break."

Blues lyrics usually follow an A-A-B format, that is, line two is a repeat of line one, and line three "answers" the first two lines (SCCJ-I-3).† For example:

> The blues is a lowdown achin' heart disease,
> The blues is a lowdown achin' heart disease,
> It's like consumption, killin' you by degrees.

---

*Certain combinations of notes, through convention, become "pleasing." In traditional harmony, certain tones in European music are designed as "keys." A key is any note now recognized as "proper" because it appears on the keyboard of the conventionalized piano. Once a key is selected, intervals of thirds, fifths, sevenths, and others, become relative to that first conventionalized note. The jump between the first and the fourth tones creates "tension." The jump between the first and fifth tones together creates "resolution." The sounding of the first, third and fifth tones together creates "fullness." In the key of C, E represents a "third." C-E-G is a tetrachord (three notes sounded together) that is pleasing to our ears. The note C is called the tonic note of the key of C. The note G is called the dominant. The note F, called the subdominant, is interesting because it creates an implied demand for a return to the tonal center C. (The note D, a second, could have performed the same function but seems too close to the tonal center for such distinction.) In order to avoid confusion, scholars refer to the chord based on the keyboard as I (since the particular root or key note is variable, that is, can be any note). D in the key of C, II, is mathematically defined as a chord based on one tone above I; III is two notes above I, and so on. (Cf. chapter 1, pages 17–18). The most common European harmonic progression is I-IV-I-V-I. This pattern creates some tension (IV) but is quickly resolved through a return to I through V. Variation of this pattern can be created by using V⁷ instead of V for resolution, that is, by piling the seventh above G, another third, on the triad V. That seventh chord generates just enough dissonance to make our ears perk up and is a common device in Western music and in jazz. In the key of C, V⁷ would be the notes G-B-D-F sounded together.

†SCCJ refers to the Smithsonian Collection of Classic Jazz. The roman numeral refers to the record (one through six in chronological order), and the arabic number refers to the "cut" or band on the LP. This form of citation will be followed throughout *The Jazz Text.* You are urged to pause and listen to this selection before proceeding.

Or:

> I'm goin' to the river, take my rocker chair,
> I'm goin' to the river, take my rocker chair,
> If the blues overtake me, gonna rock away from here.
>   (Quoted in Oliver, 1968, p. 18)

In both the illustrations above, about a measure and a half of music is left over on each line for a break. Two possibilities for the call-and-response paradigm are presented in the standard blues. The first is from the verse structure itself, where the singer has an opportunity during the twice-repeated call to think up a response. The second opportunity comes from the apposition of vocal call to instrumental response provided in each line of the stanza.

There is a formal parallel to the structure of the blues in the European ballade, which flourished in the thirteenth and fourteenth centuries. Ballades employed a three-stanza, A-A-B format. Each stanza, however, typically consisted of seven or eight lines and lacked the staccato impact of the blues. The ballade form can be found in the work of later European composers such as Schubert, Brahms, and Chopin. While no evidence exists that the medieval ballade influenced the development of the blues, the presence of this form in the European tradition once again underlines the possibility of convergence (syncretism) in European and African musical approaches (Apel and Daniel, 1961, 22–23).

Both Gunther Schuller (1968) and Wilfrid Mellers (1967) have argued that most Afro-American music (including the spirituals) prior to the Civil War was monodic, that is, not harmonic, in conception.* (Of course, the concert performances of spirituals in the eighteen-seventies and eighteen-eighties employed harmonic devices since they were performed for white not black audiences.) As blues singers began to break away from the spiritual tradition and accompany themselves on guitars, a major musical problem arose. The Afro-American song tradition—modal (not key-oriented) and oriented toward unison singing—had to be reconciled with the well-tempered (key-oriented, chromatic) European guitar (and later the piano and orchestra). The blues solution to this problem—essentially the problem of harmony—generated a whole new conception of music. The deceptively simple structure of the blues turned out to be an ingenious contribution to the world's music. Gilbert Chase has described this process.

---

* In the metaphor employed in chapter 1, nonrhythmic aspects of this music were horizontal rather than vertical in conception.

The solo voice is the "leader"; the instruments "follow the leader" but also weave semi-independent melodic lines, while at the same time filling in the harmony and marking the beat of the rhythm. When the voice ceases at the end of a melodic statement (i.e., a line of the verse), it is "answered" by the instruments, which then find themselves "on their own," free to assert their individuality boldly before the voice assumes its ascendency again in the next vocal statement. And at the end, when the voice had finished with its third line, it is the instruments that have the final say. Since each vocal statement is answered by an instrumental statement, there is a perfect antiphonal pattern that corresponds to a fundamental device of Afro-American music.

Since the instruments, in addition to "answering" the voice, also weave their melodic lines along with it, we get the element of polyphony in the blues, with a more or less complex contrapuntal texture, depending on the number of instruments involved. And since the singer will sometimes follow a melodic line independent of the underlying harmony, we also get the element of polytonality (or more accurately, bitonality), that is, the simultaneous use of two or more keys. Thus the vocal and instrumental blues, within their deceptively simple framework, are capable of considerable complexity and variety (Chase, 1966, p. 453–54).

The blues dramatically foreshadowed the collision of at least three musical trends. American folk music tended toward a free, pentatonic conception of whole-tone intervals. Western "art" music had, since the sixteenth century, moved toward chromaticism with formal complex harmonics. Afro-American song represented an accommodative approach rooted in a non-Western, rhythmically sophisticated, modal music. The human voice was the primary instrument of the blues. Under intense cultural pressure, the blues voice reconciled these divergent tendencies of American music. Formal musical instruments built to handle the twelve-tone scale were, in turn, adapted to the flexible vocal conception of the blues. Jazz, an instrumental music, inherited from the blues this nonformal sense of the musical instrument as a voice. As a result, beginning with the blues, the limitations of conventional instruments were simply set aside.

Whenever jazz moves too far from "the blues sense," it is in danger of becoming nonjazz. Returning to the language analogy of chapter 1, both blues and jazz come from the same linguistic family; there are many cognates between the two. Further, the blues are a progenitor of jazz. Rooted in black folk culture, the blues are the Afro-American touchstone of American jazz. Paradoxically, the development of the blues provided a European-oriented harmonic understructure for the Afro-American song. That understructure—jazz players refer to harmonics as "the changes" (referring to chord changes)—is carried over into jazz transformations of other forms, such as the sixteen- and thirty-two-bar A-A-B-A formats of American popular song.

THE BLUES CONTENT

Historically, the development of the blues is not surprising. A people who could create the beautiful cadences of the spiritual out of the abject degradation of slavery should also be able to create music out of the cruel and unfulfilled promise of emancipation. Rarely in the history of humankind had so much been promised to so many but yielded so little as the Fourteenth Amendment to the Constitution of the United States. The blues built slowly. Black men served time on the chain gang for minor infractions after Reconstruction. Blacks who became technically free but were locked into the wage slavery of sharecropping gave voice (often in veiled terms) to the injustice of the new order. Field hollers and work songs took on a new meaning as former slaves were left to "compete" in a market economy for which they were not equipped, having been systematically placed at a disadvantage occupationally and educationally.

An unintended consequence of emancipation was to divide the population of the United States into two castes, one black and one white, with the whites unequivocally in command. Black people found themselves defined as "niggers." (This tragic situation contributed mightily to the development of New Orleans jazz, as we shall see in the next chapter.) People with any noticeable trace of "black blood" were déclassé. The blues became their music.*

The blues did not evolve as an "art" music. While there is little direct evidence from the prerecording era, there is much indirect evidence that the standard blues form emerged slowly. At least in part, this gradual emergence was a result of the diversity of the black experience in America, both before and after the Civil War. The blues is certainly a "folk" music but not the folk music of a small, contained ethnic group.

---

* Many middle-class blacks, including intellectuals, rejected the blues. The harsh reality for most black Americans, which the blues expressed, represented a threat to the fragile status of "the black bourgeoisie," to use Franklin Frazier's apt designation (Frazier, 1957).

Rather it was (and is) the music of the black diaspora that followed the war between the states.

The black population of the United States dispersed in the late nineteenth and early twentieth centuries. The spread of the boll weevil from Mexico into southern cotton fields in the seventies and eighties affected the livelihoods of sharecroppers and small cotton producers; crops failed at an alarming rate. As one blues lyric had it, "I'm so far down, down looks like up to me." Lured by the prospect of better jobs on the frontier and in the cities, black men, and sometimes their families, left the plantations in large numbers. In noncotton sectors of the economy, there was much labor-intensive activity. Turpentine and logging enterprises needed hands; northern industry needed workers; the railroads needed laborers. In a sad pattern that was to repeat itself again and again, black workers were pressed into service until other cheap labor—European and, in the case of the railroads, Oriental—could be employed. By 1915 more than half a million blacks had migrated North, and nearly 2 million had left their home states in the South. This internal migration rivaled the Atlantic migrations in its scope and disruptive consequences.

Black troubadours captured the essence of this great movement. Using whatever expressive instruments they had at hand—voice, guitars, banjos, horns, and pianos—they telescoped their experiences into musical and poetic form. With an eclecticism born of necessity, they sang and played about the loneliness of common folk cut off from home and hearth.

The earliest blues are usually referred to as country or rural blues. They might also be referred to as transitional Afro-American secular folk music, since these songs represented a shift from stable rural to marginal urban life-styles for many black Americans. Country blues dominated black secular folk music from about 1880 to 1920. It was a period in which black Americans laid the musical foundations for the emergence of individualism in the blues form.

Wandering blues singers became legends in the black enclaves of southern and southwestern cities. Hopping freight trains from one place to another and singing on street corners or in the harsh dives and juke joints of the period, these singers, like the wandering minstrels of the Middle Ages, eased some of the pain of the black underclass by rendering that pain into song and verse. Though often filled with dark humor, the blues are unsentimental. They are about sex more often than love, about rootlessness more often than temporary loneliness, about the frustration of a "no win" political and economic system rather than about the American Dream.

De four [before] day blues ain't nuffin'
But a woman wants a man.

When a woman takes de blues
She tucks her head and cries.
But when a man catches the blues,
He catches er freight and rides.

If de blues was whiskey
I'd stay drunk all de time.

De blues ain't nothin'
But a poor man's heart disease.

I got de blues,
But I'm too damn mean to cry.
     (Quoted in Oliver, 1968, p. 30)

The country blues were never fully accepted by polite society, black or white. Elements of the blues and the designation "blues," however, did influence popular music through watered-down Tin Pan Alley versions after 1900. These blues were a pale and formalistic version of the real thing.

W. C. HANDY

In his autobiography, *Father of the Blues,* W. C. Handy presents a good example of the general resistance to authentic country blues. Although Handy was several cuts above the Tin Pan Alley tunesmiths, he makes it clear that his ambition was to be a composer of "dressed-up," European-style music using native themes. But William Christopher Handy had the good sense to let authentic Afro-Americanisms influence his compositions. His "Memphis Blues" (originally called "Mr. Crump" and written as a campaign song for a local Memphis politician) uses the twelve-bar, three-line form, as well as the basic three-chord harmonic structure of the blues in the first and last strains.* His most famous song, "St. Louis Blues," is a mixture of twelve- and sixteen-bar strains and

---

* "Memphis Blues" also employs a tango rhythm (♪♩♩♪) in the bass, a dramatic foreshadowing of the Caribbean influence on jazz. A variant of this figure (♩·♪♩) was the rhythmic basis of the Charleston, a Georgia Sea Island Negro dance popularized by stride pianist James P. Johnson (Chase, 1966, p. 457). Jelly Roll Morton was later to argue that all true jazz had "a Spanish tinge" (Lomax, 1950).

three- and four-line verses. Its pattern, by the way, was widely adopted by popular-song writers to turn out hundreds of Tin Pan Alley pseudo-blues. Handy spent most of his early musical career playing in minstrel shows and leading local march and dance bands. While doing that, he kept his ears open. He reports on his experiences in the Mississippi Delta as an itinerant musician and band leader.

A lean loose-jointed Negro had commenced plunking a guitar beside me while I slept (in a train station in Tutwiler, Mississippi). His clothes were rags; his feet peeped out of his shoes. His face had on it some of the sadness of the ages. As he played, he pressed a knife on the strings of the guitar in a manner popularized by Hawaiian guitarists who used steel bars. The effect was unforgettable. His song, too, struck me instantly.

Goin' where the Southern cross' the Dog.

The singer repeated the line three times, accompanying himself on the guitar with the weirdest music I had ever heard. The tune stayed on my mind. . . . (The singer explained that he was going to Moorhead where the Southern Railroad crossed the Yellow Dog or Yazoo Delta Railroad.)

. . . Southern Negroes sang about everything. Trains, steamboats, steam whistles, sledge hammers, fast women, mean bosses, stubborn mules—all became subjects for their songs. They accompany themselves on anything from which they can extract a musical sound or rhythmical effect, anything from a harmonica to a washboard.

In this way, and from these materials, they set the mood for what we now call blues (p. 74).

A short time later, W. C. Handy described his feelings about a local band which he saw in Cleveland, Mississippi, during an engagement there in 1903.

The music they made was pretty well in keeping with their looks. They struck up one of those over-and-over strains that seem to have no very clear beginning and certainly no ending at all. The strumming attained a disturbing monotony, but on and on it went, a kind of stuff that has long been associated with cane rows and levee camps. Thump-thump-thump went their feet on the floor. Their eyes rolled. Their shoulders swayed. And through it all that little agonizing strain persisted. It was not really annoying or unpleasant. Perhaps "haunting" is a better word, but I commenced to wonder if anybody besides small town rounders and their running mates would go for it.

The answer was not long in coming. A rain of silver dollars began to fall around the outlandish, stomping feet. The dancers went wild. Dollars, quarters, halves—the shower grew heavier and continued so long I strained my neck to get a better look. There before the boys lay more money than my nine musicians were being paid for the entire engagement. Then I saw the beauty of primitive music. They had the stuff the people wanted. It touched the spot. Their music wanted polishing, but it contained the essence. Folks would pay money for it. The old conventional music was well and good and had its place, no denying that, but there was no virtue in being blind when you had good eyes.

That night a composer was born, an *American* composer. Those country black boys at Cleveland had taught me something that could not possibly have been gained from books, something that would, however, cause books to be written. Art, in the high-brow sense, was not in my mind. My idea of what constitutes music was changed by the sight of that silver money cascading around the splay feet of a Mississippi string band (pp. 76–77).

Very few blacks, W. C. Handy excepted, achieved commercial success from the country blues. The blues had to be transformed from country to city blues and be recorded before black artists gained real recognition for this astonishing contribution. Handy's apology for authentic black folk music speaks for itself.

CITY BLUES

Most of the country blues singers were men who typically accompanied themselves on the guitar (although jug bands and string bands were used in the country blues era). The classic or city blues singers were, by contrast, women accompanied by an orchestra. The classic blues period, from 1920 to 1940, was the era of the race record.

On Valentine's Day, 1920, Sophie Tucker was scheduled to record two sides of Okeh records, but she was not able to make the date. Perry Bradford, the popular black composer whose songs were to be recorded, suggested a black woman named Mamie Smith as a substitute (Oliver, 1960, p. 1). That disk, with "That Thing Called Love" on one side and "You Can't Keep a Good Man Down," sold 75,000 copies within a few months. Less than six months later, another Bradford tune called "Crazy Blues" was recorded by Smith. "Crazy Blues" was the first recorded vocal version of the twelve-bar blues by a black artist. It sold 7,500 records a week for months. No one was more surprised at the success of these records than the Okeh executives. Soon, other companies began to employ the Okeh formula. The race record market was discovered, and it was a gold mine. Record companies catering to the black market sprang up. With little advertising and with very little overhead in artists' fees, record companies could count on thousands of blacks to plunk down seventy-five cents (not an inconsiderable sum in those days) for the latest blues hit.

In retrospect, the success of the blues was not surprising. The blues tradition was at least forty years old by 1920. Blacks, uprooted and marginal in the new industrial order, must have yearned for a way to become a part of the new technological era. The blues record and the blues star gave them "a piece of the action." The diffusion of the blues on records in turn had a profound reciprocal effect: some "raw" and "low-down" blues were cleaned up for the recording horn; protest about the American system was often disguised. Much censorship was self-imposed by those artists who knew what they had to do in order to make it and also had a sense of community standards. It might also explain why female singers were more likely than males to be recorded, even though the country blues singers were almost exclusively males (Oliver, 1960). They were less of a threat to the male-dominated social order.

It should not be thought, however, that race records were the exclusive domain of female city blues singers. In fact, from the mid-twenties onward, country blues singers such as Blind Lemon Jefferson and Leroy Carr made records that sold thousands of copies. Lonnie Johnson, a successful blues artist, recorded with Louis Armstrong's Hot Five in 1927, with Duke Ellington in 1928, and in 1929 with the legendary white jazz guitarist, Eddie Lang, who recorded under the pseydonym Blind Willie Dunn (Charters, 1975, pp. 82–83). The giants of the recording industry, Victor and Columbia, both flooded the race records market with field recordings (recordings made in improvised southern studios, not during live performances) from 1927 through the early days of the Great Depression (Charters, 1975, pp. 86–106). The depression hit the recording industry very hard and led to the collapse, or near collapse, of most record companies. Radio saved mass music but nearly dried up the Afro-American stream of mass popular culture, especially the blues.

What happened to blues during this period parallels the process of dialectic documented by Berger (1947) and Leonard (1962) for jazz and later by Kamin (1974) for rock and roll. In briefest terms, this process involved the resistance to black culture in its most vital manifestations by white America. The black experience had to be "sweetened up" for public consumption. Although aspects of the minstrel show filtration of black life can be found in the classic blues, there is one important difference: most blues records and virtually all country blues records were made for blacks, not for whites. Certainly the mask slipped a little.*

The collaboration of blues singers and jazz musicians was crucial to the development of both forms. The twelve-bar, three-chord, and three-stanza form of the blues strengthened the harmonic underpinnings of jazz and provided a structural unity that allowed formal composition and arrangement a place in jazz improvisation. For blues singers, orchestral accompaniment meant that musical discipline became as important to a good blues performance as emotion. The collaborations of Lonnie Johnson and the greatest of all classic blues singers, Bessie Smith (not related to Mamie), with jazzmen Louis Armstrong and Fletcher Henderson are evidence of this assertion. In fact, Gunther Schuller has argued that the blues craze of the twenties and early thirties may have saved jazz from the gimmickry of the jazz craze of the late teens and early twenties.

> But it has never been emphasized sufficiently that the blues craze, following on the heels of the novelty-jazz fad, served to clarify the distinctions between a deeply felt musical expression of a certain ethnic group and a rather superficial, derived commercial commodity. In the process, the blues craze may even have saved jazz from oblivion. Perhaps King Oliver's Creole Jazz Band of 1923, and the subsequent efforts of Armstrong and Morton, would have saved jazz anyway. But already in 1922, the blues recordings of Mamie Smith and the hundreds of other girls who were keeping the recording studios busy were providing abundant evidence that there was a wide gulf between the blues and its attendant instrumental style, and the tricky slapstick music that was being passed off as New Orleans jazz. At the same time, the blues made quite clear the musical distinctions between it and the commercial world of dance bands with their smoothly insipid saxophones and unimaginative stock arrangements (Schuller, 1968, p. 252).

During the period of the classic blues, Chicago and New York became major blues centers, in large part because of the location of record-

---

*As Paul Oliver rightly points out, blues research is at a serious disadvantage because of censorship. Our knowledge of the form and content of the blues is based almost entirely on recorded output. We have evidence from interviews and from more recently recorded material that themes of protest, for example, were indeed employed by the country blues singers (Oliver, 1960, p. 7). Classic blues singers became "creatures" of the music industry and the record business. That some of them, such as Bessie Smith, transcended this bondage is testimony to their strength, not a credit to the system.

ing studios in those cities. Both cities had black populations of considerable size. Chicago, however, provided continuity with the past since the city (along with a host of regional centers such as Memphis, Houston, and other middle-sized places) had also been an important center of blues throughout the country blues era. Situated near the headwaters of the Mississippi, and the gateway to the West, Chicago had long been a center of black migration from the South.

After 1940, urban blues supplanted classic blues. Male singers again became dominant, with electric guitars and the familiar rhythm-and-blues mélange of saxophones and drums backing the vocalist. Charles Keil (1966) has suggested that the urban blues fused the older "preaching" tradition with a secular context on the contemporary scene.

> In spite of the fact that blues singing is ostensibly a secular, even profane, form of expression, the role [of blues singer] is intimately related to secular roles in the Negro community. Second, the role is all-encompassing in nature, either assimilating or overshadowing all other roles an adult male may normally be expected to fulfill (Keil, 1966, p. 143).

Older country blues singers such as Leadbelly (Huddie Ledbetter) and Big Bill Broonzy were rediscovered. Younger blues singers went back to the roots of the blues in the black experience. Still later (in the mid-fifties), urban blues infused rock and roll with vitality. And eventually rock and roll created broader interest in jazz in a manner analogous to the revitalization of early jazz by blues during the classic blues period.

Paralleling the development of the blues in the prejazz era, an instrumental form deeply rooted in Afro-American tradition emerged. Ragtime music was a response to the same conflicting tendencies in popular American musical culture that produced the blues. It also responded to the boom in the manufacture of pianos just before the turn of the century.

A NOTE ON RAGTIME

For most of us, the essence of ragtime music is syncopation. In chapter 1 (pages 15–16) syncopation was defined. But ragtime is more than just syncopated music. Ragtime built upon the great popularity of minstrelsy and the "coon song" as well as upon march and cakewalk cadences in America just before the turn of the century. This was the era of John Philip Sousa and the marching band. Sousa's famous "Washington Post March" was used as a two-step cakewalk dance.

The popular dance in two-four time transmitted through marches was an important influence on ragtime. Schafer and Riedel suggest:

> The dance feeling in ragtime cannot be overemphasized. It is clear that it was the single most vital impulse behind the creation of ragtime, and it is the source of the complex rhythmic pulse in the music (Schafer and Riedel, 1973, p. 8).

The most important difference between ragtime, the blues, and jazz is that ragtime is not improvised. Instead, it is a composed genre with from three to five themes in sixteen-bar strains (Schafer and Riedel, 1973, p. 55 ff.).

> The problem that both listeners and performers faced at the turn of the century was that ragtime was poised between two traditions—that of nineteenth-century sentimental parlor music and that of rough, black, country folk-dance styles. The white would-be ragtime pianist had a background in one tradition but not in the other; while the black performer, coming to a rather difficult and exactingly precise score, would hear the outline of the folk style in it but not see the decorous modifications Joplin had imposed (Schafer and Riedel, 1973, p. 89).

Scott Joplin, composer of the all-time rag classic, "Maple Leaf Rag" (SCCJ-I-1), along with James Scott and Joseph Lamb, made ragtime an art form of great beauty and dimension. But ragtime lent itself to expurgation, and Tin Pan Alley was prepared to schematize it.

A ragtime craze in America predated the era of the phonograph. Rudi Blesh and Harriet Janis suggest that the public was aware of raglike music as early as 1893, but they define the ragtime era as the period of massive sheet-music and piano-roll sales from 1897 to 1917 (Blesh and Janis, 1966, pp. 4–6). Ragtime music was (and is) rooted in the division between rhythmic and melodic elements. The rhythmic or bass portion is a "rolling" figure (*basso ostinato*) in two-four time. The treble melody is played against this steady bass figure with unexpected accents and "fills." Dynamic tension is therefore created in two parts. Ragtime music originated in the competition between rhythm and melody in folk-guitar duets and duets between instrumental sections, as well as between vocal and instrumental collusions. The piano keyboard tended to diminish this duality because of its (relatively) broad range across the musical spectrum.

Unlike the blues, which has shown great tenacity in clinging to its Afro-American roots, ragtime broke away from those roots and developed into a form easily packaged for the commercial market. Ragtime is fun. It presents a technical challenge to would-be virtuosos and easily lends itself to formal elaboration. It is gay, happy music; the dimension of unsentimental melancholy, so important to the blues, is missing. There is something disquietingly mechanical about much popular ragtime music—the perfect vehicle for the mechanistic piano roll.

Black ragtime composers such as Scott Joplin were so caught up in the formal potential of ragtime that they expended great energy seeking acceptance as "legitimate" composers, basing their work on folk themes à la Dvořák.* Racism, of course, made that a tragically futile enterprise. Coon songs, minstrel routines, and ragtime had to be happy, light and—most of all—comforting music about well-adjusted, grateful ex-slaves. That Scott Joplin spent a large portion of his fortune and much effort to get his ragtime opera *Treemonisha* produced legitimately (and ragtime recognized as a legitimate art form) is bittersweet testimony to this problem (Blesh and Janis, 1966). The Tin Pan Alley view of ragtime as exploitable, happy music defeated Joplin's view of ragtime as American "classical" music.

Two other forms of Afro-American piano music became especially important influences in the development of jazz, in spite of Tin Pan Alley bowdlerization. In the West and Southwest, boogie-woogie, or the "fast Western," developed as a powerful and percussive underpinning to instrumental Afro-American music. In the East, ragtime was transformed into Harlem stride. Both were piano music, and both extended the potential of Afro-American music.

Boogie-Woogie

Boogie-woogie is a piano style that is perhaps closest to the vocal blues in conception and execution. Although most often characterized as a type of ragtime (Chase, 1966, p. 463), boogie-woogie avoided the pretentiousness of much formal ragtime and is much closer in spirit to the improvised blues than to composed ragtime. It developed in the same western and southwestern contexts as the country blues. Typically employing the twelve-bar structure and blues harmonics, boogie-woogie relied on a persistent, percussive, *ostinato* (repeated) bass figure in the left hand of "eight beats to the bar." In the right hand (treble), interesting cross-rhythms and melodic invention struggled against the steady pulse of the left.

---

*Dvořák, universally respected as a composer, spent a considerable period of time in the United States, and his well-publicized championing of European folk themes and American Negro music had considerable impact in musical circles.

So the music played on barrelhouse pianos naturally represented the triumph of the guitar's percussion over the vocal lyricism of the country blues. The pianist's left hand becomes kinetic rhythm, creating, with complete denial of pianistic sophistication, a thick chugging of low-spaced triads in crotchets, then in quavers, then in the thrusting dotted rhythm of boogie-woogie. Against the remorseless bass, played without variation of dynamics, is the treble, usually widely spaced, and often in complex cross-rhythms, pulling against the rhythmic-harmonic drive that apportions two chords to the bar, one on the first beat, the other on—or sometimes just before—the third. Fundamentally, barrelhouse piano is a two voiced music for the player's left and right hand (Mellers, 1967, p. 273).

Boogie-woogie was an important influence on early jazz performers in Kansas City, Chicago, and New Orleans. Especially in Kansas City, this piano style became transformed into the orchestral "riff" (the repetition of a musical phrase over and over). Later, in the hands of a master like William "Count" Basie, the boogie-woogie/blues conception of percussive impulse transformed big band jazz.

Harlem Stride

Somewhere on a continuum between commercial ragtime and the "gutsy" style of boogie-woogie lies the piano style that came to be known as Harlem stride. The country blues never gained the kind of popularity along the East Coast that they had in the rest of the country. Instead, a sophisticated blues and ragtime crossover piano music developed out of the syncopated orchestras, marching bands, and cabarets of East Coast cities.

Along the East Coast, Eubie Blake, Willie "The Lion" Smith, James P. Johnson, and others, pioneered a fusion style of piano playing. In ragtime, the left hand (bass) typically altered octaves (C and C one octave above) with chords to establish the rolling bass. In stride, tenths and other less conventional intervals and combinations of notes were played against the syncopated right hand. A broken rhythm became characteristic of this style, which distinguished it from both ragtime and boogie-woogie. It should be noted that many stride pianists also studied classical music.

Stride was more open to improvisation than either ragtime or boogie-woogie and deeply influenced later generations of jazz piano players in the New York City area. Stride piano transformed the two-handed duet format of boogie-woogie into an orchestral conception. The left hand became truly contrapuntal rather than just sustaining right-hand syncopation and improvisation. Willie "The Lion" once told me that the real test of piano playing was a "two-independent-handed approach."

Influences

New York City, of course, dominates the eastern coast of the United States, and it has always acted as a magnet for the most sophisticated aspects of popular culture. By the turn of the century, music publishing and popular song production were centered in New York. More European in orientation, pianistic and orchestral traditions in New York tended to be eclectic and technically sophisticated. Without doubt, this tradition was authentic and even expected in the abolitionist North, but it did lack the genuine sadness and poignancy of the southern blues. The eventual union of southern blues and ragtime construction was a critical factor in the development of true jazz.

Up to this point, I have discussed musical influences on early jazz. The musical threads that must be woven together are diverse in origin; the pattern in which they were woven together is complex. Three crazes figure prominently in the jazz mix. The first was the turn-of-the-century ragtime craze, followed by the early Dixieland jazz craze, which, in turn, was followed by the blues craze of the twenties. Each made accommodations to mass taste; each brought an element of Afro-American influence into the mainstream of popular American musical culture.

EARLY JAZZ

Jazz was associated with New Orleans* in the beginning, although there was other jazzlike music in different parts of the country. Too many

---

*At the turn of the century, New Orleans was musically alive with marching bands, Caribbean voodoo music, ragtime, and European salon music—a veritable crazy quilt of music. Out of this came the distillation of the "classical" New Orleans marching jazz group: a front line composed of cornet, clarinet, and trombone. The banjo (an African-derived instrument) or tuba and, later, drums, usually provided a straight four-four rhythm accompaniment. The cornet (or trumpet) played the melody because of its acoustic power, and New Orleans cornet players soon learned to embellish in order to capture audience attention (especially important in "street competitions"). The clarinet played harmony above the cornet or trumpet melody line with complex "fills" to generate excitement. The trombone player gave "bottom" to the front-line ensemble by playing the most important note in each chord change. Although limited initially, improvisation evolved as the bands became stationary. In the next chapter, New Orleans music will be considered in some detail.

migrations of bands and blues singers, piano players and minstrel shows were taking place to limit the development of early jazz to New Orleans. Martin Williams has written:

> The truth is that jazz started in New Orleans, depending entirely on what you mean by "jazz." . . . But, if we admit that this jazz music is clearly a kind of African-American music, then we are already in trouble. For all African-American music did not start in New Orleans. To put it another way, only New Orleans African-American music came from New Orleans (Williams, 1967a, p. 11).

One reason for the New Orleans focus is the fact that the first jazz recording labeled as a jazz recording was made by a New Orleans band in 1917—the all-white Original Dixieland Jazz Band. With that recording, the jazz age was ushered in. More and more musicians began to call themselves jazz musicians and were recognized as such by others. It is impossible to overestimate the importance of the phonograph record and New Orleans in the spread of this phenomenon and to the breaking down of clear distinctions between jazz and the regional music that had been developing for some time. As I have emphasized, the late 1800s and early 1900s were a time of great mobility for musicians, since music was linked to the whole circuit notion of traveling entertainment in America (Truzzi, 1968, pp. 314–22).

The one clear impression gained from reading early jazz musicians' biographies is that of mobility. The South and Southwest were filled with traveling bands, and so were the North and East. Music that would now be called jazz was being played by bands in carnivals and circuses, many rag- and blues-oriented musicians accompanied blues singers and comedians as part of the show. Musicians went wherever they thought they could get work. In addition, early jazzmen were often not fully professional; many worked at some other trade in addition to playing music. As Hentoff says in *The Jazz Life:*

> In the earliest years of jazz, however, few of the players took the music that seriously. The "musicianers" of the South and Southwest at the beginning of the century regarded the need to work at another trade during the day as a matter of course (p. 29).

Early jazz was most often incidental music. The tradition, for example, still survives in New Orleans of hiring a band to open a new drugstore, to celebrate a holiday, or to play for a dance, wedding, or funeral. The musicians, who were required to play long hours, were often short on formal training and fell back on the folk idioms that served them best. Standard tunes were repeated over and over; improvisation relieved boredom and "filled time."

Early jazz was close to being a music of the people—a music to dance to. It was the beginning of an evolution rather than a revolution into a genre. It offered some hope to those whose occupational mobility was limited. It was a job, a chance to earn money, and, perhaps, to enjoy oneself. We all take origins too seriously. It is doubtful that early jazzmen were thinking in terms of "founding schools." They were just expressing natural feelings and "making it." "The majority of the early jazzmen, however, were relatively responsible citizens who, in their roles as musicians, were playing thoroughly functional music. . . . The only critics were the dancers and drinkers" (Hentoff, 1961, p. 30).

The "functionality" of the music was universal. It was music "to do things by." Playing the music was a job. The flavor of these early "occupational structures" was captured by Willie "The Lion" Smith as he talked about the way he broke into the business in Newark around 1911.

> As you walked around the Coast (the entertainment section of Newark, New Jersey) you could always hear the tinkling of the pianos from behind the swinging doors and the banging shutters of those houses they called buffet flats, or just plain cat houses. There was action and music at any time of the day or night. That was where those "Around the Clock" blues came from. And when they opened up a new saloon they made a ceremony out of throwing away the key.
>
> I was brave and cocky enough to walk right into the saloons and go into my dance, and then pass around my derby to collect the loot. It not only got me to wearing a hat again, but gave me an opportunity to sneak some tunes on the stomp box when the regular player wasn't looking, or was at the bar taking on a load (Smith and Hoefer, 1965, p. 28).

Willie "The Lion" discussed in the same way other early jazzmen whom he met in his travels and theirs. Music in America at the turn of the century was on the move. For the black musician whose opportunities were limited and for whom music was a way out of a life as a shoeshine "boy" or porter, travel was a necessity and became a way of life. It was a chance at professional status. Speaking of Jelly Roll Morton, Alan Lomax says:

> He could not be content with his music, because jazz for him was power, a way out of a narrow valley of Jim Crow and Creole prejudice. He began to look away from New Orleans, wondering if he had the key to a larger world. After 1904 he was constantly on the prod, using New Orleans only as a base of operations (Lomax, 1950, p. 109). . . .

But well before the birth of jazz, other black entertainers were on the move in America, and they carried their roots—the blues tradition—with them. In explaining how professionalism got into the folk tradition of the blues, LeRoi Jones (Imamu Amiri Baraka) has said, "This professionalism came from the Negro theater: the black minstrel shows, traveling road shows, medicine shows, vaudeville shows, carnivals and tiny circuses all included blues singers and small or large bands" (Jones, 1963, p. 82). Although gravely constricted in their work, black performers were not all restricted to black audiences. Racism notwithstanding, Americans of African origin were part of the entertainment world and helped shape its future. The black jazzman was certainly not the first black performer to reach a large American audience.

> In 1898, Will Marion Cook, a talented composer, director and syncopater, whose "Clorindy: The Origin of the Cake-Walk" revealed the composer's recognition of the serious potentialities of Negro ragtime, won instant recognition as a pioneer in serious Negro musical comedy. John Isham, the enterprising Negro to whom the Negro theater is indebted for the break from minstrelsy to musical comedy (insofar as Negro talent was concerned), was responsible as inspiration and impetus for operettas such as Black Patti's Troubadours, which repudiated the minstrel tradition. During those same years, Bert Williams, actor and humorist, was an idol of the vaudeville stage. A sensitive and brilliant performer, a true comic artist, and one of the first Negroes to be accepted in the legitimate theater (Butcher, 1956, p. 152). . . .

It is not surprising that in 1917 James P. Johnson (SCCJ-II-4), who was to have such a profound effect on early jazz (especially in the East), could be described by Hadlock in this way:

> He was married and settled into a reasonably prosperous life of café jobs, songwriting, making piano rolls, Broadway stage work, vaudeville tours on the TOBA [the all black Theater Owners' Booking Agency] circuit, and, eventually, coaching promising youngsters like Thomas Wright Waller (Hadlock, 1965, p. 148).

Theorists would attempt to identify all the various strands that contributed to the development of jazz styles. The growth of transportation, mass media (phonographs and radio), and urbanization mixed everything together in a potpourri of styles and influences. Nat Hentoff quotes Garvin Bushell, a well-known black musician, who catches the flavor of the early commingling of styles and influences.

Ragtime piano was the major influence in that section of the country [Ohio]. Everybody tried to emulate Scott Joplin [the great ragtime composer]. The change began to come around 1912 to 1915 when the four-string banjo and saxophone came in. The players began to elaborate on the melodic lines; the harmony and rhythm remained the same. The parade music in Springfield was played by strictly march bands, but there was instrumental ragtime— and improvisation—in the dance halls.

I started on piano when I was six and continued for four years. I took up the clarinet at thirteen. Another uncle was a pianist, a devotee of Scott Joplin, and Maple Leaf Rag was one of the first things I heard. People then were also playing the fast western, what later came to be called boogie woogie. It meant a fast bass, and it was said to have come out of Texas.

We first heard instrumental ragtime in the circus bands which usually had about fourteen men—brass, clarinets and rhythm. They were Negro bands; the players improvised; and they played blues. They traveled all over the country, but the men in the band were mostly from Florida, Georgia, Tennessee, Louisiana. I don't know how my uncle got in there. I don't know when they started, but in 1912 my uncle was in his thirties and he'd been playing in circus bands nearly all his life (Hentoff and Shapiro, 1965, p. 72).

SIDNEY BECHET: AN ILLUSTRATION OF ARTISTIC FRUSTRATION

Sidney Bechet (SCCJ-II-2 and 3) is generally acclaimed as one of the great early jazzmen, and his influence on later instrumentalists is widely recognized. Up until 1919, Bechet's influence was restricted to the small coterie of musicians with whom he played in various New Orleans-based bands. Then Bechet's career took a rather interesting turn.

Bechet was heard by Will Marion Cook. . . . Cook was a violinist who had been taught the instrument since childhood and raised with the promise and strict training of a virtuoso. In young manhood, however, he was abruptly and cruelly told that there was no chance for a Negro classical violinist to succeed. Thus, Cook's Southern Syncopated Orchestra.

Cook was so impressed with Bechet that he asked him to join him, and thus it was that Bechet went East to New York and thence on his first trip to Europe in 1919 (Balliett, 1959, p. 143). . . .

But the music of Bechet was not an entirely novel phenomenon in France. The way had been heralded by an American who enjoyed a considerable reputation as a "legitimate" composer, Louis Moreau Gottschalk. Gottschalk had studied in Paris in the mid-nineteenth century and was admired by Liszt, Chopin, and Berlioz for his use of native American folk material. Gottschalk, whose mother was a Creole of color, was from New Orleans. His music was firmly rooted in the black music of Congo Square.* Various black bands had toured Europe before, but Bechet captured the attention of serious musicians and composers in the 1919 tour. Swiss conductor Ernest Ansermet, upon hearing Bechet in London in 1919, called him

> an artist of genius . . . [and described his musical inventions as] . . . admirable equally for their richness of invention, their force of accent, and their daring novelty and unexpected turns. . . . These solos already show the germ of a new style. Their form is gripping, abrupt, harsh, with a brusque and pitiless ending like that of Bach's Second Brandenberg Concerto. . . . Bechet's own way would be the highway along which the whole world will move tomorrow (Balliett, 1962, p. 136).

But the world did not move as quickly as Ansermet had thought. Bechet did not prosper. It was not until the late 1930s and early 1940s that Bechet received the acclaim at home that insured him a place in the gallery of American jazz giants. By the time he had achieved recognition in the United States, Bechet was living as an expatriate in France. As Whitney Balliett points out:

> For, by the early forties, Bechet had been elevated to the aerie occupied by men like Louis Armstrong, Bunny Berigan, Art Tatum, and Coleman Hawkins. This was brought about by an obfuscating swarm of praise (from the moldy figs) and dismissal (from the modernists), which appeared to enlarge him, the way a fog seems to swell a house or a ship (Balliett, 1962, p. 163). (In France in the fifties, Bechet became a popular cultural hero and a considerable financial success.)

* Congo Square was an area in New Orleans where African music was tolerated. I shall discuss the phenomenon at some length in the next chapter.

chapter 4

A Tale of Four Cities I Jazz as City Music and New Orleans Origins

American music in the post-Civil War period underwent sweeping changes. The importation of different musical traditions from Africa and Europe, together with the growth of a native entertainment industry, generated a volatile atmosphere for musical production. Changes in the size, composition, and distribution of the population of the United States and the development of new transportation and communication technologies meant that the potential for a mixing together of musical elements reached a state of "critical mass." The ensuing musical chain reaction took place in big cities, which provided the opportunities for important developments.

Modern cities are a consequence of **(1)** the rapid growth of specialization of activity (the division of labor) and **(2)** the technology that makes such specialization pay off in increased productive capacity. The modern city is, first and foremost, a marketplace. Goods, services, and ideas are traded for other goods, services, and ideas. The city is not only a place of struggle but also the place of opportunity, of upward mobility, for those equipped to compete in its markets.

But modern city life often creates a sense of disjunction and uprootedness, and prompts a search for meaning. Members of modern urban societies are forced to accept solidarity despite dissimilarities. City dwellers must learn—often painfully—to seek commonality.

Jazz symbolically fused many of the contradictions of modern society within itself. (Indeed, jazz is a metaphor for urban existence.) Jazz was created by an outcast minority, yet it appealed (albeit in modified form) beyond that minority. Jazz embodied the dynamic tension at the very core of modern life, the tension between the individual creator (the soloist) and the group (the ensemble), with its need for discipline and coor-

84

dination. While its most important inspiration, the blues, was rural in origin, jazz was—and is—city music. Moreover, jazz shares with the modern city a most important characteristic: both are based on exchange. The canons of jazz (outlined in chapter 1) permit it to encompass an enormous range of musical traditions; it transforms their diversity into a commonality of form and feeling.

An expanded music market allowed increasingly sophisticated musicians to present their music as a commodity to be exchanged with a larger audience for fame and fortune. That larger audience ranged from a small segment who saw the new music as an emergent art form to the drinkers and dancers who saw it simply as happy, bouncy music. Jazz players served these and many other clienteles.

As jazz emerged, it pulled together blues and popular American song structures, military and marching band cadences, and piano and dance band styles into an integrated whole that made sense musically in its own terms. As Gunther Schuller correctly points out, the earliest jazz was based on melodic embellishment and therefore was within the American tradition of melodic emphasis (Schuller, 1968, p. 65). It was surely shaped as much by its audiences as it was by its players. Those audiences were "tune oriented." Schuller says, "The music played depended almost entirely on for whom it was played" (p. 70). The market for music controlled, muted, and transformed jazz into an element of popular entertainment and culture. As an instrumental music, moreover, jazz was less threatening than, say, the vocal blues to conventional white and middle-class-black values.*

JAZZ AS CITY MUSIC

Jazz players came from all over but made their reputations in cities. Jazz, as we have come to know it from recordings and from lore and legend, came out of certain cities such as New Orleans, Kansas City, Chicago, and New York. Other cities—Detroit, Indianapolis, Newark—

---

*Based on the research of Berger (1947), Leonard (1962), and others, it is clear that jazz *was* perceived as a real threat by those who decried the devolution of European "art music" standards through the mass acceptance of popular musical forms and by those "moral entrepreneurs" who saw jazz as opening the door to primitive sexual licentiousness. The analysis by Berger and Leonard of the establishment reaction to jazz is a dramatic foreshadowing of a similar reaction some decades later to rock and roll (Kamin, 1974). As instrumental music, however, jazz was a much less direct assault. One had to know a great deal about music theory, for example, in order to perceive blue notes as an assault on the well-tempered scale.

produced important jazz players, but whether the very best jazz musicians made it to the jazz capitals, or whether they were recorded, is a moot point. The focus of jazz history must be on what was, not on what could or should have been. The story of jazz is the story of recorded jazz and has been for some time.

The big city provided an anchor for jazz because it had a population large enough and diverse enough to support new musical forms. Throughout history, cities have always been the center of the arts and especially artistic innovation. The patterns of entertainment circuits and the mass market model established in the latter part of the nineteenth century vitalized Afro-American music insofar as it transformed it into a universalistic (that is, widely accepted) and sophisticated city music. It was also necessary for each jazz capital to have a substantial black population receptive to a jazz elite. Black audiences provided a home base for budding jazz players.* (Significantly, there was no black population in far western cities to provide the springboard for a jazzlike tradition. This explains, in part, why jazz was an eastern, southern, and midwestern phenomenon.)

The large American city in the early twentieth century came to dominate its surrounding area, including smaller cities and towns, both economically and culturally. As the United States became a national society, it also became a nation of regions. Regions, however, became less and less "self-balanced" (see the discussion in chapter 2 and Mills, 1953, pp. 9—59) and more interlocked. Such interlocking, moreover, was not an even and easily understood process. In retrospect, it is possible to see how certain urban centers came to preeminence. Some had the advantage of being deep-water ports; others were near areas rich in natural resources.

Each major American jazz center was also a regional urban center. New York and, later, Chicago were superdominant and major centers for entire sections of the country. It is easy to understand how they grew into the main centers of jazz. New Orleans, the most cosmopolitan of Ameri-

---

*The whole argument about jazz as black music gets tangled, shrill, and even pointless in this regard. While whites are always converts to jazz, blacks quite naturally see the music as another form of Afro-American art or entertainment. (Blues and jazz represent one of only two authentically native, folk-based musical forms in America. The other is, of course, country and western music.) One can hardly dispute the Afro-American origin of jazz. However, once it passes into the general consciousness through mass entertainment mechanisms, such as recording, it is susceptible to a host of other influences. These influences are reflected back on the originators of the music and on the music itself. Feedback just as surely shapes jazz as it does any other communication.

can cities until well into the twentieth century, was also a superdominant regional city. There, the most direct confrontation of Afro-American and Euro-American subcultures occurred. Kansas City represented a special case as a jazz center; its eventual development into a "wide open" town encouraged a nonstop entertainment industry to flourish. Kansas City was also the gateway to the Southwest territory, a particularly fertile area for blues-based music. Other cities produced important jazz, but New York, Chicago, New Orleans, and Kansas City represent four major types of jazz centers. A significant amount of important jazz came out of these cities.

Both New Orleans and Kansas City lost their position of preeminence when the recording and radio industries gained control over popular musical entertainment. Chicago and New York, and finally New York alone, accounted for most jazz output. Specialization and the growth of a national hierarchy of urban dominance—abetted by radio—affected jazz, as it did many other areas of American life and culture (Hawley, 1950). A great deal of jazzlike music came to be perceived as part of a style understood to be *the* jazz style. This style might change, but at any given time, the media-based style of jazz predominated over other variations.

An apparent paradox seems to emerge on the origins of jazz. Jazz is big-city music, yet many of the most important early jazz players learned the style and served apprenticeships in so-called territory bands. These bands played in small towns and traveled extensively in all parts of the country. They represented an earlier preradio form of mass entertainment (see chapter 2) and persisted well into the radio era. The key to the apparent paradox can be found in several factors: **(1)** style setting occurred in urban not rural areas; **(2)** local status hierarchies emerged with the most prestigious players and bands located in major cities; **(3)** a national hierarchy finally emerged, which subsumed the local status groupings. Big money and national exposure were reserved for those who were recorded and played in big city clubs and dance halls. Everybody knew the difference between the major and minor leagues in the entertainment industry. Thomas J. Hennessey points out that by the mid-thirties this process was well established.

Thus, by 1935, the band business had become a highly structured institution dominated by large impersonal entities and organized on a national basis. It had thus moved a considerable distance from 1917 when it had been a collection of local territories where business was conducted on an informal basis by individual bandleaders and locations owners (Hennessey, 1973), p. 491).

Our concerns go back well before 1935, however, in order to see how this state of affairs came about.

> The reality of early jazz history is the emergence in several parts of the country of independent popular musical styles, all linked by the common bonds of a mixed Euro- and Afro-American musical parentage and a performance orientation. They developed in response to specific situations and thus each strain had its particular mixture of individual elements. In the Southwest, the blues and piano ragtime had a strong influence on the style. In the Midwest and Southwest, the brass band tradition of the circus and tent show musicians emerged in an instrumental ragtime style. In Chicago and New York, established black communities sought legitimacy with a style heavily-weighted with Euro-American elements. In the Northwest and West Coast, the lack of any strong input from black folk tradition saw a very weak musical style develop, closely tied to brass band and dance music tradition. In New Orleans, two very strong traditions, (a) the classically-influenced Creole and (b) the blues and church music-shaped uptown tradition, developed and intermingled (Hennessey, 1973, p. 170).

In order to avoid the simplistic popular notion of how jazz developed (see chapter 1), I am suggesting another model here, a model of *dominance*. Well before the turn of the century, musical elements such as polyrhythm, syncopation, improvisation, and the use of blue notes were coming together in many contexts throughout America (for example, the whole Ethiopian and "coon song" tradition that led directly to the establishment of minstrelsy). Music that would certainly be labeled today as jazz or near-jazz appeared as part of many Afro-American subcultures. Once fused with other trends under the umbrella of popular mass audience entertainment (for example, Tin Pan Alley) however, it tended toward standardization. The music that was labeled as jazz on records and on the radio became the yardstick against which other related forms came to be judged. Other types of jazzlike music may even have been more authentic, but they did not survive.

Our focus on cities in this and the next chapter must be understood as a concession to a view of jazz from a contemporary perspective. Certain cities became jazz centers because of their dominant position in other areas of American culture and commerce. One might even have limited the discussion to Chicago and New York only, since all the well-known jazz players made their national reputations in those cities. Other cities are included in the discussion because of their historic importance in contributing to and influencing the Chicago and New York scenes.

NEW ORLEANS

New Orleans is unlike any other American city. Founded in 1718 as the southern anchor of a great semicircle of French settlements stretching all the way into Eastern Canada, New Orleans became the point of transfer for goods into and out of the interior of North America. Situated just south of Lake Pontchartrain and near the mouth of the Mississippi River, New Orleans struggled for survival in the early years under its founder, the French Canadian Jean Baptiste le Moyne, Sieur de Bienville. During his forty years as leader, Bienville tried to stabilize his tiny community by excluding undesirables and encouraging the development of family life. He was greatly aided in this effort by the generous land-granting policies of the French government. Colonizers were given large blocks of land.

With the importation of slaves, the estate pattern of inherited wealth through land ownership was established as the basis for a New World aristocracy. Other colonizers, including a small group of German immigrants and Arcadians from Nova Scotia,* arrived, adding to the cosmopolitan flavor of the city. Growth, however, was very slow. In order to understand Bienville's problem in attracting a stable population to his settlement, it is necessary to know something about the topography of the area. That topography also had an important impact on subsequent social developments.

If you were to look at a map of the United States and acknowledge the critical importance of deep-water ports in the prerail era, the location of the city of New Orleans seems to be a natural for urban growth. If, however, you were given other information, you might change your view. Climate is an important factor. New Orleans is hot and humid in the summer and cold and damp in the winter. The semicircular bend in the river where the city is located—hence the nickname for New Orleans, the "Crescent City"—ranges from two feet below to fifteen feet above gulf level. At the time of settlement, the highest ground was along the banks of the river and on a ridge running out toward Lake Pontchartrain. Away from this high ground, the land was swampy and insect- and reptile-infested. This unusual topography meant that the most desirable land

---

*The odyssey of the French Canadian Arcadians was made famous by Longfellow in his poem "Evangeline." These settlers were the ancestors of the Cajuns of Louisiana, a distinctive ethnic group with an interesting folk tradition and music of their own. Even now, many traditional New Orleans jazz groups find employment in Cajun dance halls, and Cajun music has certainly had an influence on New Orleans jazz. The Cajuns were French ethnically but were different subculturally from the Creoles, whom I shall discuss below.

lay out from the center of the city along the narrow Esplanade Ridge. The higher elevations to the east and west along the Mississippi were also an attractive alternative to the swampy areas in between.

These ridges form a crude inverted T, with the earliest settlement at the point where the crossbar joins the stem. This area became the famous French Quarter or Vieux Carre of New Orleans. Unlike most other cities less constricted by topography, the downtown area of New Orleans has remained vital. With twentieth-century drainage systems in place, minor elevations within the city became unimportant, but by that time nostalgia and tradition kept the French Quarter alive.*

In 1743 Bienville was succeeded as Governor of Louisiana by Pierre de Rigaud, Marquis de Vaudreuil-Cavagnal, who came to the provincial capital, New Orleans, from the elegant royal courts of France. He and his Marquise initiated a sparkling social life patterned after that of the French court. Music, dance, balls, parades, parties, and, of course, the pre-Lenten Mardi Gras made the Crescent City the center of gaiety in the New World. A style of life emerged that involved vice on a scale that would have (and later did) shock the most wayward of Puritans.

In 1762 New Orleans passed to Spanish control; Louis XV gave Louisiana to his cousin, Charles III of Spain. The Spanish made a few attempts to make New Orleans more Spanish than French, but the cultural life of the city was too firmly established and the Spanish adapted to established customs. (There were, however, sporadic outbreaks of violent conflict between the Spanish and the French in New Orleans, and General Alexander ("Bloody") O'Reilly was sent at one point by the Spanish government to suppress a major revolt.) Napoleon forced Spain to cede Louisiana back to France in 1800, and in 1803 he sold the entire area to the United States.

With the Louisiana Purchase, cultural as well as political conflict engulfed New Orleans. Viewed as a frontier area by entrepreneurial Americans (who had been kept from establishing themselves earlier because of the hostile policies of the Spanish government), New Orleans became a boom town. New wharves and warehouses sprang up. Banks, brokerage houses, and other commercial enterprises grew. From a population of 10,000 in 1803, New Orleans grew to 20,000 by the time of the

---

*A typical pattern is for zones to develop outward as a city grows. Newer groups move in behind those who, as they become affluent, move farther out from the central part of the city (Hawley, 1950). The center of the city is reserved for commerce and business activities with a zone of cheaper real estate separating the business district from the suburbs. New Orleans simply did not follow this pattern. Instead, the relatively narrow ridges of higher land radiating out from the center retained a mixed residential/business character.

1810 census. Unable to acquire land in and around the French Quarter, the Americans built their homes and businesses to the west along the high ground near the Mississippi. This area became known as the Garden District, and the homes rivaled those of the older Vieux Carre in their splendor. To the east, where the land was less attractive, truck farmers and less affluent white immigrant groups settled. Under both arms and along both sides of the inverted T created by this pattern of settlement was a fringe of black residences.

New Orleans operated under the Latin Catholic *Code Noir* of 1724 until it came under American control in 1803 and for a time unofficially after that. Free blacks lived and worked in New Orleans as servants and on the docks under the rule of manumission. Toleration of free blacks lasted until the Civil War and its aftermath. In fact, New Orleans had attracted blacks from all over the New World throughout the eighteenth and part of the nineteenth centuries. The side-by-side presence of African-Americans with widely different levels of assimilation into the dominant culture, some free and some bonded, created a unique situation. The "place" of blacks in New Orleans was a very complex matter.

Conflict between those of French and Spanish ancestry, who clung to the life style of a landed aristocracy, and the Americans, who were interested in the commercial potential of New Orleans, had led, in 1836, to the establishment of three separate municipalities. The city had been reunited in 1855, but the district boundaries for the French, American, and truck-gardening sections were firmly established.

In 1840 New Orleans had replaced New York as the nation's leading seaport (and even today ranks as the nation's second largest behind New York). By 1850 New Orleans had a population of more than 100,000; it was the fifth largest city in the United States. New York, Baltimore, Boston, and Philadelphia were larger. Of these cities, however, only New York City was significantly larger with a population approaching 700,000. Chicago, by contrast, had a population of less than 30,000 in 1850.

Another status group, the Creoles, emerged in New Orleans and played a vital role in the life of that community. Over the years, it became customary for French and Spanish men of means to keep and sometimes to marry women of African ancestry. It also happened that these women and their offspring could, and did, inherit wealth—including plantations and slaves of their own. The children of these liaisons were known as Creoles of color, *gens de coleur* or simply Creoles.* The Creoles became

* Originally, the word "Creole" referred to anyone born in a Spanish or French colony of nonnative descent, that is, of French or Spanish parents. In more recent times, it has come to mean one who has some French or Spanish ancestry, including those who also have African forebears. Although it seems strange

important artisans, craftsmen, and small businessmen in New Orleans and enjoyed a social status well above that of the slaves, free blacks, and many whites. Later legislation passed by the Louisiana legislature (1861) and by the City of New Orleans (1894) led to a sharp decline in status for Creoles. These statutes defined as Negro those of African ancestry and took away their rights. The *Code Noir* was dead.

Just before the turn of the century, New Orleans consisted of a patchwork of subculturally and ethnically distinct neighborhoods linked together through an exquisite sense of who belonged where according to a most peculiar set of historical and ecological circumstances. Linking all these diverse elements together was the spirit of the city, a spirit that included gaiety, vice, and, above all, a love of music.

THE MUSIC OF NEW ORLEANS: BLACK, BROWN, AND BEIGE

Three groups are of primary interest to those concerned with the development of New Orleans jazz: (**1**) the Euro-Americans, (**2**) the Afro-Americans, and (**3**) the Creoles. Unencumbered with the musical conflicts of the British colonies, operatic, salon, and formal dance music flourished within the white ethnic communities of New Orleans.* Talented musicians of color were easily incorporated into the "highbrow" musical life of the city. French, German, and Italian professors of music taught talented children of mixed parentage the fundamentals (and beyond) of European music. In an ambience more akin to the French royal court prior to the revolution than a grim English parsonage, music for the sake of music itself was encouraged.

Until the racist whirlwind swept through the United States in the middle of the nineteenth century, slaves and freedmen of African ancestry enjoyed a unique cultural freedom in New Orleans. Evidence of this can be found in the toleration of voodoo (or vodun) and the famous dances of Congo Square.

to most Americans, who have been conditioned to think solely in racial terms of black and white, old New Orleans categorized persons in terms of the proportion of their African heritage. Those who were one-eighth black were called octoroons; quadroons were one-fourth black. Octoroon and quadroon women were highly prized, and mistresses were often selected by men of means at special Quadroon Balls, which were held quite frequently.

* "New Orleans opera, was for forty years [in the beginning of the nineteenth century], the standard to be emulated in America" (Burkle and Barker, 1973, p. 6).

Before the Civil War the Congo Dances (Congo Square is today called Beauregard Square) were one of the unusual sights of New Orleans to which tourists were always taken. At times almost as many white spectators as dancers gathered for the festive occasions. That the Negroes had not forgotten their dances, even after years of repression and exile from their native Africa, is attested by descriptive accounts of the times. Gaily dressed in their finest, many of the men with anklets of jingles, the Negroes rallied at the first roll of the bamboulas, large tom-toms constructed from casks covered with cowhide and beaten with two long beef bones. . . .

Though discontinued during the war, the Congo Dances were again performed after the emancipation and were not entirely abandoned even two decades later. . . .

Voodoo incantations, brought over on slave ships, were the foundation for religious chants and songs of consolation of those who felt the weight of the "Black Man's Burden" and the sting of their master's lash (Ramsey and Smith, 1939, pp. 8—9).

On some of the plantations near New Orleans, the slaves heard little European music. Blacks recently arrived from Africa and the Caribbean kept their own cultural traditions alive. Freed slaves absorbed European musical traditions without sacrificing their own heritage. Of course, one must not be too sanguine about the level of tolerance in New Orleans; there were many periods of suppression. Voodoo was illegal. African music and dance were often ridiculed, and both were often tolerated only as a means of social control—keeping the "natives" happy and productive. Yet Africanisms had a better chance of survival in and around New Orleans than elsewhere in the United States; their suppression, for the reasons outlined above and elsewhere in this book, was—at best—halfhearted.

For the Creoles, the situation was different. This was a group that, over the course of the nineteenth century, suffered a severe decline in status. Looked upon as a special caste with its own aristocracy, Creoles came to be defined as Negroes when racial polarization swept the country. Creoles lost their lands, their jobs, and their privileges and were forced to compete with blacks in the lower reaches of the social hierarchy. For those who made music this meant a shift in place of employment from the salons to the saloons. Many Creoles, looking backward to better times, were less than enthusiastic about becoming blacks.

At the same time that elitist sources of employment were drying up, bawdy entertainment was flourishing. From the mid-nineteenth century onward, New Orleans became a boom town. Rough and tough rivermen (referred to as "Kentucks" by the natives) and wanderers of every description came to New Orleans to gamble and to partake of the "sporting life" of the city. Things were so wide open that in 1897 the moral entrepreneurs, represented by city councilman Sidney Story, passed legislation to create a red light district in the city. Informally named Storyville (much to the consternation, one may presume, of Mr. Story), this section became the vice and entertainment capital of the United States. Creoles who wished to pursue a musical career found work in Storyville. Alan Lomax has written:

> By and large these black Americans were common laborers or service workers. They were not trained musicians, but won their Storyville jobs by sheer talent. Creoles who wanted to work in Storyville, had to play in the bands with them. So for the first time since reconstruction, Creoles were compelled to accept blacks as equals and this was bitter medicine. As the mulatto group had been forced down, its caste prejudice had mounted. "The mulattoes were actually more prejudiced than the white people at that time," dark-skinned Johnny St. Cyr [a premier banjo player of the era] somberly remarked, and his comment was confirmed every time a Creole opened his mouth. Invariably, in describing someone, a Creole would begin, "He's kind of light brown . . ." or, "He's real black, got bad (kinky) hair . . ." or, "He's a real nice-lookin' light fellow . . ." A man's pigmentation was his most significant human attribute in New Orleans.
>
> Light-skinned Downtown shared the bandstand with "real black and nappy-headed" Uptown. There was fear and hate on both sides; but jazz demanded cooperation (Lomax, 1950, p. 80).

Lomax, a few pages later, quotes the brother (a respected Creole dentist) of legendary jazzman Sidney Bechet (whom we encountered in the last chapter) in one of the most moving passages of jazz—or the humanist—literature:

> When the settled Creole folks first heard this jazz, they passed the opinion that it sounded like the rough Negro element. In other words, they have the same kind of feeling that some white people have, who don't understand jazz and don't *want* to understand it. But, after they heard it so long, they began to creep right close to it and enjoy it. That's why *I* think this jazz music helps to get this misunderstanding between the races straightened out. You creep in close to hear the music and, automatically, you creep close to the other people. You know?" (pp. 88—89)

For black New Orleans, the growth of prostitution and gambling represented an employment potential. Playing a musical instrument was an attractive alternative to driving a coal wagon or sometime employment as a stevedore on the waterfront. Music was a step up in the status hierarchy. Rough and tough as it all must have been, playing music for any social function was easier and more "natural" than struggling in the humiliating world of industrial "free" labor. With an African sense of the functional nature of music, these musicianers bent the music they played to the needs of the marketplace. Brown-skinned players slipping in status met blacks creating a musical niche for themselves in the famous marching bands of New Orleans.

The marching band was the key to the development of New Orleans jazz. Since the Napoleonic era, military bands had flourished in the Crescent City. The Mediterranean tradition from Spain and Southern France of funeral bands, popular even today, blended easily with the marching band tradition. Encouraged further by the American marching band craze of the nineties and an incredible number of social organizations and secret societies that provided sponsorship, New Orleans supported a large number of such bands.

Traveling through America in the early part of the nineteenth century, the French historian Alexis de Tocqueville characterized the United States as a nation of joiners. Nowhere was this tendency toward voluntary association more evident than in New Orleans. The city's social life was filtered through a honeycomb of lodges, fraternities, and funeral societies. This tendency was doubly reinforced by the common African custom of forming secret societies (Stearns, 1956).

A unique musical blend emerged, then, with the Creoles, who were more likely to have had formal and European-based training, joining blacker and more African-oriented colleagues as they were pushed together by market demands. Certain compromises and adjustments had to be made by both groups. They had to learn each other's musical language and accommodate to what was, after all, two different subcultures. A new set of "social facts" arose, which we now identify as the structure of New Orleans jazz. The crucible where the "mix" was fired was in the streets, in the marching bands of New Orleans. With a musical conception unlike other marching bands and hired for a variety of reasons in a city that had a voracious appetite for music of all kinds, the march musicians of New Orleans adjusted their repertoire accordingly. For example, funeral conventions grew up that were an amalgamate of European and African customs: the band played a slow dirge based on well-known hymns on the way to the cemetery and joyous upbeat music on the way back.

The bands also contracted to play for dances, picnics, parties, and other social occasions. The competition for jobs was fierce, and leaders used every trick to get the best players into their bands. Bands competed with each other in the now legendary "cutting contests."

Bands would literally drum up support by marching through the streets or riding in wagons that proclaimed an upcoming event with placards affixed to the wagons' sides. The bands often confronted one another in the streets or in the parks. Contests would arise on the spot. Highly valued in such contests were the famous cornet and trumpet players of New Orleans, such as Buddy Bolden, who could "call the children home" with their powerful sounds. Because of the ability of these players and their potential loudness, trumpets or cornets dominated New Orleans and, later, Chicago bands.

The bands of New Orleans adopted certain conventions that set them apart from other bands and permitted further evolution. First and foremost, they exploited rather than suppressed the individuality of more talented members. Trumpets or cornets forcefully carried the lead melody within the relatively slow-paced four-four tempo of march time. Trombones and tubas doubled the melody line in the bass. Clarinets, the classic Creole instrument, embellished the melody line in the high register. Drums were relegated, for the most part, to the traditional time-keeping function of the marching band.

As this practice became common, the bands began to evolve toward more work in concert settings. Trimming the large marching aggregation to a five-, six-, or seven-member "sit down" ensemble made this style of playing more efficient without disturbing newly agreed-upon conventions. (In concert the banjo was often substituted for the tuba as a "bottoming" instrument in order to provide a fullness to the melodic line.) Other combinations, such as the addition of a second trumpet (cornet), were also common. All in all, great emphasis came to be placed on instrumental virtuosity. Reputations were made and unmade on the individual musician's ability to stir an audience. Novelty and the development of a distinctive sound (the field holler tradition) became important.

While the marching band was being transformed, other trends were also under way in New Orleans. Ragtime and blues, especially as pianistic traditions, were undergoing change in the sporting palaces of the city. Establishments such as Lulu White's Mahogany Hall (perhaps the ultimate whorehouse of all time in the New World) were noted for their extravagant decor. Just as in the lobby of a fancy hotel, the "parlor" of such establishments required not a loud trumpeted band but the talents of a piano "professor" to entertain the guests before and after activities upstairs (Morgenstern, 1977). In the bars and juke joints, both the piano and band traditions intermingled. All kinds of music and a dizzying number of traditions and styles were mixed together helter-skelter in the Crescent City. While Storyville has captured everyone's imagination as the section of New Orleans where jazz was played day and night, the truth of the matter is that the demand for music and the commingling of styles occurred all around the city and its environs.

COLLECTIVE IMPROVISATION: THE ESSENCE OF NEW ORLEANS STYLE

Those in New Orleans closest to the Afro-American conception of music used a vocal approach to music. If, as Gunther Schuller has argued (1968), the blues are sung speech, then New Orleans jazz was instrumental speech. Musical instruments, widely and cheaply available after the Civil War from demobilized military bands, were used as extensions of the human voice. Trumpets and trombones—often revealing uncertainties about tonal centers—sang, grunted, and growled in the hands of New Orleans jazz players. Smears, slides, and quavers were all indicators of a musical attack that differed significantly from the formal European approach. While it is true that many New Orleans musicians may have had scant formal training, it is romantic or stereotypical (or both) to suggest that these early jazz players did not comprehend how band instruments were properly played. Many New Orleans musicians in reality simply chose to subordinate whatever instruments they had at hand to a particular conception of music. And that conception was blues-based (see chapter 3).

Another characteristic of folk-oriented music is its functional nature, that is, the use of music as expression and as release in work, play, and in political and social contexts. As jazz was drawn into the maelstrom of big-city, media-oriented popular entertainment, it adapted to the functional demands of those circumstances. The black-Creole confrontation in these surroundings was a recapitulation of the folk music—art music and popular music—proper music dialectics discussed in chapter 2.

The Creoles were a *force de frappe* in New Orleans jazz. Diatonically and chromatically conceived European music and musical instruments, together with melodically oriented hymns and popular songs, increasingly played in popular entertainment contexts, were mediated by the Creoles in their forced cooperation with their darker uptown brothers. White musicians, too, learned from and contributed to the musical open-city atmosphere of New Orleans. This heady mix of styles and traditions generated a formidable musical problem: how to blend so many cultural

influences and play music together. This musical problem was made doubly difficult by the pressures for rugged individualism that developed as
music became a market commodity. The ingenious solution to this problem was collective improvisation.

Collective improvisation is very difficult to bring off. But doing it,
even once, unified the diverse elements of jazz into a cohesive whole.
Collective improvisation demanded a dense, vertical, harmonic, and
polyphonic approach to music. Polyphony was critical to the development of New Orleans jazz (Schuller, 1968). Polyphony is the production
of several interrelated, yet independently important, melodic lines. All are
closely related to a theme and complement each other. The technique of
counterpoint, which is employed to create a polyphonic context, reached
a high point in the Western tradition with the work of Bach and other
masters of the Baroque period. Employing heterophony—a primitive
form of polyphony*—as well as polyphony, New Orleans jazz musicians
were able to bring great discipline to their collective improvisations.

> Certain writers have said that it requires as much musical train-
> ing and intellect to listen with understanding to a New Orleans en-
> semble improvising collectively as it does to listen to a Bach fugue.
> One has only to listen to a great deal of both kinds of counterpoint
> to know that these writers have understated their case. It is easier to
> follow and understand a Bach three-part fugue (or, for that matter,
> any premeditated, composed fugue) than a collective improvisation
> because the trained composer is concerned with keeping the various
> strands independent of each other; he knows that comprehension
> comes from the listener's being able to distinguish each part from the
> others. Since rhythm impresses itself on most listeners before pitch,
> the simplest music to understand is homophonic or chordal, where,
> despite the use of three or more individual voices, there is really only
> one part, one rhythm to follow.
>   . . . Despite the advantages of having three distinctive tone col-
> ors to distinguish its lines, New Orleans heterophony is more difficult
> to follow and comprehend than a Bach fugue. The reasons are not
> difficult to understand when we consider three individuals trying to
> achieve on the spur of the moment, often publicly, what the com-
> poser is able to calculate privately and at his own pace. It is no won-
> der, then, that much of what is created by the New Orleans en-

---

*Heterophony is a form of polyphony in which two or more performers produce
 nearly the same melody, with modification in one part usually consisting of the
 addition or subtraction of some notes.

semble, when they are improvising collectively, is, so to speak, heavy, dense, not easily penetrated, and often without apparent direction. If one is to understand the structure and design of New Orleans jazz—and there is a design—one must hear it as a chiaroscuro: as a pattern of light and dark sections, what Italians call "clear dark" (Ostransky, 1977, pp. 135–36, passim.).

Two things, then, were essential in the development of collective improvisation in New Orleans: **(1)** musicians who understood one another perfectly and were willing to subordinate their talents and creative impulses to a group conception; **(2)** a strong leader who could provide a worthwhile unified conception and a strong enough lead to weld the parts together. The later integration of New Orleans jazz players, such as Joe "King" Oliver and Louis Armstrong, into the Chicago and New York scenes added an important and essential element to the already extant jazz styles that had been developing independently.

It is a stubborn part of the New Orleans myth that jazz moved up the Mississippi River after Secretary of the Navy Franklin D. Roosevelt closed down Storyville in 1917. The truth is that many New Orleans jazz players and jazz groups traveled widely throughout the first quarter of this century. Perhaps the coincidence of the ODJB recording in 1917 and the closing of Storyville that same year reinforced that myth. The New Orleans conception of jazz shaped and molded other regional styles and led directly to the establishment finally of a national style. Three major figures stand out in this process: Jelly Roll Morton, Joe "King" Oliver, and Louis Armstrong. Brief biographies of each of these men appear on the following pages.

JAZZ / The Personal Dimension

Jelly Roll Morton (Frank Driggs Collection)

JELLY ROLL MORTON

When writers describe Jelly Roll Morton, the following words inevitably appear: braggart, hustler, liar, musical genius, dandy, brilliant composer. Indeed, his complex personality was a cause for controversy among those attempting to assess the musical contributions of the man who claimed he "invented jazz in 1902."

Born into a Creole family in Gulfport, Louisiana, in 1885, Morton received his first exposure to music in the "sporting houses" of the Storyville district of New Orleans. Always on the move, Morton spent many of his early years on the road, not only as a pianist, but also as a pool shark. From 1917 to 1922, his activities were centered in California, where he prospered as a musician and composer. He also tried his hand at other professions, including that of boxing promoter. From 1923 to 1928, Morton used Chicago as home base, and his first recordings were a series of sessions with the New Orleans Rhythm Kings, his own groups, and piano solos made there in 1923 and 1924. His most famous recorded works, however, were those done for Victor beginning in 1926 with his group, the Red Hot Peppers (SCCJ-I-7 and 8; II-1).

In 1928 Morton decided to follow the growing numbers of musicians, Louis Armstrong and King Oliver among them, who were moving to New York. At first he continued to record successfully and maintained his flashy image. But by 1930 the expiration of his recording contract, the depression, and some business setbacks combined with changing musical tastes to reduce Morton's popularity. He continued to lead bands in New York and on tour in the early and mid-thirties, but by 1937 he had settled in Washington, D.C., where he ran a nightclub. Although living in relative obscurity, Morton was sought out by collectors and students of jazz history who were aware of his important role in the development of the music.

In 1938 folklorist Alan Lomax recorded an extensive series of interviews with Morton for the Library of Congress (SCCJ-I-2). These reminiscences and musical demonstrations comprise a unique historical document of Morton—the man and his music, and the places and the era that shaped him. Partly as a result of the new historical interest in him, Morton returned to New York in late 1938, where he made some recordings and organized a publishing company. Poor health forced him to curtail his activities, however, and in 1940 he moved to California. Although he was involved in some musical work in his last year, his health continued to decline, and he died in July, 1941.

Morton may not have invented jazz, but he was one of the earliest original jazz composers, a seminal arranger with an "orchestral" concept, and a soloist who brought many musical elements together to form his own unique style.

Recordings

Jelly Roll Morton 1923–24, Milestone M-47018 (2 records). (Solos and groups, Chicago, 1923–24.) Several reissues are expected from the French RCA Black & White Series, Bluebird, 1926–30, Red Hot Peppers, and the Library of Congress Series from 1938.

Reading

Biography   Lomax, Alan. *Mister Jelly Roll: The Fortunes of Jelly Roll Morton, New Orleans Creole and "Inventor of Jazz."* New York: Duell, Sloan & Pearce, 1950 (also in paperback).

Biography and Criticism   Williams, Martin. *Jelly Roll Morton.* Kings of Jazz series. New York: A. S. Barnes, 1963 (paperback).

Discography   Davies, John R. T., and Wright, Laurie. *Morton's Music.* Essex, England: Storyville Publications, 1968 (paperback).

King Oliver (Frank Driggs Collection)

KING OLIVER

The history of jazz is filled with tragic tales, but the story of King Oliver ranks among the saddest. Born in New Orleans in 1885, he received his earliest musical training in a neighborhood youth band when he was fourteen. Soon after, he began playing in some of the many brass bands in the city, including the Melrose, Olympia, Onward, and Eagle. As was often the case with musicians of that era, Oliver had a day job as a butler. Oliver was soon challenging Freddie Keppard as the premier cornetist in the city. In 1914 Oliver joined a band led by trombonist Kid Ory, who was the first to call him "King."

Early in 1918, Oliver traveled to Chicago, where he played with the bands of Bill Johnson and Lawrence Duhe. In 1920 he led his own band in Chicago until he received an invitation for an engagement in San Francisco. (Oliver had been recommended by Kid Ory, who had been in California for some time.) Returning to Chicago in 1922, he opened at the Lincoln Gardens with King Oliver's Creole Jazz Band. Later that year, Oliver hired young Louis Armstrong as second cornetist, and the band's popularity reached a new peak. During a tour of the Midwest in 1923, the band was recorded in Richmond, Indiana, by Gennett Records. Other historic sessions followed, featuring for the most part, along with Oliver and Armstrong on cornet, Honore Dutrey (trombone), Johnny Dodds (clarinet), Lil Hardin, who was to become Mrs. Armstrong (piano), and Warren "Baby" Dodds on drums (SCCJ-I-6). The repertoire included New Orleans standards, blues, and originals by Oliver, Armstrong, and Hardin.

It was during this period that Oliver had a profound influence on the jazz world. There are numerous accounts of musicians, both black and white, flocking to Chicago to hear the exciting musical innovations of the Creole Jazz Band. Particularly thrilling were the two-cornet breaks developed by Oliver and Armstrong. By 1924, Armstrong, although still devoted to his idol, was persuaded to move on, eventually to New York and Fletcher Henderson's band. Oliver continued to lead his own groups in Chicago with various musicians. In 1926 Oliver's band, now called the Dixie Syncopators, established residency at Chicago's Plantation Café. The orchestra, which had expanded to three reeds, included Kid Ory on trombone, Albert Nicholas and Barney Bigard (reeds), and Luis Russell (piano). Oliver signed a recording contract with Brunswick, and for the next two years his Dixie Syncopators produced numerous records in the Vocalion Records "race" series.

In 1927 Oliver accepted an engagement at the Savoy Ballroom in New York. After a moderately successful beginning, Oliver found it difficult to find steady engagements. "He had come to New York too late, and found that his imitators had preceded him, leaving no openings for the King. He did not have the reputation in New York that he had in Chicago, hence had difficulty finding work at his terms" (Allen and Rust, 1958, p. 23). After Syncopators disbanded in 1927, Oliver was sustained financially by his recording contract and whatever playing dates he could find, which often included the anonymous backing of blues singers. He managed to land a new contract in 1928, this time with Victor, for whom he recorded until 1930.

From 1931 on was a period of continuing decline for Oliver, both physically and professionally. He suffered from heart disease and other illnesses, but, worst of all, he began to lose his teeth to pyorrhea, which severely limited his playing. After 1935 he was unable to play at all. Nevertheless, he continued to lead a band, composed of unknown younger musicians, throughout the South and Southwest. This seven-year period was a nightmarish tale of transportation, personnel, and financial problems. Finally, Oliver ended up in Savannah, Georgia, in 1937, without a band and in declining health. The former "World's Greatest Jazz Cornetist" was forced to take various odd jobs that included running a fruit stand and working as a janitor in a pool hall. Always a proud man, Oliver was saving for a return to New York, anticipating a comeback, when he died in Savannah in April, 1938.

Recordings

King Oliver's Jazz Band, 1923, Smithsonian P2 12744, LPs. (1923 Chicago recordings with Armstrong and blues accompaniments 1924–28 issued together on this LP.)

Reading

Biography and Discography   Allen, Walter C., and Rust, Brian. *King Joe Oliver.* London and New York: Sidgwick and Jackson, 1958.

Biography and Criticism   Williams, Martin. *King Oliver.* Kings of Jazz series. New York: A. S. Barnes, 1961 (paperback).

LOUIS ARMSTRONG

Perhaps the single most influential figure in jazz history, Louis Armstrong was born in New Orleans on July 4, 1900. He received his earliest musical training in the Waif's Home to which he was sent after firing a gun in celebration of New Year's Eve, 1913. After release from the home in 1915, Armstrong worked at several jobs, both musical and nonmusical. During this period he became acquainted with King Oliver, the reigning New Orleans trumpet master, who became Louis's teacher and the only significant musical influence in his life. In 1918 Armstrong re-

Louis Armstrong (Ed Berger)

placed his idol in trombonist Kid Ory's band, when Oliver moved on to Chicago. During the next few years, Armstrong gained experience in several local bands, as well as through a stint on the riverboats. Until 1922, when he was summoned by his mentor, Oliver, to Chicago, he was considered the top cornetist in New Orleans. As second cornetist in Oliver's band, young Louis's musical horizons were greatly expanded as he was exposed to a new type of music and an exciting cosmopolitan environment. It was with Oliver's band that Armstrong made his recording debut in 1923 (SCCJ-I-6). The young musician developed so rapidly that he was soon rivaling the master.

By 1924 he was ready for the challenge of a new musical format and accepted an invitation to join the highly respected Fletcher Henderson Orchestra in New York, creating a sensation among musicians. Armstrong recorded with Henderson, as well as accompanying blues singers (SCCJ-I-5; II-2). The next year he returned to Chicago where, over the next three years, he made a series of recordings with studio groups called the Hot Five and Hot Seven that were to revolutionize the concept of the jazz solo (SCCJ-II-5 through 9; III-1). By 1929 Armstrong was already a celebrity and began to cater to his ever-increasing legion of admirers. He abandoned the small-group format and, for the next seventeen years, fronted big bands that served primarily to showcase his talents (SCCJ-III-2 and 3). His repertoire also changed to include popular songs and "novelties," and his singing began to play a greater role in his performances. He appeared in films, on Broadway and, later, on television.

In 1947 Armstrong returned to leading a small group, his All Stars, which included, at various times, pianists Earl Hines and Billy Kyle, trombonists Jack Teagarden, Trummy Young, and Tyree Glenn, clarinetists Edmond Hall and Barney Bigard, and drummers Sid Catlett and Cozy Cole, among others. Louis traveled with his group on nonstop and often grueling tours almost until his death in 1971. He earned the title "Good Will Ambassador," played before royalty, made triumphant tours of Europe and Africa, and even challenged the Beatles' supremacy on the charts with a hit record of "Hello Dolly" in 1964.

Armstrong combined a physique perfectly designed for playing the trumpet with natural showmanship, boundless energy, and musical genius. Although he most directly influenced a generation of trumpet players (as well as other instrumentalists), Armstrong's innovations established basic concepts of jazz improvisation that were essential to the development of even the most recent styles. These qualities included a new rhythmic relaxation and melodic freedom—in short—swing. As a vocalist he is owed a debt by almost every popular singer.

In spite of his contributions, many purists tended to dismiss his work after 1930 as musically unimportant. It must be remembered, however, that Armstrong had ceased to be solely a jazz figure, and, in a sense, belonged to the world. He considered himself an entertainer first, devoted to pleasing his public. He also came under fire at times for not speaking out more on political issues, although on several occasions he took a strong stand on civil rights. His commitment to his music was total; it left little opportunity for other concerns.

Fortunately, Louis Armstrong's career is well documented on record, and these recordings attest to his achievements. Although often saddled with inferior sidemen, Louis himself was seldom less than inspired. Time and again he managed to transform even the most banal material into works of art. There is almost always something of interest in an Armstrong performance, not only in his "classic" early period, but throughout his career.

Recordings

Louis Armstrong and King Oliver, Milestone 47017 (2 records). (1923–24 Chicago period; 1924, New York.)

The Louis Armstrong Story, vols. 1–4, Columbia CL851-854. (1925–31; records cover Hot 5, Hot 7, Armstrong's collaborations with Earl Hines, and early big band works.) Also on *Louis Armstrong and Earl Hines,* 1928, Smithsonian P2 12753.

The Genius of Louis Armstrong, vol. 1, Columbia G30416 (2 records). (Anthology of 1923–33 recordings.)

Louis Armstrong, July 4, 1900–July 6, 1971, RCA VPM 6044 (2 records). (Big band records for Victor, 1932–33, 1946, 1956; famous 1947 All Stars' Town Hall Concert.)

Young Louis Armstrong, 1932–33, Bluebird AXM2-5519 (2 records). (More extensive collection of 1932–33 Victor recordings.)

From the Fifties *Louis Armstrong Plays W. C. Handy,* Columbia Special Products JCL-591.

Satch Plays Fats, Columbia Special Products JCL-708.

Satchmo—A Musical Autobiography, MCA 10006 (4 records). (New versions of his early classics with commentary by Armstrong.)

From the Sixties *Hello, Dolly!* MCA 538.

The Essential Louis Armstrong, Vanguard VSD 91/2 (2 records). (1965 Paris concert.)

Reading

Autobiography Armstrong, Louis. *Louis Armstrong—A Self-Portrait.* New York: The Eakins Press, 1971 (also in paperback).

———. *Satchmo: My Life in New Orleans.* New York: Prentice-Hall, 1954 (also in paperback).

———. *Swing That Music.* London and New York: Longmans, Green, 1936.

Biography and Criticism Goffin, Robert. *Horn of Plenty: The Story of Louis Armstrong.* New York: Allen, Towne & Heath, 1947.

Jones, Max, and Chilton, John. *Louis: The Louis Armstrong Story.* New York: Little, Brown, 1972.

McCarthy, Albert J. *Louis Armstrong.* Kings of Jazz series. New York: A. S. Barnes, 1961 (paperback).
Panassie, Hugues. *Louis Armstrong.* New York: Scribner's, 1971.

Discography   Jepsen, Jorgen Grunnet. *Discography of Louis Armstrong.* 3 vols. Copenhagen, Denmark: Debut Records, 1960.

chapter 5

A Tale of Four Cities II Chicago, Kansas City, and New York

In the earlier chapters of this book, I emphasized predispositions in American musical life, such as folk pentatonicism (music based on the five-note scale), which prepared the seedbed for the emergence of jazz. The unique coincidence in America of deeply rooted African musical elements and urban industrialism, in addition to other elements, spurred the development of popular music. Finally, the emergence of market-sensitive mass communications, represented by the radio and the phonograph industries, created large commercial markets for music. The tendency toward the consolidation of music production began in the Tin Pan Alley era, and the model of mass distribution was developed from the sale of sheet music and piano rolls. Following the pattern set in other major American industries, that of monopolistic capitalism, the modern music business took off in the 1920s. Records and the radio generated stars who owed their national popularity to an ability to attract large segments of the listening, dancing, and buying public. Local musicians were drawn into the vortex of big-time mass commercial music production. A national status hierarchy emerged, providing mobility for individual players and linking local territories together. Of course, this process was not without artistic and personal cost. Often, players had to conform to the demands of mass taste and the thirst for novelty in order to make it in the big time. Some jazz musicians, such as Louis Armstrong, moved gracefully between the worlds of commercial music and jazz. Some played pure jazz and were rewarded, if at all, posthumously. Most, however, played the music of their time and left the problem of labeling their music to others.

Chicago and New York drew musicians from all over the country in the late teens and early twenties. During this period, Chicago provided a volatile mix of musical elements that was parallel to, but strikingly different from, the musical blend in New Orleans in the two previous decades.

CHICAGO: ON THE MAKE

In 1850 Chicago ranked fifteenth in size among American cities and had a population of only 30,000 people. By 1900 Chicago had grown into a city with a population of nearly 1,700,000 and had become the second-largest city in the United States. Chicago's nearly sixfold growth from the middle of the nineteenth century to the beginning of the twentieth was the result of several factors. The explorers Marquette and Jolliet visited the present site of Chicago in 1673, and just before the American Revolution, a trading post was established. Fort Dearborn was created in 1803. The completion of the Erie Canal in 1825, which linked the Hudson River to Lake Erie, provided a thin highway of water that flooded the Midwest with commerce and immigration. The Erie was part of an elaborate canal system spreading westward during the nineteenth century across New York State, Pennsylvania, and Ohio, linking the Eastern seaboard to the Great Lakes. The completion of the Chicago Sanitary and Ship Canal in 1900 reversed the flow of the Chicago River away from Lake Michigan and toward the Mississippi through the Des Plaines River, creating a new waterway that linked the Great Lakes to the Gulf of Mexico. Harbor improvements, lake traffic, and the settling of the prairies brought prosperity.

The remarkable growth of the railway just before and after the Civil War also made Chicago, because of its fortunate location, a major transshipping and industrial center. Following the Great Fire of 1871, a new sprawling city of stone and steel rose from the ashes and radiated out from Lake Michigan, attracting a flood of laborers. Labor troubles followed this human tidal wave, and Chicago became notorious for the bloody Haymarket Riot of 1886 and the Pullman strikes of 1894. It was a city of violence and unrest, a city of action. No one has captured the spirit of this lusty city better than Carl Sandburg in his famous poem, "Chicago."

> Hog Butcher for the World,
> Tool Maker, Stacker of Wheat,
> Player with Railroads and the Nation's Freight Handler;
> Stormy, husky, brawling,
> City of the Big Shoulders: . . .

Phenomenal growth made Chicago a jumble of ethnic and racial subcultures, each competing for a place in the sun. Chicago became a city of zones and neighborhoods, with the Loop (downtown) at the center of a great semicircle. It was a boom town without the civilizing effects of having had a history. Raw, vulgar, and sprawling out from Lake Michigan into its hinterland, the Windy City developed ethnic enclaves of considerable size. Among those attracted to this northern industrial mecca were thousands of blacks from all over the South and Midwest. They poured into the area south of the Loop and bounded on the west by the stockyards, creating the South Side, which is to Chicago what Harlem is to New York. From 1910 to 1920, the black population of Chicago jumped from 40,000 to 100,000, a two-and-one-half-fold increase in absolute size and a proportional growth of 2 percent to 4 percent of the city's population. Their minstrels, the blues singers, followed this mass migration to the South Side. By 1920 Chicago was a blues town as well as a boom town. Loneliness, uprootedness, and alienation—all perennial blues themes—were part of the Chicago experience. But robust affirmation of life and love also fit in with the exuberant optimism that is so much a part of Chicago's character as a city.

Night clubs, vaudeville houses, theaters and, above all, dance halls sprang up to meet the demand for entertainment from both blacks and whites. Luxurious resorts along the fashionable North Shore, as well as South Side cabarets, meant jobs to large numbers of musicians. Until the advent of the talkies in 1927, many musicians were members of theater pit orchestras. In the words of Karl Fisher's 1922 song hit, the Windy City had become "Chicago That Toddlin' Town."

Rapid growth, the demand for services, and the need for social order, together with such factors as the unenforceable Volstead Act (Prohibition) created a situation in Chicago that encouraged both the political machine based on ethnic politics and mob control. Long before the advent of official welfare programs, local political bosses, through district leaders, provided special help in finding jobs for the party faithful and saw to it that a ton of coal was delivered to those who were in need (Merton, 1957, pp. 72–82). In other areas, where the political machine was unwilling or unable to supply goods and services, gangsters found opportunities to exercise control (Bell, 1961, pp. 127–50). Both Kansas City and Chicago were excellent case studies of this pattern of machine and/or mob control. In both cases, a corollary of this kind of political system encouraged a wide-open attitude toward all kinds of vice, deviance, *and* entertainment. Jazzman Art Hodes recalled a wild and woolly evening in a Chicago cabaret:

Another time the night club was full, people getting drunk and celebrating. Upstairs, unknown to the customers (many of them) was a gambling joint. You could lose plenty up there. Johnny Craig, a drummer, and myself were playing downstairs. When all of a sudden, pop, pop—the Fourth of July, pistols and all. And me with my back turned! Man, I was scared! I ducked. Some guy was celebrating, shooting at the ceiling, and it was made of tin. Those gamblers upstairs must have done some moving around. Well, this celebrator couldn't have shot all his bullets away when the boss came out of the kitchen, fit to be tied, picked up a heavy water bottle, walked up to this guy with the gun in his hand, and stretched him cold with one blow on the top of his skull. And if it hadn't been for some gal pleading with the boss to let him be, he would have kicked and beat the celebrator to pieces—he was that mad (Hodes in Gleason, 1958, pp. 42–43).

Like a cow town without a sheriff in a Grade B Western, Chicago two-stepped toward Prohibition, the depression, and mobster control throughout the twenties.

THE SOCIAL CONTEXT

Although unburdened by the quasi-aristocratic caste/estate system of New Orleans, the music of Chicago was nonetheless burdened with a tendentious dichotomy between the music of moral uplift and music that satisfied "base" desires. This split was reflected on all levels of the class structure. Within the music of popular entertainment, self-conscious moral entrepreneurs took it upon themselves to protect the public from licentious, undisciplined sounds, such as jazz. While much of this activity represented either foolish or malicious posturing, it tended to suppress some of the more earthy and folklike aspects of both blues and jazz in favor of smoother and more conventional sounds and cleaned-up lyrics. This struggle and its effects on jazz have been well documented in the jazz literature (Cf. Berger, 1947; Leonard, 1962). While it is not necessary to repeat that entire discussion here, it is useful to keep it in mind insofar as it shaped the music of Chicago in the twenties.

In New Orleans, white jazz players were, by and large, on the side lines and incorporated the new spirit into their music in much the same way that Afro-American influences had always penetrated mass American music: pragmatically, through mass audience acceptance. If it sold, use it. The Tin Pan Alley treatment of ragtime and blues at the turn of the century provided the model. However, much Afro-American music remained

as unassimilated folk music before the influence of phonographic recording. The runaway success of the Original Dixieland Jazz Band's recording
in 1917 changed everything. Something called jazz had mass commercial
potential. Adam Smith's "invisible hand of the market" reached out.
Wild claims about "inventing" jazz by ODJB members (and others) generated controversy (Schuller, 1968, pp. 175–87). Such claims and coun-
terclaims all became part of the hype as jazz became a fad. The faddish
aspects of jazz included the most embarrassing barnyard imitations (a
devolution of trumpet growls and slurs based originally on vocal imitation) and crazy "nut" jazz à la Spike Jones. Jazz musicians and serious
jazz listeners found themselves, as early as the mid-twenties, tilting at the
twin windmills of properly attributing creative origins and assigning
proper credit for invention. Meanwhile, real responsibility for shaping
what was to be played and preserved on records fell to the music brokers, those who packaged and presented music to the public. For many
of these brokers, green dollars were infinitely more important than blue
notes.

A mass (that is, undifferentiated) buying public has no sense of itself,
of belonging to a group, although individuals in a mass are members of
groups. The broadest appeal across groups, rather than narrower appeals
within groups, however, is the secret of mass marketing. This creates a
situation where the tyranny of the majority is always a threat. The mass
has no need for a history or for truth. Rumor, fable, and simplified sets of
facts, some true and some false, are turned into history.* The story of jazz
in Chicago in the 1920s was the story of struggle for market shares, and it
broke along lines shaped by larger American class and racial antimonies.

When New Orleans jazz players (and players from other parts of the
country as well) arrived in Chicago, they found two music establishments
in formation: one black and one white. Both were, in important respects,
creatures of the burgeoning music industry and both appealed to well-
established Protestant ethic norms for ideological support. These "establishments" looked to European "art" music as the standard. In a
country without an aristocracy, upward strivers gained some pseudodis-
tance from their agricultural and mercantile roots through the borrowed
status of "classical" European music.

The course of musical evolution in the nineteenth century was
determined by the European bourgeois community that set the cul-

---

* In *Improvised News,* Tamatsu Shibutani argues that rumor is, by and large, a
substitute for the factual information needed by any acting group. By extension,
I would argue that authenticity and a sense of history are packaged by sellers for
an aggregate of consumers only insofar as they are needed to sell product.

tural tone of the time. Evolution today is determined by an audience, not of thousands or hundreds of thousands, but of hundreds of millions. And the cultural tone of the time is set by what hundreds of millions of people like.

Today's serious music audience flatters itself that in perpetuating the European tradition it improves the cultural tone of the time. Many of its members, particularly in the United States, are members for no other reason. Subscribing to symphony concerts and community recital series is widely regarded as evidence of the subscriber's good citizenship.

In the sense that this audience supports and encourages ideal performances of European musical masterpieces, the claim of a cultural contribution is justified. But it is a contribution to the nineteenth century in the form of a historical summing up rather than a contribution to the twentieth in the form of a twentieth century music. The occasional performance of a new composition cannot disguise the autumnal flavor of the spectacle (Pleasants, 1955, p. 169).

Given the nature of popular music* a dialectic tension between jazz and blues-based entertainment music, as well as less authentic (wholly market determined) mass market music, grew up. Mass market music producers often employed classical themes and substituted lush-sounding, but simplified, arrangements (for example, heavily augmented reeds) for the real complexities of European art music. "Jazzin' the classics" became a kind of cottage industry for big band arrangers in the late twenties and thirties. Some harmless and even good-humored pop classics resulted, such as Freddy Martin's big band theme "Tonight We Love," based on Tchaikovsky's First Piano Concerto. The name of Paul Whiteman, the "King of Jazz," became synonomous with this procedure. Enormously successful, Whiteman was famous in the twenties and into the thirties for symphonic jazz. While the gentle irony of the name "Whiteman" can hardly be missed, some extraordinary white jazz players such as Bix Beiderbecke were at one time or another part of the Whiteman orchestra. His fine arrangers, such as Bill Challis and Ferde Grofé, who wrote the evocative "On the Trail," lent real musical merit to the band's output. Whiteman, to his credit, commissioned George Gershwin in 1924

---

* "Pop" music in the American context meant (and still often means) short melodic phrases of four or eight bars varied slightly through simple harmonics with little emphasis on rhythm and an avoidance of chromatic complexity. Tin Pan Alley formulas froze the popular-song format into sixteen- and thirty-two-bar constructions early in the century. In short, many people growing up in this culture acquire a feeling for tunes and a feeling for how long any song should last.

to write "Rhapsody in Blue." While this piece has little to do with jazz, it is an American pop classic.

CHICAGO JAZZ: BLACK AND WHITE

Nowhere was the conflict between "good" and "bad" music more evident than among blacks in Chicago in the twenties. Jelly Roll Morton had come up to Chicago in the early teens to play and settled there in the early twenties. Freddie Keppard, Joe Oliver's immediate predecessor and the legendary Buddy Bolden's immediate successor as the king of New Orleans trumpet players, came to Chicago around 1920. (Keppard had at first refused to record his music because he feared that it might be stolen.) Oliver brought a group into Lincoln Gardens, a major South Side dance hall, in 1922. A veritable flood of Crescent City musicians created in Chicago a "New Orleans music in exile" in the late teens and early twenties. While the playing of these exiles was often hotter and more inventive than the music they found, their playing created a new set of tensions in popular music. The conflict noted in the last chapter within the black population of New Orleans between Creoles and Negroes was repeated in Chicago. Many blacks who had achieved some modicum of social mobility (within the limits of racism) adopted an attitude of disdain for lower-class black culture.

Several sociologists have noted that the unusual racial situation in the United States yielded up a dual (or caste) class system (Dollard, 1937). E. Franklin Frazier, who labeled those in the upper levels of the black class system the "black bourgeoisie," pointed out that the top status positions among blacks were, by and large, far below the prestige, occupational, and wealth levels available to whites. With a rather precarious hold on "respectability" and with a constant fear of slipping back into a lower status, the black bourgeoisie tended to be intolerant of, and hostile to, characteristics perceived as part of the life of common black folks. Instead, they emulated the presumed values, attitudes, and life-styles of upper-middle-class whites, creating a "world of make-believe" (Frazier, 1957).

More germane to Chicago, however, is *Black Metropolis,* a large-scale study of Chicago's South Side published in 1945 by St. Clair Drake and Horace Cayton. Unlike the patchwork pattern of segregation found in New Orleans, blacks in Chicago were restricted, for the most part, to one area. This led to great population density and crowded conditions. It also provided a political base for black politicians and created a market for goods and services, including a market for entertainment. Under the hothouse conditions of the South Side, various attitudes, values, and life-styles came into direct confrontation. Sharp conflicts arose as Drake and Cayton illustrate in their complex picture of South Side life. One such conflict was between the "shadies" and the "respectables." Small businessmen, white-color workers, and the pillars of the local churches (of which there were, and are, many) had a tenuous grip on the fringes of a lower-middle-class life-style because of their color. Filled with Booker T. Washington-like notions of industriousness and being a credit to their race, these blacks tried to put as much psychological and social distance as possible between themselves and the shadies. The shadies, on the other hand, were out to enjoy life and beat the system whenever possible.

By the time Louis Armstrong arrived in Chicago in 1922 to join King Oliver, the tension between blues-oriented musicians and the "Chicago Establishment" (Hennessey, 1973) was tangible. Well-established black Chicago bandleaders such as Doc Cooke and Dave Payton viewed their musical mission as one of uplift. Not unlike the studio musicians of a later era (those who play for radio and TV commercials, for example), these musicians prized the craft aspects of playing popular music, such as facility in sight-reading, as well as neatness and punctuality. Payton wrote a column for the Negro newspaper, *The Chicago Defender,* for many years, which appealed directly to the sensibilities of the respectables.

> The day of clown music is over. . . . It was the custom about five years ago for the leader of the dance band to yell out the key and stomp off the tempo, and every one in the band would fake his own part, and when all was over the dance fans would yell for more. But since that time the dance music has journeyed through a real revolutionary stage until now it requires real, first class musicianship to line up in the first rank (*Journal of Jazz Studies,* vol. 2, no. 1, p. 17).

Hot players from New Orleans must have had a sense of *déjà vu.* The sweet versus hot orientations in Chicago and New York paralleled the Creole versus Negro conflict of a generation earlier in the Crescent City. While many creative jazz players failed to achieve the recognition they deserved, this stage of the jazz dialectic did raise the general level of technical competence among jazz players.* First of all, many players, such as Louis Armstrong, saw the handwriting on the wall and learned to

---

*New Orleans players such as Freddie Keppard and Jimmie Noone did manage to cross over and play with establishment groups. Keppard, for example, was a featured soloist in Doc Cooke's band. The lines were not always firmly drawn, although the generalization is, I believe, correct.

read music well. Second, there was a selection process, whereby better-trained and well-disciplined musicians got jobs (Shih, 1959).

The basic ability to read music well became crucial as the big band era was ushered in. Bands were a business, and the businessmen who ran the bands wanted disciplined musicians and a skilled labor pool from which to recruit. Jazz players from New Orleans and elsewhere found new pressures awaiting them as they became part of the music industry. Even the technology of the 78 rpm record "rationalized" music making. Each side of a 78 rpm record permitted only about three minutes of recording; everything had to be compressed into that time frame. As circuits of traveling entertainers crossed America from coast to coast in the twenties, an elaborate scrollwork of networks led to dance halls and theaters based in major metropolises. The super cities—Chicago and New York—brokered music along with textiles and sides of beef.

Across the caste line, some extraordinary young white musicians also learned about jazz. Two groups of musicians are most often mentioned in the context of white Chicago jazz, the Wolverines and the Austin High School Gang. Both groups were noted for their "hot" playing. They were influenced by the ODJB (which had played in Chicago in 1916 prior to its triumph in New York in 1917) and by a group of white New Orleans musicians, playing in Chicago called the New Orleans Rhythm Kings. The NORK had a conception of music that was very close to that of the best black groups. The Wolverines and the Austin High School Gang produced many important white jazz musicians, including Benny Goodman and Bix Beiderbecke.

> It was the start of "white" jazz in the Midwest. . . . Unlike New Orleans style, the style of these musicians—often and confusingly labeled "Chicago"—sacrificed ease and relaxation for tension and drive, perhaps because they were mastering a new idiom in a more hectic environment. They had read some of the literature of the twenties—drummer Dave Tough loved Mencken and the American Mercury—and their revolt against their own middle-class background tended to be conscious. The role of the improvising—and usually non-reading—musician became almost heroic (Stearns, 1956, p. 129).

The phonograph was the rage, and college kids from Yale, Princeton, and other schools who wanted to be "with it" formed jazz clubs, collected records, brought jazz groups to campuses, and began to imitate the hot jazz players in their own amateur playing. Other white youngsters began to be influenced by the tide of jazz recordings. The young Leon "Bix" Beiderbecke, who later became a legendary figure in jazz, acquired a cornet in high school in Iowa and discovered the recordings of the Original Dixieland Jazz Band. He also heard Louis Armstrong and other New Orleans musicians on the riverboats while living in his hometown of Davenport, Iowa.

Biederbecke migrated to Chicago and joined other young white people who were discovering the music of the South Side.

> The Chicagoans represent the coming together of two provincial forces—the New Orleans musical fraternity and the Chicago jazz gang. . . . It is no longer possible for one self-contained group of jazzmen to find direct inspiration in the work of another self-contained group imported nearly intact from a different part of the country. (Mezzrow and Wolfe, 1946, p. 149).

Going down to the South Side cabarets and listening to records were the major ways that young white Chicagoans learned about jazz. They were rebels. Often from nice middle-class homes, launched on classical music by their parents, the young rebelled by discovering black jazz. For them, it was an answer to the horrors of World War I and the Darwinistic cruelty of the robber baron era. Chicagoan Muggsy Spanier described his vocational cornet training this way:

> As a kid (and Louis always called me Kid Muggsy, inscribing my prized pictures of him that way), I would go down to the South Side and listen hour after hour to those two great trumpeters, Joe King Oliver and Louis. That's when they were at the old Lincoln Gardens. It got so that I knew every phrase and intonation they played, just from listening, so that, in spite of myself, I was doing the same things—as nearly as possible, of course (Hentoff and Shapiro, 1955, p. 110).

Jimmy McPartland, who played with the Wolverines, described the other major avenue of vocational training this way:

> What we used to do was put the record on—one of the Rhythm Kings', naturally—play a few bars, and then all get our notes. We'd have to tune our instruments up to the record machine, to the pitch, and go ahead with a few notes. Then stop! A few more bars of the record, each guy would pick out his notes and boom! We would go on and play it. Two bars, or four bars, or eight—we would get in on each phrase and then all play it (Hentoff and Shapiro, 1955, p. 113).

The die was cast. Musicians were hearing each other in person and on the phonograph record. The music that had started in New Orleans,

Chicago, and other local centers had now spread nationwide. Jazz had burst onto the national scene and had become, if not interracial, at least biracial. But all this became a threat to morals. As Neil Leonard (1962) suggests, opposition to jazz began to form in the 1920s. Jazz was too secular and too Negro for the institutional critics of American life. And jazz was unprotected from the attacks of its critics.

The attack ended in the compromise of the 1930s, as we shall presently see, when the institutional critics exerted enough pressure to clean up jazz and make it sweet. Two strategies were developed in the 1920s (Peterson, n.d.). One was containment. Statutes were actually passed outlawing jazz in some major communities. These were, however, unworkable and so the effort was shifted toward keeping jazz out of the home, the school, and off the concert stage. Jazz was confined to nightclubs, which were evil anyway. "Jazz, like the Negro, was all right in its place" (Peterson, n.d.).

The second strategy was that of modification. This effort to modify the excesses of jazz resulted in the great compromise of the 1930s. By making jazz white, this second strategy also had the effect of keeping blacks in their place. The second strategy worked and ironically also accomplished the goal of containment for much real jazz. But this strategy was effective only because of the development of the radio and phonograph, which could be controlled even though the jazzman could not. Outsiders had control of the mass media, which the jazzman needed in order to work. Jazz had to be marketable in the developing media.

This process did not involve a dark conspiracy. Much of this modification came from audience demands, for example. The promoter, too, who hired the bands for dance dates was also responsible, but he had to make a living. American racism did have an important impact on the development of jazz, although it was often subtle and, perhaps in some cases, unintentional.

Other factors were also important. Leonard's major thesis in *Jazz and the White Americans* is that those who had a commitment to other forms of music (for status or financial reasons) attempted to suppress jazz as soon as they realized its impact on American popular music. He argues that by the time those whom he refers to as "traditionalists" (those who wished to stop jazz) realized what was happening, it was too late. The accommodation, according to Leonard, was a compromise to clean up jazz and make it respectable. Against the backdrop of the depression, popular or commercial jazz became primarily white jazz, and black music was driven underground, as was the jazz of the creative hot white players. In any event, "in the twenties, most of those who listened at all regarded jazz as merely an energetic background for dancers" (Hadlock, 1965, p.

9). The connection between jazz and popular dance was critical, more-over, because it provided more work for dance musicians who had been influenced by jazz. It brought about the real possibility for large numbers of would-be musicians of playing music professionally. To other dance musicians, the creative jazz musician had become a hero, even though they might regard their own work as something less than heroic.

> Gradually, in the second decade of the century, it became pos-sible for more players to make the music a full-time career. But none of the early travelers was ever allowed to forget that he was primarily an "entertainer. . . ." The jazzmen who gained their basic experi-ences in the 1920s and 1930s operated under the same contract (Hentoff, 1961, p. 30).

The depression and the end of Prohibition brought the jazz age to a close. By 1930 phonograph record sales had been cut in half, and more people were standing in breadlines than in ticket lines for the dance halls and nightclubs. Radio continued to grow, however, as did other aspects of the music business, and many musicians began to head East to find work. This was especially true of many jazz players, primarily blacks, who had been frozen out of the traveling dance bands. New York and Harlem beckoned.

There is little dispute, however, that while all this was going on, jazz had already been co-opted by the big popular dance bands as far back as the 1920s. Paul Whiteman represented "nice jazz" to a large proportion of the American public. Whiteman managed to combine dance music with just a dash of hot jazz and the trappings of the classical music con-cert in order to make his music palatable to the masses. Whiteman's ca-reer, which spanned three decades of jazz, is an interesting illustration of Leonard's thesis.

> By the time the Big Band Era had begun, Paul Whiteman was approaching his twentieth anniversary as a famous bandleader. Na-tional recognition began coming to him as far back as 1918, and for almost a full generation he had been leading a colorful and distin-guished career during which he had pioneered a symphonic ap-proach to dance music and had gained the misnomer of the King of Jazz. For a true jazz band he never really had. And yet within his usually pompous arrangements he did sometimes feature some of the era's top [white] jazz soloists (Simon, 1967, p. 71).

If they accomplished nothing else, these big bands of the 1920s at least made many people aware of a new music called jazz. Most people may have had a faulty view of what jazz really was, but they knew that it was around.

CHICAGO: THE MUSICAL CHALLENGE

Each jazz generation faces a new set of musical challenges. The challenge for the Chicago jazz fraternity in the 1920s revolved around the issue of improvisation. Those involved in the jazz subculture during this period were learning about the music more and more from phonograph records. To a much greater degree than in New Orleans, Chicago meant a comprehension of jazz for a wider variety of people. In the last chapter we saw how collective improvisation solved the problem of jazz ensemble for musicians with a considerable range of talents and with diverse musical origins. But polyphonically conceived collective improvisation turned out not to be a final solution. That kind of playing depends, as we have seen, on unity of musical conception and subordination to a strong leader that can come only from long association. While groups of musically talented monks in Europe in the fourteenth century and King Oliver's group in the early twentieth achieved phenomenal unity of conception and purpose, the demands of popular music production made such stability virtually impossible. The Chicago solution was a dramatic return to the solo break as a device.

The importance of the break in blues construction was discussed in chapter 3. Everywhere and at all times, the ability to solo and take a solo break has been essential to the jazz performer's playing. However, the discipline needed to make jazz a truly collective music subordinated this characteristic to the twin needs of technical (especially music reading) sophistication and ensemble playing during the first decade and a half of this century. Here again the Oliver band is significant (SCCJ-I-6).* When Louis Armstrong joined Oliver in Chicago, it was clear to everyone involved that the two men would be rivals. Armstrong's obvious affection and respect for Joe Oliver as a musician and as a man kept the competition within bounds. But within the Oliver group, the relationship between

---

* The Oliver band's stability and its acceptance by both musicians and audiences gave it a particular potential for leadership in the jazz world. The unequaled genius of Jelly Roll Morton in solving many of the problems of an evolving form must also be noted. But Morton, for a variety of reasons, did not have the impact on jazz development that Oliver and Armstrong did. His genius, in fact, is only now being fully realized (SCCJ-I-7 and 8; II-1; Schuller, 1968, pp. 134–74).

Louis and Lil Hardin, who later became Mrs. Armstrong, was to have a lasting influence. Lil Armstrong eventually encouraged Louis to leave Oliver and join Fletcher Henderson in New York. It was she who helped Louis to become a better music reader and it was she, with her formal training and broad knowledge of musical form, who realized his enormous talent. While a clinical psychologist might have a field day with this situation, our interest is limited to the musical implications of how Louis Armstrong handled the difficulties involved.

> When I joined the band on second trumpet I made the seventh member. Those were some thrilling days of my life I shall never forget. I came to work the next night. During my first night on the job, while things were going down in order, King and I stumbled upon a little something that no other two trumpeters together ever thought of. While the band was just swinging, the King would lean over to me, moving his valves on his trumpet, make notes, the notes that he was going to make when the break in the tune came. I'd listen, and at the same time, I'd be figuring out my second to his lead. When the break would come, I'd have my part to blend right along with his. The crowd would go mad over it!
>
> King Oliver and I got so popular blending that jive together that pretty soon all the white musicians from downtown Chicago would all come there after their work and stay until the place closed. Sometimes they would sit in with us to get their kicks. . . .
>
> The funny thing about it is that King Oliver had been kidding me that he was my stepfather for years and years (Hentoff and Shapiro, 1955, pp. 99–100).

It was not long before the genius of Armstrong asserted itself. His work apart from the Oliver group in various Chicago clubs, such as the Sunset, and, later, his classic recordings with his own Hot Five and Hot Seven groups (SCCJ-II-5 through 9) made it clear that his talent* vigorously reasserted the fundamental truth of the blues: individual expression.

---

* In discussing the work of Louis Armstrong, it should be made clear that there were many other players of genius who made major contributions to the jazz genre. For example, Earl "Fatha" Hines assimilated the new conception of jazz most effectively (SCCJ-III-1). Hines revolutionized the jazz piano by converting the piano into a lead instrument. He played, and still plays, the piano as if it were a lead trumpet. Hines represents the fusion of instrumental and piano styles and the potential of "displacing" the usual role of particular instruments, the innovative and improvisational use of pure sound.

In Oliver's Creole Jazz Band we have already observed the twenty-three-year-old cornet player skillfully treading the fine line between the functional requirements of second cornet to King Oliver and his own burgeoning solo tendencies. In even these earliest Armstrong recordings, tiny phrase-cells began to appear and recur, which seen in retrospect, became the standby devices of his solos. This is not to say that they were mechanically delivered clichés. They were for the most part original with Louis (a few seem to have come from Bunk Johnson and Oliver), and they were fundamental manifestations of Armstrong's particular brand of lyricism. They became the pivotal points upon which a solo was constructed, and through the years they were expanded in expressive scope and function until entire solos could be constructed from them (Schuller, 1968, p. 90).

While the blues indeed fulfilled the need for individual expression, they introduced a complex set of musical problems as well. The solution to those musical difficulties, such as the use of the call and response form to "partial" the vocal and the instrumental into a musical dialectic, was carried over in jazz with the contrapuntally organized solo and ensemble structure. A cyclical emphasis on the solo or the ensemble characterized early jazz. In Chicago the individual soloist took command and became identified with true jazz. Even to the present day, jazz buffs pay closest attention to the solos of black players such as Armstrong and white players such as Beiderbecke and consider these solos the very essence of the musical form.* Yet a larger problem asserted itself. Making a living in popular music meant, for the most part, playing in dance orchestras. And the essence of the big dance band was ensemble work. The public needed a tune to identify with.

Enter the arranger as the key figure. The jazz arranger, like the composer in European classical music, had to have a holistic conception of the musical material with which he was working. And it was the arranger who solved the problem of the ensemble versus the solo in larger musical aggregations. Arrangers such as Don Redman, Benny Carter (an outstanding musician as well as arranger) and Fletcher Henderson set the structure within which the solo/ensemble dialectic was played out. Henderson is nearly prototypical of this development (SCCJ-III-6 and 7).

Those interested in jazz and its development have available to them one of the most detailed and scholarly works ever compiled about an art-

---

*While both musicians were truly extraordinary in their attack, Bix represents precision and Louis represents abandon in their respective temperamental approaches to the jazz idiom. Both men had perfect control of their instruments and clear perceptions of what they were about musically.

ist. The late Walter C. Allen's *Hendersonia* is the ultimate biodiscography. * In this work we learn that Fletcher Henderson was a bright and talented student who began a scientific career that was simply overtaken by a love of music. At first, he played the piano and pursued a musical career as an avocation. Because he was black and because of the exigencies of the world of entertainment, he became involved with the blues. As the pianist for (among others) the "Empress of the Blues"— Bessie Smith—he was forced to accommodate his playing to a singer and to learn the nuances of the vocal versus instrumental dialectic that the genre demands.

Henderson represented the new generation of musicians who influenced jazz. Shih's hypothesis that the new bandleaders and band arrangers were middle class and that they had substantial formal training in music is clearly borne out in the case of Fletcher Henderson (Shih, 1959). Furthermore, he used sophisticated technical devices while remaining true to the spirit of jazz. Generally, show bands had emphasized brass; the jazz leadership in New Orleans had always belonged to trumpet players. In dance bands the emphasis shifted to reeds with their smoother and more fluid sound. As guitars replaced banjos and string basses replaced tubas, the whole sense of smoothness and fluidity became a threat to the fire that trumpets gave to jazz bands. The shift from two-four to four-four time in jazz was part of the same development.

Henderson and others, Duke Ellington among them, settled this conflict by making the call and response pattern internal to the band through alternation of brass and reeds within musical phrases. (One can recognize this immediately as a blues solution to the problem.) In an eight-bar section, for example, the reeds would take the first six bars and the brass the last two. Structurally faithful to the standard blues format, this organization sound provided a nearly perfect foil for soloists. It was the perfect musical canvas upon which Louis Armstrong could paint his magnificent solos after joining the Henderson band.

When Armstrong came into the Henderson band after leaving Oliver, the center of jazz shifted from Chicago to New York. Whereas jazz in New Orleans and Chicago tended to represent a paternalistic attitude on the part of sympathetic whites toward black music, the growth of big

---

* As jazz begins to receive the kind of mature scholarship it deserves, others are beginning to study its development with the same dedication that has characterized the study of European masters of music. Morroe Berger and James Patrick are now tracing the biographical and musicological career of another giant, Benny Carter. The first fruits of this monumental enterprise have appeared in the pages of the *Journal of Jazz Studies.* (*Journal of Jazz Studies,* vol. 4, no. 1; vol. 5, no. 1).

money commercial possibilities made race relations in this field much more competitive (Van den Berghe, 1967).

The emergence of the soloist in the disciplined context of the larger band and the stabilization of sections into reeds, brass, and percussion with specific functions laid the groundwork for swing. In chapter 1, I suggested that there were two different meanings for the term "swing" in jazz. Musically, the term means a fulcrum sense of musical tempo. This sense is enhanced by the flexibility of bass, drums, and piano—but especially the bass—providing a heartbeat for a musical group. In its second sense, the term "swing" became a synonym for well-organized yet jazz-related big band music.

Jazz continued to flourish in Chicago into the thirties but two developments, mentioned earlier, demonstrated that Chicago was, after all, only a provincial capital. These were the talking motion picture, which reduced the need for theater pit orchestras drastically after 1927, and the extraordinary growth of radio, which, together with the depression, brought the jazz age to a close.

SWING

In the 1930s almost everyone became aware of jazz as an influence on American music. While there is little consensus among jazz scholars about why the word "swing" replaced "jazz" as a label, it is probable that many people felt more comfortable when popular instrumental music was "born again" with a more neutral name. But much swing was jazz, although swing had two aspects: hot (more jazz-oriented), and sweet (less oriented toward true jazz, more oriented to smooth music for dancing). Whatever else swing meant, however, it meant big band music.

The primary setting for jazz had become the dance hall. This was an outgrowth of a tradition in America originating in the early territory bands, as well as long-standing big band traditions in vaudeville, pit bands, and circus bands. Americans had become aware of jazz and indeed some of them were interested enough in it to lay the foundations for a jazz cult in the United States. This cult, which started among musicians themselves in the 1920s, had by the 1930s spread beyond the musicians. A broader audience, complete with nonplaying "technical" critics, developed. Jazz had become part of the music business, and in order to function effectively, it had to focus its attention on New York. The dance tradition had so diffused jazz specialization that many creative jazz artists needed a new context for performing.

NEW YORK

New York had long been the center of music publishing, recording, and, with the growth of broadcast networks, radio. Jazz—black and white—already had a long-standing tradition in New York. I have already mentioned Willie "The Lion" Smith who, together with James P. Johnson, Thomas "Fats" Waller, and others, made piano playing a vital and separate tradition in New York. During the depression, rent parties were popular social events, and it was easier and cheaper to hire a piano player than a band. But the piano player was expected to make as much music as a whole band (it should be noted, however, that piano playing was important almost everywhere in jazz). Willie "The Lion" has described how it was:

> Sometimes we got carving battles going that would last for four or five hours. . . . We would embroider the melodies with our own original ideas and try to develop patterns that had more originality than those played before us. Sometimes it was just a question as to who could think up the most patterns within a given tune. It was pure improvisation.
>
> You had to have your own individual style and be able to play in all the keys. In those days we could all copy each other's shouts by learning them by ear. Sometimes in order to keep the others from picking up too much of my stuff I'd perform in the hard keys, B major and E major.
>
> The rent party was the place to go to pick up on all the latest jokes, jive and uptown news. You would see all kinds of people making the party scene: formally dressed society folks from downtown, policemen, painters, carpenters, mechanics, truckmen in their workingmen's clothes, gamblers, lesbians, and entertainers of all kinds. The parties were recommended to newly arrived single gals as the place to get acquainted (Smith and Hoefer, 1965, p. 555–56).

Negro folk music had an independent effect on the great black pianists of the 1920s and 1930s; other elements were there before and after the arrival of the big bands. James P. Johnson spoke of the influences on his playing:

> The people who came to the Jungles Casino [in the 1920s] were mostly from around Charleston, South Carolina, and other places in the South. Most of them worked for the Ward Line as longshoremen or on ships that called at southern ports. . . . The

Charleston, which became a popular dance step on its own, was just a regulation cotillion step without a name. . . .

From listening to classical piano records and concerts, from friends of Ernest Green such as Mme. Garret, who was a fine classical pianist, I would learn concert effects and build them into blues and rags (Hadlock, 1965, p. 146–47).

Jazz did not come to New York from Chicago. A more accurate statement might be that jazz centered in Chicago and later in New York. Jazz and jazzlike music were being played all over the country, but recording and the radio made jazz appear to the public to come first out of Chicago and later New York.

New York represented a coming-together of several streams that had flowed out of New Orleans and other points South and West. When the Chicagoans and other "hot" musicians got to New York, they found jazz already there, and a new fusion began to occur. We have spoken of the piano tradition that was so strong in New York, but there was also a longstanding big band tradition, heavily influenced by the universally popular ragtime tradition.

As far back as 1912, a major concert of syncopated music led by three black conductors took place at Carnegie Hall. The black regimental bands of World War I became famous throughout America and the world. James Reese Europe, a leader of one of these bands, became the toast of New York in the teens. He also played for and developed the music for the dance team of Irene and Vernon Castle, who epitomized the 1911 to 1917 dance craze (Whitcomb, 1973). Even then, during the dance-craze period, the New York scene represented a smoothing and sweetening of dance into easily learned steps. It was a taming process. As Whitcomb has suggested, the essence of pop is the art of producing "the vaguely familiar."

The brilliant work of Eubie Blake with his partner, bandleader/lyricist Noble Sissle, and countless others created a great tradition of Afro-American contributions to American popular music. Fletcher Henderson gave to the entire big band what Jelly Roll Morton had given to the piano/orchestra earlier. The point to be made, though, is that much of this music, as good as it was, was urbane and sophisticated but lacking in the truly blues-based and gutsy element that was the hallmark of, for example, New Orlean jazz. Just as the flow of illegal slaves revitalized the African sense of music for black Americans throughout the latter half of the nineteenth century, the shift to New York of Chicago jazz players in the twenties and thirties revitalized Afro-American roots in that city two generations later.

White bands of the 1930s were successful because of the demand created by radio; less black jazz and blues were heard over the radio. Radio was largely airing sweet "potted palm" music. The situation had not improved much by the mid-1930s, but with a union-enforced ban on playing canned music, which began in 1922, the bandleader became important and, in fact, was the forerunner of the modern disk jockey. In the 1930s bandleaders jumped on the radio bandwagon, and the air waves were filled with live big band shows. Radio made bands. Some bands were named for commercial products, for example, B. A. Rolfe's Lucky Strike Orchestra. The new working site for mass-appeal popular jazz became the recording studio. The radio did not, however, open up equal opportunity for black bands. There was great pressure on the sweet radio bands to produce hits. The modern pop music era was born, and those who made a living in the music business were not particularly interested in creativity. They were interested in selling songs and the right formula.

Entertainers from vaudeville (and other types of show business) fronted radio bands. From Jimmy Durante, who once played with a jazz band, to Ozzie Nelson, entertainers built careers on song plugging and commercial (formula or sweet) jazz. Some gifted white players, such as Benny Goodman, did make it, but by and large real jazz was hard to find. Jazzmen relied on college kids, jazz cultists, and the more aware dancers for an audience. Real jazzmen had a difficult time competing in the electronic media.

White jazz-oriented musicians either modified their music and went commercial or they starved. Most white jazz players of this era contented themselves with occasional hot licks in the rather stifling musical contexts in which they found themselves. When they wanted to play real jazz, they went uptown to Harlem. There they could sit in with and listen to the black bands that did not have to compromise as much because they had been safely "contained." But what about the black jazzman? What was happening uptown?

From the turn of the century onward, Harlem has been the symbolic and cultural center of life for black people in America. This was due in part to the various "Harlem Renaissances" in the arts beginning in 1898 (Cruse, 1967). So even when the black musician could not succeed on the national scene, he still had the option of "going home" to Harlem, where he was sure of an appreciative audience. The nightclub remained the mainstay of the black musician even as his white counterpart was moving into radio.

But the black musicians also had to accommodate to the popular swing era. The wide-open New Orleans style fell into a decline; jazz was modified to please the dancers. The pressures from black audiences were different from those of white audiences, however, and the black band leaders found a less drastic solution, which left a strong and lasting imprint on jazz style. It does not detract from Benny Goodman's achievement to recognize, for example, that his style depended heavily on the arrangements of black men such as Fletcher Henderson, whom he employed as an arranger. Goodman simply had the good sense to be color-blind when it came to real talent.

The big band movement had been gathering steam through the late 1920s and into the 1930s. The pioneers were the black big band leaders. This was due in large measure to the demand created by dancers in the black community. The black bands had to play music that was both hot and danceable. Here again historical forces were at work. There had been important early breakthroughs by blacks into American musical comedy. The emphasis, however, in the black Broadway shows was on dance, whereas white musical comedy had treated dance as incidental to the art form (Stearns and Stearns, 1968). Black audiences were knowledgeable about the dance and demanded more sophistication (from the jazz perspective) than white audiences.

The Stearnses carefully documented how American popular dances, from the cakewalk to the boogaloo, have generally shown a lag between the white and the black dancers, with the black dancers performing them first. Nightclubs, dance halls, and cabarets were considered sinful anyway by puritanical America, and what went on there was of little concern, as long as it was contained. So these places became the settings where the fusion among professional dancers, the dancing public, and the big bands took place. As George Simon says: "With almost all the best hotel rooms and vaudeville houses reserved for white bands, these spirited, pre-swing-era outfits blew their wares mostly in ballrooms. . . ." (Simon, 1967, p. 25). By the time the swing era was ushered in by Benny Goodman (for most of the American public), it was well established in the black community. It is also of more than passing interest that for most Americans the swing era was ushered in on the mass media, that is, radio. All agree that the stage had been set by other bands (notably the popular Casa Loma band), "but early in 1935 came Goodman's big chance, a weekly Saturday-night appearance on a coast-to-coast radio show" (Simon, 1967, p. 27). The official swing era was a child of radio.

From 1935 until World War II, competition grew among bands, and both swing and nonswinging sweet music filled the airwaves, with the sweet bands getting the lion's share. When the war began, many band-leaders and bands enlisted, usually amid great publicity, and swing began to wane. The American Federation of Musicians' recording ban of 1942, which stopped all recording by AFM members because of the use of "canned" music on radio, and the rise to prominence of vocalists, finally killed swing (Simon, 1967, p. 33–39).

In order to understand what was happening with the black bands in the 1930s, it is necessary to know something about the context—the ballroom or nightclub—in which most of the music was heard. Speaking about the Jimmie Lunceford band, a black band, discographer Albert McCarthy succinctly sums up what these bands had to do:

> To begin with, the Lunceford band, almost more than any other, found the secret of pleasing several audiences at once without, except in a few instances, lowering musical standards. To the dancers it was a fine dance band; to the people who went to see a show it was a good theatrical spectacle; to the jazz fan it was a good jazz group. I don't think any other band succeeded so well in engaging diverse audiences. I am concerned with it as a big band from a jazz viewpoint and, leaving out Ellington and Henderson, I don't think it was equalled (McCarthy in Williams, 1962, p. 136).

In the 1930s jazz had split along racial lines. Up until the introduction of the phonograph record and the radio, jazz was considered, for the most part, a form of black music, although many white musicians played it. In the teens and twenties it came to the attention of white musicians and a hip white audience, and they were attracted to it because of its vitality and the challenge it offered.

Real jazz was not protected from popular musicians the way that "real" classical music was, because it had neither high-status patrons nor academicians to enclose it and control access to the places where it was professionally played. Classical music tended to be restricted to the concert stage; it was not "functional," although it once had been. Negro jazz was originally functional as folk music and later as incidental music in a myriad of entertainment settings. The radio and phonograph, and the short life of the hit tune, forced popular music to devour new sources of sound; jazz was used to vitalize popular music in the United States. The "cost" to jazz was enormous. Even the race records, a marvelous source of real jazz in America, either collapsed during the depression or were permitted to die by their parent companies.

Most writers on race relations in the United States agree that there was a growth of anti-Negro sentiment in the post-World War I period due, in part, to the wave of black immigration into urban centers (Marden and Meyer, 1978, pp. 136–55). Although the connection with jazz is indirect, it seems reasonable to assume that some aspects of the containment of jazz were part of this larger phenomenon. A few black bands, of course, did gain general popularity during the swing era—Ellington and

Basie, for example. But many black bands were forced to remain where they had always worked. Integrated public appearances did occur, however, and jazz broke the major-league color line long before baseball.

Many younger black musicians grew restive under this "contract." They felt overly restricted by playing in big bands. They tended to be better educated than their musical "fathers" (in order to play in a tightly knit big band, as we have demonstrated, it was necessary to read music well) and more conscious of the fact that they were not reaping the enormous financial rewards that recording and the radio offered.

By the end of the 1930s, unlike earlier periods, conditions for perceived and resented discrimination were present within jazz. With the outbreak of World War II, it was no longer a case of jazzmen against institutional criticism of their art form, but rather a case of black musicians realizing that they could not make it. And the reason they could not make it was not because of prejudice against jazz (although that was present also) but because of racial prejudice.

KANSAS CITY

In the musical *Oklahoma!* we all laugh at the country bumpkin who tells us "Everything's Up to Date in Kansas City." Yet, in historical perspective, that perception appears much less laughable. Well into the 1930s, Kansas City remained a true provincial capital. While many American cities were losing their regional "self-balanced" character to national integration, Kansas City remained not only a major commercial center but also "the city" for ten states and one-sixth of the country. Located west of the Mississippi River, Kansas City's beginnings can be traced to a French trading post established in 1826. Situated at the confluence of the Missouri and Kansas (Kew) rivers, it became an important trade and transportation center at the start of the Oregon and Santa Fe trails. The whole West was Kansas City's territory during the period of great westward expansion. It is still a major agricultural center with grain elevators and stockyards brokering southwestern agricultural products. For the same reasons that Chicago gained a substantial black population—employment opportunities—Kansas City attracted blacks.

A relatively isolated provincial center, Kansas City fell under the control of a corrupt political machine. Combining criminal activities with ethnic politics and a strong power base in the city's First Ward, Boss Tom Pendergast solidified his control of the city after the passage of the Volstead Act in 1919. Beating back every good-government challenge, the Pendergast machine controlled "Kaycee" until 1938, when Tom Pendergast was indicted for income tax fraud. No one has better described this politics/crime syndrome in American life than Daniel Bell in *The End of Ideology*. In the chapter entitled, "Crime as an American Way of Life," he says:

> Americans have had an extraordinary talent for compromise in politics and extremism in morality. The most shameless political deals (and "steals") have been rationalized as expedient and realistically necessary. Yet in no other country have there been such spectacular attempts to curb human appetites and brand them as illicit, and nowhere else such glaring failures. From the start America was at one and the same time a frontier community where "everything goes," and the fair country of the Blue Laws. At the turn of the century the cleavage developed between the Big City and the small-town conscience. Crime as a growing business was fed by the revenues from prostitution, liquor, and gambling that a wide-open urban society encouraged and that a middle-class Protestant ethos tried to suppress with a ferocity unmatched in any other civilized country. . . .
>
> Crime, in many ways, is a Coney Island mirror, caricaturing the morals and manners of a society. The jungle quality of the American business community, particularly at the turn of the century, was reflected in the mode of "business" practiced by the coarse gangster elements, most of them from new immigrant families, who were "getting ahead," just as Horatio Alger had urged (p. 128).

Both Chicago and Kansas City were examples of Bell's insights. But the very isolation of Kansas City made it controllable in a way that Al Capone could only dream about in the more cosmopolitan Chicago. Kansas City became a magnet for ragtime, blues, and jazz musicians because they were protected from moralistic harassment and could play their music in cabarets and in after-hours jam sessions just as long as they brought in the drinkers and the dancers.

From the point of view of jazz history, there was a lack of commercial pressure in Kansas City evident in both New York and Chicago, which were struggling for national dominance of the new mass media. The position of Kansas City as a wide-open town and as the big city at the head of the Southwest territory helped to encourage the emergence of a jazz style consonant with, yet exhibiting considerable independence from, national jazz development. Two strong musical traditions existed in the Southwest that both retarded and contributed to the evolution of jazz there. One was the existence of a hot and dusty blues tradition out of Texas and Oklahoma. The other was the powerful grip of ragtime (Scott

Joplin established ragtime out of Sedalia, Missouri) on the entire area long after it had faded elsewhere. (Both of these traditions are touched upon in chapter 3.)

Throughout the twenties and thirties territory bands* emerged in cities and towns with substantial black populations that wanted music in their cabarets, dance halls, and other places of socialization such as parks and picnic grounds. These bands were local and often made up of semi-professional musicians. Good players drove out those of lesser talent or persistence, and avocation turned into vocation. A kind of Darwinian selection process was at work. If the population expanded, as it often did in the period of rapid industrial expansion, and if the opportunities for entertainment grew, outside groups with reputations would be called in. While people took pride in their local groups, they also made greater demands for excellence as they grew more knowledgeable from hearing a variety of bands. Some local bands stayed close to a home base and were content to satisfy their patrons, although they might lose the best players to more aggressive units. Other bands began to travel farther afield, and territorial invasions often took place.

Enterprising promoters recognized the natural appeal of pitting local champions against outsiders with larger reputations. The famous "battles of the bands" took place. A visiting band was booked opposite a local one. Like similarly organized carnival boxing matches, these battles generated great public interest. After these titanic struggles, the best musicians from each competing group would gather, often in smaller clubs, to exchange musical ideas. A great sifting and sorting took place; new groups formed in a kaleidoscope of changing leaders and players. One-night stands and road bands entered the American lexicon. The competition was fierce and often the money was relatively good. Locals turned into cosmopolitans in a virtual parody of the classical market paradigm (Russell, 1971).

The process described above went on in all the territories to a lesser or greater degree. It also was repeated in Chicago and New York in such places as the Savoy Ballroom in Harlem and in band battles between

---

*As discussed in chapter 4, territories and territory bands developed independently in several parts of the country (Hennessy, 1973). Hennessey's work in this area is monumental. The purpose of the discussion here is simply to emphasize the model he developed. It must be recalled that the various territory bands were ultimately drawn into a national hierarchy and tended to lose their regional flavor in favor of an emerging national style. Those who chose not to play the national game—or were found wanting in the big time for one reason or another—simply faded into oblivion. The Southwest territory and its capital, Kansas City, retained an independent status longer than the others and provide a perfect case study for the process of development and decline.

black and white groups in places like the famous Roseland Ballroom in Manhattan. Not unlike the cutting contests among the street bands in New Orleans, the competitive nature of music and musicians jostling for places in the consciousness of the public reflected the struggle for a market share found throughout American economic life in this era. The stick of obscurity and poverty and the golden carrot of stardom were incentives for everyone. A genuine quest for artistic excellence, of course, also contributed to rivalry.

People in the Southwest, conditioned to the authentic ragtime of Scott Joplin and James Scott in Kansas City and the earthy bluesmen out of Texas, demanded hot playing. Out of this mingling of styles, the famous Kansas City riff was born. The riff is a short incessant refrain repeated over and over, serving a musical function akin to the mantra in meditation. At its best, it produces an ecstatic state. Derived from the intense repeated phrase common to the blues, the big band riff simplified the ensemble problem and provided counterpoint to the improvised solo break.

Exceptional bands in this tradition, such as the ones led by Andy Kirk (The Clouds of Joy), Walter Page (and his Blue Devils), and Bennie Moten, became Kansas City legends. Many musicians trained in the Southwest tradition brought real fire to better known bands in Chicago and New York. On the increasingly sophisticated and disciplined template that Chicago and New York bands repesented, New Orleans, Kansas City, and other "provincial" musicians kept etching authentic blues-based strokes.

Sometimes entire bands would invade the big time and remind jazz musicians and listeners alike of the roots of jazz. The Moten band, for example, was taken over by William "Count" Basie following Bennie Moten's death in 1935; it was brought East and recorded (SCCJ-V-7 and 8). The band had enormous impact on the New York scene. A gentle irony here, of course, is that Count Basie—the best known of the Kansas City band leaders—was from Red Bank, New Jersey. Basie is a living example of the anthropological truism that cultural production, with the aid of modern transportation and communication, knows no well-defined boundaries and is differentially shared across traditional geographic lines.

The Count Basie orchestra developed several important musical devices; each had a significant impact on later jazz developments. Jo Jones, Basie's drummer, shifted the emphasis of jazz drumming away from straight timekeeping. Cymbals, and especially the bass drum, were used to accent rhythm with great dramatic effect. (In the next chapter the critical importance of this shift will become clear.) Basie himself used the piano to accent rather than to carry either the melody or rhythm of the band. The strong bass work of Walter Page, of course, made this possible. Additionally, Count Basie melded together the basic blues shouting vocals of singers such as Jimmy Rushing and the light minimlist instrumental brilliance of players such as Lester Young—an extraordinary feat that demonstrated the possibilities of combining diverse elements in jazz.

In Kansas City, the Jay McShann band took on the mantle of the Basie band, and Charlie Parker, a key figure in the bop era, played with McShann's band. Other important bop players also came from the Southwest.

The swing era will be considered again in the next chapter from the point of view of what was to follow it. Implicit in that discussion is the idea that swing did not die, but rather became a part of subsequent jazz developments. In fact, each era in jazz broadened and integrated what had gone before.

CODA

In listening to jazz of the thirties and in reading about it, the term "Dixieland" jazz is often used. Dixieland is an elusive label. Sometimes it is used to refer to derivative white jazz from the earliest New Orleans groups (Schuller, 1968, 165—87) through the "happy music" played by contemporary amateur and professional musicians who have not elected to adopt the complexities of bop (Tanner and Gerow, 1973, pp. 41—62). Sometimes all jazz prior to 1940 is referred to as Dixieland. As long as one is aware that the label is loosely and variably applied, one is aware that any semantic defense of this label (and others such as swing and bop) may generate more heat than light.

Another troublesome label in the jazz tradition is boogie-woogie. Characteristics of the boogie-woogie style were discussed in chapter 3. The popularity of the style bridged the twenties and thirties and peaked in the depression years of the early thirties. (After all, piano players were cheaper to hire than bands. Both bogie-woogie and Harlem stride piano represented a lot of music for a little money.) Many jazz pianists include boogie-woogie numbers in their repertoire, and in 1938 there was a major revival of this style (Tanner and Gerow, 1973, pp. 63—67). Important boogie-woogie players such as Jimmy Yancey, Pine Top Smith and Meade Lux Lewis (SCCJ-IV-2) were active in Chicago at the same time that city blues and Chicago jazz were in their heydays. Each of these styles influenced the other and had common ancestors.

JAZZ / The Personal Dimension

Bix Beiderbecke (Frank Driggs Collection)

BIX BEIDERBECKE

The life of Bix Beiderbecke is the stuff of legend. A brilliant musician with an attractive personality, he developed self-destructive habits that resulted in his death before his twenty-ninth birthday. The cult that has arisen around him has made an objective assessment of his contributions difficult.

Leon Bix Beiderbecke was born in Davenport, Iowa, in 1903, the son of a businessman. He seemed to have a natural gift for music and, as a child, was drawn to the piano. But formal lessons had little effect on him. Because of his musical instincts and fine ear, he progressed in his own way. At age fifteen, he heard a record by the Original Dixieland Jazz Band and soon acquired a cornet, which he taught himself to play. Using unorthodox fingering, he achieved effects that conventionally trained players would have found difficult if not impossible to realize. By 1919, Beiderbecke was also playing piano in bands with his fellow high school students. Around this time, he also began to hear some of the music from the Mississippi riverboats and, on one such occasion, met Louis Armstrong, who was then playing with Fate Marable's Mississippi riverboat band. By 1920, Bix had become proficient enough on cornet to play it publicly, and began to devote so much time to his music that his schoolwork suffered.

In 1921, his parents enrolled him in Lake Forest Academy, a private school near Chicago, but he was dismissed the following year for his poor academic showing. Musically, however, his stay was a success. He played with the school orchestra, sat in with various groups in Chicago, and became known in musical circles. One group that impressed Bix was the New Orleans Rhythm Kings. After some engagements in Chicago and on the riverboats, Bix joined the Wolverine Orchestra, which played mostly in Indiana and Ohio. In 1924, he made his first recordings with the Wolverines for Gennett Records in Richmond, Indiana, and later that year the orchestra traveled to New York where they played at the Cinderella Ballroom. Returning to the Midwest, Bix briefly joined a Jean Goldkette unit in Detroit. (Goldkette was a musician/entrepreneur who often fielded several musical groups simultaneously.) After an abortive attempt at college (he lasted eighteen days), he withdrew from the University of Iowa.

Soon afterward he met saxophonist Frankie Trumbauer, whose orchestra he joined in St. Louis. Trumbauer was a highly skilled musician and helped Bix with reading scores. In 1926 both men were signed to play with Jean Goldkette's primary orchestra. The Goldkette band was advanced musically, with a number of jazz players, and an arranger, Bill Challis, who was far ahead of his time. Although Bix performed with the Goldkette orchestra on records his most significant recordings from this period are those he made with Trumbauer in 1927 (SCCJ-III-4 and 5). During that same year, Bix recorded a piano solo of "In a Mist," a piece he had composed several years earlier and was constantly reworking. This composition, along with three others by Bix, was eventually written down by Bill Challis and published as *Bix Beiderbecke's Modern Piano Suite.*

After the Goldkette band folded in 1927, several members, including Bix, Trumbauer, and Challis, were hired by Paul Whiteman for his large, "symphonic" ensemble. Bix was prominently featured and well paid by Whiteman, but this period marked the beginning of the end. He began to drink heavily, his health deteriorated, and he was forced to take an extended leave. During this time, Bix began to question his own musical direction and developed a new interest in piano and classical music. "As Bix's interest in piano and composition deepened, it led to ever bolder explorations of his own musical frontiers—and ever more acute awareness of their limitations" (Sudhalter and Evans, 1964, p. 255). By mid-1929, his poor health, in addition to the strenuous schedule of the Whiteman orchestra, forced Bix to leave the band. He returned to Davenport, where he rested, and received hospital treatment for his growing alcohol problem. His health continued to decline, and he spent the final two years of his life playing intermittently, traveling between his home town and New York City. He died in August, 1931, in New York, of lobar pneumonia.

His death affected only a small group of his fellow musicians at the time. It was only later that the legend grew, nurtured by such works as Dorothy Baker's novel *Young Man with a Horn* (a fictionalized account of Bix's life) and some nonfiction accounts, which were no less fantastic. In recent years, writers such as Richard Sudhalter and Gunther Schuller have succeeded in separating the facts from the legend. Beiderbecke's career has been placed in some perspective.

One incontrovertible source in understanding Beiderbecke as a musician are his recordings. They reveal that his approach to the music he played was a true departure from what had preceded him. His lyrical and logical conceptions, pure, light tone, and advanced harmonic thinking inspired a whole school of trumpet players, most notably Red Nichols, Jimmy McPartland, and Bobby Hackett.

Bix Beiderbecke had musical aspirations that, had he lived to realize them, might have taken him beyond jazz. His piano compositions only hint at what that direction might have been.

Further Information

Biography/Criticism   Berton, Ralph. *Remembering Bix: A Memoir of the Jazz Age.* New York: Harper & Row, 1974.

James, Burnett. *Bix Beiderbecke.* Kings of Jazz, no. 4. London: Cassell, 1959 (also in American paperback).

Sudhalter, Richard M., and Evans, Philip R. *Bix: Man and Legend.* New Rochelle, N.Y.: Arlington House, 1974.

Wareing, Charles H., and Garlick, George. *Bugles for Beiderbecke.* London: Sidgewicke & Jackson, 1958.

Discography   Castelli, Vittorio; Kaleveld, Evert; Pusateri, Liborio. *The Bix Bands; A Bix Biederbecke Disco-biography.* Milan: Raretone, 1972.

See also "Bix Beiderbecke on Record: A Comprehensive Discography" by Philip R. Evans and William Dean-Myatt in Sudhalter and Evans, listed above.

Bix Beiderbecke on LP   *Bix Beiderbecke and the Chicago Cornets,* Milestone M-47019 (2 records). (1924, with the Wolverines and other groups.)

The Bix Beiderbecke Story, vol. 1, *Bix and His Gang,* Columbia CL-844 (1927—28, groups led by Bix and Frankie Trumbauer); vol. 2, *Bix and Tram,* Columbia CL-845 (1927—28, with Trumbauer); vol. 3, *Whiteman Days,* Columbia CL-846 ("In a Mist" piano solo, 1927; 1928–29 with Whiteman Orchestra).

Benny Goodman (Frank Driggs Collection)

Benny Goodman

Few figures in music have achieved Benny Goodman's popularity, but this recognition has gone hand in hand with consummate musicianship.

Born in Chicago in 1909 of Russian Jewish parents, he began studying the clarinet at the age of ten in a synagogue. He continued his studies with a classical teacher, Franz Schoepp (who also taught jazz clarinetists Buster Bailey and Jimmy Noone). In high school Goodman played with some of his fellow students who shared his growing interest in jazz music—among them cornetist Jimmy McPartland. They patterned their playing after artists they admired on record. Benny was particularly impressed by clarinetist Leon Rappolo, of the New Orleans Rhythm Kings, and by Jimmy Noone.

Goodman turned professional quite early, joining the musicians' union at thirteen, when he began working with Charles "Murph" Podolsky's band. For the next three years he played intermittently with Podolsky and other local groups. In 1925, at the age of sixteen, Goodman was recruited by Ben Pollack, who had heard of the youngster's talent. Goodman joined Pollack's band in California, and returned with him to Chicago, making his first appearance on record at a September 1926 session there. He went to New York with Pollack's band, remaining with it until 1929. The Pollack period was one of great musical growth for Goodman.

In the early thirties he worked primarily in New York radio and recording studios and Broadway shows. During this time he made many jazz-flavored recordings, including some with Red Nichols, Ben Selvin, and Ted Lewis, as well as a few under his own name. Among the latter were several "all star" dates arranged by budding producer John Hammond. Leading black artists, such as Coleman Hawkins, Teddy Wilson, and Billie Holiday, took part in these sessions, although integrated studio groups were still a rarity at the time.

In 1934, Goodman formed his first big band and, after a successful audition, began an engagement at Billy Rose's Music Hall. This band, using arrangements by Fletcher Henderson, Benny Carter, and Dean Kincaide among others, was also featured on NBC radio's "Let's Dance" series. Through broadcasts and records, the orchestra began to attract a following. Its popularity crystallized during a tour of the western states. If one date can be designated as the start of the swing era, it is August 21, 1935, when Goodman opened at the Palomar Ballroom in Los Angeles to a wildly enthusiastic reception. During the next few years, such musicians as drummer Gene Krupa, trumpeter Harry James, and pianist Jess Stacy were featured, and Fletcher Henderson's arrangements were played; the band's fame skyrocketed.

Meanwhile, Goodman inaugurated an equally important series of trio and quartet appearances and recordings featuring an interracial group made up of himself on clarinet, Gene Krupa on drums, Teddy Wilson on piano, and Lionel Hampton on vibes (SCCJ-IV-3). In 1938, the Goodman band, along with several guest artists gave a widely acclaimed concert at Carnegie Hall. Goodman formed a new small group in 1939, a sextet, which included the brilliant young guitarist Charlie Christian (SCCJ-VI-2 and 3). Throughout the forties Goodman led big bands from time to time, while continuing his small-group activities. During the fifties, sixties, and seventies, he appeared mainly with small groups, occasionally assembling a big band for special events.

He has made many tours abroad, including an important State Department-sponsored trip to the U.S.S.R. with a big band in 1962. Since the late thirties, Goodman has also made a number of appearances as soloist with classical ensembles. In 1978, he performed in Carnegie Hall to mark the fortieth anniversary of his historic first concert there.

As an instrumentalist, Goodman set new standards for clarinet technique, and created a style that was widely imitated. As a bandleader, he succeeded for a time in bringing jazz to the forefront of popular music in America. He also contributed to the removal of racial barriers in the music industry.

Today, approaching his seventies, Goodman remains what he has always been: a fine musician, a taskmaster, and an enigmatic personality regarded by some as generous and by others as aloof.

Further Information

Autobiography   Goodman, Benny, and Kolodin, Irving. *The Kingdom of Swing.* New York: Stackpole Sons, 1939.

Biodiscography   Connor, D. Russell, and Hicks, Warren W. *B.G. on the Record: A Biodiscography of Benny Goodman.* New Rochelle, N.Y.: Arlington House, 1969.

Benny Goodman on LP   *Jazz Holiday,* MCA 4018 (2 records). (1928–34, with Red Nichols, Joe Venuti and Eddie Lang.)
The Complete Benny Goodman, vol. 1, Bluebird AXM2-5505 (2 records) (1935); vol. 2, Bluebird AXM2-5515 (2 records) (1935–36); vol. 3, Bluebird AXM2-5532 (2 records) (1936); vol. 4, Bluebird AXM2-5537 (2 records) (1936–37).
Carnegie Hall Jazz Concert, vols. 1–3, Columbia CL-814/815/816 (1938). *Solo Flight,,* issued with Charlie Christian as leader, Columbia CG-30779 (2 records)
Benny Goodman Presents Eddie Sauter Arrangements, Columbia Special Products JGL-523 (early forties).
Bebop Spoken Here, Capitol M-11061 (late forties).
On Stage, London 44182/44183 (2 records). (Recorded live in Copenhagen, 1972, wtih Zoot Sims.)
In addition to these LPs, Sunbeam records had isued an extensive Goodman series, including many air checks and other noncommercial material.

Duke Ellington (Frank Driggs Collection)

DUKE ELLINGTON

Edward Kennedy Ellington was born in Washington, D.C., in 1899. His family was relatively well off, and as a child Ellington was, by his own admission, "spoiled rotten." His father worked as a butler and, later, as a blueprint maker for the Navy. Although Ellington began piano lessons at twelve, he was more interested in athletics. It was not until he heard some local piano players and a young Philadelphian, pianist Harvey Brooks, that he began to apply himself seriously. He received help from several of the musicians he admired, but he singled out Doc Perry, a well-known Washington, D.C., pianist of the twenties, as a primary source of inspiration.

While in high school, Duke (who received his noble title from a schoolmate) began to play for money, sometimes as a solo pianist, sometimes putting together small groups for dances, and occasionally even acting as a booking agent for other bands. Ellington was also talented in the visual arts and turned down a scholarship to the Pratt Institute of Fine Arts.

In 1923, Ellington, along with two of his sidemen, drummer Sonny Greer and saxophonist Otto Hardwicke, went to New York. Through Greer, they had been signed to play in Wilbur Sweatman's vaudeville orchestra. But when work became scarce, the young musicians had to hustle to survive. Finally, they returned to Washington. During the months he had spent in New York, however, Ellington got to know some of the leading piano stylists, including Willie "The Lion" Smith, James P. Johnson, and Fats Waller. "The Lion," Ellington recalls, was especially kind to him. Later in 1923, Fats Waller convinced Duke to try again in New York, and Ellington's group, the Washingtonians, eventually landed a residency at the Hollywood Club (later called the Kentucky Club). There the young leader made several important additions in personnel and began to shape his orchestral concepts. In 1927 the band played an engagement at the Cotton Club, which lasted, with interruptions for tours, until 1931. During this residence the band received wide exposure through radio broadcasts and recordings (SCCJ-VI-4) and attained international popularity. In 1933, Ellington made a highly successful tour of Europe, the first of many trips abroad.

In 1943, with a performance of *Black, Brown and Beige,* Ellington initiated a series of annual concerts at Carnegie Hall, presenting a number of his longer works over the next few years.

Ellington continued to lead his orchestra throughout the forties, fifties, sixties, and into the seventies, enjoying great success, even though many other big bands had disbanded or were struggling for survival. He constantly expanded his musical horizons by such new ventures as his first religious-music concert in 1965.

The late sixties and early seventies were a time of undiminished musical creativity for Ellington, as well as a time for enjoying the recognition due him. He received countless awards, many honorary degrees, and other distinctions. His seventieth birthday was celebrated at the White House. In early 1974, suffering from lung cancer, he was forced to restrict his appearances, although he continued to compose right up until his death on May 24 of that year.

Ellington was one of the most prolific composers of this century. He wrote his first composition, "Soda Fountain Rag," in 1914 and hundreds of compositions after that, many of which became popular hits as well as jazz standards. He also composed the scores for several films and shows. Another facet of his genius was his extended works, whose themes often reflect places he had seen (*Far East Suite*), famous figures (*Portrait of Ella Fitzgerald*), and many other subjects.

Ellington the composer cannot be separated from Ellington, the bandleader, since he used his orchestra as a vehicle for his writing. Musicians stayed with his bands for many years, a continuity unequaled by any other group in jazz. Ellington wrote many works to feature the special talents of his soloists (SCCJ-VI-8). Through the years he skillfully applied to his musical canvas the unique tonal colors of such players as alto saxophonist Johnny Hodges, trumpeters Bubber Miley, Cootie Williams, and Rex Stewart, tenor saxophonist Ben Webster, Paul Gonsalves, and baritone saxophonist Harry Carney. Many of his men were with him for decades, and if they left, they usually returned to the fold eventually. Ellington was willing to endure whatever hardships were required to keep a band together, so important was it to him to be able to hear his new works performed immediately. "I keep these expensive gentlemen with me to gratify that desire," he said (Hentoff, 1976, p. 29).

Ellington, the pianist, is often overlooked in the light of his other accomplishments, but he evolved a singular style and distinctive touch that did not go unheeded by younger musicians such as Thelonious Monk.

Always suave, unruffled, and articulate on stage, Ellington insisted that his private life remain his own. He was always understanding of his musicians and loyal to them to such a degree that he was reluctant ever to fire anyone, no matter how great the transgression.

No discussion of the career of Duke Ellington would be complete without mentioning Billy Strayhorn, who, from 1939 until his death in 1966, served Duke as composer, arranger, and occasional pianist. He and Ellington enjoyed total musical rapport, and often it was impossible to tell where the work of one ended and where the other began, so successful were their collaborations.

Another important figure in the Ellington musical family is Duke's son, Mercer, who played trumpet from time to time in the band as well as serving as its road manager and arranger. After his father's death, Mercer assumed leadership of the Ellington orchestra, which is now composed of talented younger musicians. The band carries on the Ellington legacy by including some of Duke's lesser known works as well as his classics in its repertoire.

In addition to the recordings cited above, the Smithsonian collection contains several other examples of Ellingtonia (SCCJ-VI-5, 6, and 7; VII-1, 2, and 3).

Further Information

Autobiography   Ellington, Duke. *Music Is My Mistress.* New York: Doubleday, 1973.

Biography/Criticism   Dance, Stanley. *The World of Duke Ellington.* New York: Scribner's, 1970.

Ellington, Mercer, with Dance, Stanley. *Duke Ellington in Person: An Intimate Memoir.* New York: Houghton Mifflin, 1978.

Gammond, Peter, ed. *Duke Ellington: His Life and Music.* New York: Roy Publishers, 1958.

Jewell, Derek. *Duke: A Portrait of Duke Ellington.* New York: Norton, 1977.

Lambert, G. D. *Duke Ellington.* Kings of Jazz, no. 1. London: Cassell, 1959 (also in American paperback).

Ulanov, Barry. *Duke Ellington.* New York: Creative Age Press, 1946.

Discography Aasland, Benny H. *The "Wax Works" of Duke Ellington.* Stockholm: published privately, 1954.

Bakker, Dick M. *Duke Ellington on Microgroove,* vol. 1, 1923–1936. Alphen aan den Rijn, Holland: Micrography, 1977. (Vol. 2 forthcoming.)

Jepsen, Jorgen Grunnet. *A Discography of Duke Ellington,* vol. 1 (1925–37), vol. 2 (1937–47), vol. 3 (1947–59). Copenhagen: Denmark: Debut Records, 1959.

Massagli, Luciano; Volonte, Giovanni M.; Pusateri, Liborio. *The Duke Ellington Story on Records.* Milan, Italy: Musica Jazz. In progress. To date, eleven volumes up to 1958. Complete with soloists, thematic sources, as well as all standard discographical data.

Timner, W. E. *Ellingtonia: The Recorded Music of Duke Ellington. A Collector's Manual.* Montreal: n.p., 1976. A chronological listing of all known Ellington recordings, commercial and noncommercial, issued and not issued. Includes date, personnel, matrix numbers, and original label, but does not list releases.

Duke Ellington on LP: *The Ellington Era,* vol. 1, Columbia C3L-27 (3 records) (1927–40).

Duke Ellington 1938, Smithsonian P2-13367 (2 records).

Duke Ellington 1939, Smithsonian P2-14273 (2 records).

This Is Duke Ellington, RCA VPM-6042 (2 records) (1927 45).

Carnegie Hall Concert, January 1943, Prestige 34004 (3 records).

Hi-Fi Ellington Uptown, Columbia Special Products JCL-830 (1952).

Piano Reflections, Capitol M-11058 (trio, 1953).

Newport '56, Columbia CS-8648.

Such Sweet Thunder, Columbia Special Products JCL-723. (Musical vignettes of Shakespearean characters, 1957.)

The Great Paris Concert, Atlantic SD2-304 (2 records) (1963).

Second Sacred Concert, Prestige 24045 (2 records) (1968).

Latin American Suite, Fantasy 8419 (1968).

70th Birthday Concert, Solid State 19000 (2 records). (Live in England, 1969.)

New Orleans Suite, Atlantic SD-1580 (2 records) (1970).

Duke's Big Four, Pablo 2310703 (quartet, 1973).

Both French RCA and French CBS are in the process of issuing multirecord series containing Ellington's entire output for these companies (Victor and Columbia) from the twenties to the forties. These LPs are widely available in larger record stores.

Count Basie (Institute of Jazz Studies)

COUNT BASIE

Since the mid-thirties, Count Basie has led, almost continuously, the most powerfully swinging of the big bands. Although closely associated with—if not the personification of—Kansas City jazz, William Basie was born in Red Bank, New Jersey, in 1904. His mother taught him piano, and he also studied with a teacher. By the time he finished high school, he had begun to work professionally in New York clubs, including engagements with the bands of Elmer Snowden and June Clark. At this time (the early twenties) he came in contact with the giants of New York stride piano. Young Basie was particularly influenced by Fats Waller and received some musical assistance from him. In 1923 Basie replaced his idol in a vaudeville troupe, Kate Crippen and Her Kids, and spent the next four years touring with similar acts.

It was on one such tour in 1926 that he first heard a Kansas City group called the Blue Devils, led by bassist Walter Page. Basie was impressed by the band's music and joined the group in 1928. Page was a skilled musician and talent scout, and the Blue Devils became the seed from which the classic Basie orchestras of the thirties grew. "By 1928, the

Blue Devils were considered the best band in a territory that included Texas, Oklahoma, and Kansas, and Page was eager to challenge the Bennie Moten Band, which monopolized the best jobs in Kansas City" (Hsio Wen Shih in Stewart, 1972, p. 198). Moten was a combination pianist/bandleader/politician and businessman. After an unsuccessful attempt to take over the Blue Devils as a group, he managed to persuade individual members, including Basie, to join his band (Shih, p. 199). By 1931, several other key members of Page's band including Page himself, had joined Moten. Basie continued as pianist for the Moten band until the leader's death in 1935.

Soon afterward, he formed his own small group, which he later expanded to nine men, including the Blue Devil/Moten nucleus. Producer John Hammond heard this group on a radio broadcast from the Reno Club in Kansas City in 1936. Convinced of the band's potential, Hammond persuaded Basie to expand to fourteen pieces and obtained some engagements for the orchestra. After some initial failures and reshuffling of band members, the Basie orchestra scored a major triumph at New York's Savoy Ballroom in 1938.

The band reached a peak in the 1938–39 period with such illustrious soloists as Lester Young and Herschel Evans on tenor, Buck Clayton and Harry "Sweets" Edison on trumpet, Dicky Wells on trombone, and vocalists Jimmy Rushing and Helen Humes. But the heart of the Basie organization was its rhythm section, composed of the leader on piano, guitarist Freddie Greene, drummer Jo Jones, and bassist Walter Page. The total empathy and subtle interplay of this foursome provided an effortlessly swinging rhythmic bass that to this day remains a model for swing groups. Basie's recordings from this period are among the most durable jazz classics (SCCJ-V-7 and 8).* Many of the arrangements were written by band members such as guitarist/trombonist Eddie Durham and trumpeter Buck Clayton. The band's most characteristic arrangements were built around the informal and exciting blues-based riff passages that were a legacy of its Kansas City origins.

In the forties, Basie managed to compensate for some key personnel losses with fine musicians such as tenor saxophonists Don Byas and Buddy Tate and trombonist Vic Dickenson.

By 1950, economic pressures forced Basie to disband, and he toured for the next two years with a small group. He re-formed his orchestra in 1952, and by the mid-fifties the new Basie unit rivaled the thirties band in popularity. With virtuoso soloists such as trumpeters Thad

---

*In addition to this Smithsonian recording, Count Basie may be heard on SCCJ-VI-2 and 3.

Jones and Joe Newman, trombonist Benny Powell, reedmen Frank Foster and Frank Wess, and scores by Foster, Neal Hefti, and Ernie Wilkins, the band of this period combined precision with power. Collaborations with singer Joe Williams produced many hits, and the band made several highly successful European tours.

In the sixties, Basie began to incorporate more popular material into his repertoire and recorded with Frank Sinatra and Tony Bennett. Purists accused him of going commercial, but the band retained a number of top jazzmen, including saxophonist Eddie "Lockjaw" Davis.

The mid-seventies were a period of revitalization for Count Basie and his orchestra. Important additions included Jimmy Forrest on tenor and trombonist Al Grey (who had been with the band in the late fifties). Basie was signed by the Pablo label, and producer Norman Granz recorded him in several new and challenging contexts, including duets with fellow pianist Oscar Peterson, trio and quartet dates, and informal small group "jams," as well as with the full band (Basie won a Grammy award for *Prime Time* in 1978).

In his solos, Basie has distilled his playing to the bare essentials, using a spare, single-note style that relies on his delicate touch and perfect rhythmic placement for effect. For contrast, he can still erupt into two-handed passages, evoking the memory of his early mentors.

As an accompanist, Basie is a master at "feeding" chords to a soloist. Not a showman, he is almost self-effacing on stage, yet he manages to control and direct the powerful musical force behind him with the most subtle messages from his piano.

Further Information

Biography/Criticism   Horricks, Raymond. *Count Basie and His Orchestra: Its Music and Musicians.* London, Victor Gollancz, 1957.

Discography   *A Discography of Count Basie, 1929 - 1950.* Compiled by Bo Scherman and Carl A. Hällstrom. Copenhagen: Knudsen, n.d.
A Discography of Count Basie, 1951 - 1968. Compiled by Jorgen Grunnet Jepsen. Copenhagen: Knudsen, 1969a.

Basie on LP   *Best of Count Basie,* MCA 4069, 2 records (1937−39).
Good Morning Blues, MCA 4108, 2 records (1937—39).
Super Chief, Columbia CG-31224, 2 records. (First recordings, 1936; famous Basie soloists in the big band, small groups 1937−42.)
One O'Clock Jump, Columbia Special Products JCL-997. (Big band 1942−51; octet 1950.)

16 Men Swinging, Verve 2517, 2 records (mid-fifties).

The Kid from Red Bank, Roulette 42015 (late fifties).

Kansas City Suite: Easin' It, Roulette 124, 2 records. (1960, arrangements and compositions by Benny Carter and Frank Foster.)

Echoes of an Era: The Best of Count Basie, Roulette RE-118, 2 records. (1958–61, includes one album of arrangements and compositions by Benny Carter.)

Echoes of an Era: The Count Basie Vocal Years, Roulette RE-107, 2 records. (Late fifties and sixties with vocalists Joe Williams, Billy Eckstine, Sarah Vaughan, Tony Bennett.)

Kansas City 7, Impulse 15. (Small group, 1962, with Basie on organ for some tracks.)

Afrique, Flying Dutchman 10138. (1970, contemporary material, including arrangements and a suite by Oliver Nelson.)

Trio: For the First Time, Pablo 2310712 (1973).

Satch and Josh, Pablo 2310722 (1974 duets with Oscar Peterson).

Count Basie and Zoot Sims, Pablo 2310745 (1976, quartet).

Prime Time, Pablo 2310797 (1977, big band).

Basie Jam, Montreux '77, Pablo Live 2308209.

See also LPs under Lester Young, p. 152.

Lester Young (Frank Driggs Collection)

LESTER YOUNG

Although Coleman Hawkins may have "invented" the saxophone as a jazz instrument, Lester Young pointed it in a new direction. He created a new sound and style that affected a generation of players and changed the course of the music.

Born in Mississippi in 1909 (his family soon moved to New Orleans), Young received his early musical training from his father, who introduced him to several instruments. The whole Young family was musical and had their own band, in which Lester played drums. The family moved to Minneapolis in 1920 and traveled throughout the West. When a southern swing was scheduled, Lester left the band. He joined Art Bronson's Bostonians on baritone saxophone, touring with them off and on from 1928 to 1930. Young had been working in various Minneapolis clubs when, in 1932, he was recruited by the Blue Devils. In 1933, he and several other members of the Blue Devils joined Bennie Moten in Kansas City. While based in Kansas City, he worked in a variety of musical settings, including a stint with King Oliver. He joined Count Basie in 1935.

Within a few months, he was asked to replace Coleman Hawkins in the Fletcher Henderson band. Already playing in his own style, Young was ill at ease with Henderson's New York-based band, where he felt pressure from other musicians to play like Hawkins. He played briefly with Andy Kirk and then rejoined Basie at the Reno Club in Kansas City in 1936, making his recording debut that year with a small group of Basieites in Chicago. He remained with Basie until 1940, and many feel that this was his most productive period. He was featured on many Basie recordings (SCCJ-V-7-8; VI-1), and it was at this time, as well, that his special musical relationship with Billie Holiday flowered. Their artistic rapport is well documented on recordings considered among the most durable of jazz classics (SCCJ-IV-6 and 7). It was from Billie that Young received the nickname "Pres" (for the "President") while he, in turn, named her "Lady Day."

After leaving the Basie band, Young worked in a variety of short-lived groups, both in New York and on the West Coast, one of which he led with his brother, drummer Lee Young. Lester rejoined the Basie band in 1943, where he remained until his induction into the army in October 1944. For Young, always a shy and sensitive man, the army was a devastating experience. Those who knew him claim that he never fully recovered from the racial prejudice and assault on his individuality to which he was subjected in the military. This nightmare culminated in a court-martial and a one-year detention sentence. Fortunately, he was released for medical reasons in June 1945, and moved to California, where he resumed playing. The following year he joined impresario Norman Granz's touring Jazz at the Philharmonic, and subsequently made several overseas trips with various JATP troupes, in addition to leading his own groups and working as a soloist.

In the late forties and early fifties, Young, although plagued by poor health, was still capable of fine performances, evident in some of his recordings from this period. His last three years were marred by drinking problems and a nervous breakdown. On March 15, 1959, within hours of his return from a Paris engagement, Lester Young died in his New York hotel room.

Young, as well as several other prominent jazzmen, cited saxophonist Frankie Trumbauer (SCCJ-III-4 and 5) as one of his primary influences. Young's airy sound and understated attack, foreshadowing the "cool" approach, were in direct contrast to the prevailing sonority of tone created by Coleman Hawkins. Young's style created a sensation, inspiring a whole generation of imitators, as well as those who used his style as the takeoff point for their own development. Among the latter were Charlie Parker and Stan Getz.

Young was almost as influential in his personal style as he was musically. As Dan Morgenstern writes, "Lester was a prototypal hipster.

He walked on crepe soles, gliding through life like a graceful sleepwalker. Porkpie hats became fashionable long after he had introduced them. His detached yet knowing attitude became a model for a generation of 'cool' people" (Morgenstern, 1977, p. 63).

Further Information

Discography   Jepsen, Jorgen Grunnet. *A Discography of Lester Young.* Copenhagen: Knudsen, 1968.

Lester Young on LP   *The Lester Young Story,* vol. 1, Columbia CG33502 (2 records). (First recordings, 1936, with Billie Holiday, 1937.)
The Lester Young Story, vol. 2, Columbia CG33503 (2 records). (With Billie Holiday, 1937—38.)
The Lester Young Story, vol. 3, Columbia JG 34840 (2 records). (With Billie Holiday, Basie, 1938—39.)
Aladdin Sessions, Blue Note LA456-H2 (2 records). (Late forties, Young's own groups.)
Pres & Teddy & Oscar, Verve 2502 (2 records). (Small groups, fifties.)

Benny Carter (Ed Berger)

BENNY CARTER

Few people in the history of jazz have made so many substantial contributions in so many varied areas as Benny Carter. Born in 1907 in the San Juan Hill area of Manhattan, he received his first music lessons from his mother, who taught him piano. Later, influenced by two trumpet players—his cousin, the legendary Cuban Bennett, and a neighbor, Bubber Miley—he decided to play trumpet. He worked in a laundry for months, saving his money to buy an instrument. After failing to master it over a weekend, he exchanged it for a C Melody saxophone, which he learned to play through self-study and with several teachers. By age fifteen he was jamming at various clubs without pay.

His earliest professional experience came with the bands of June Clark, Billy Fowler, Billy Paige, and Charlie Johnson. During this period (1924–1928), he became a well-known sideman in various orchestras, including a brief period in Pittsburgh with Earl Hines (where he played baritone), after which he joined Horace Henderson. An early influence was Frankie Trumbauer (SCCJ-III-4 and 5). In 1928 he made his recording debut (with Charlie Johnson) and led his own band at the Arcadia Ballroom in New York. Later that year he achieved the goal of aspiring young jazz musicians of that time; he joined Fletcher Henderson's orchestra, the training ground for many of the soloists who shaped jazz's future. In 1931, he took over the leadership of McKinney's Cotton Pickers. By 1933, he was already a well-known leader whose bands included such top musicians as Chu Berry, Teddy Wilson, and Sid Catlett. Meanwhile he had also mastered the trumpet and recorded his first solo on that instrument.

Carter traveled to Europe in 1935, working first in Paris with Willie Lewis's band and later becoming staff arranger for the British Broadcasting Corporation (BBC) dance band in London. He played an essential role in the development of jazz in Europe. After his return to New York in 1938, he led another big band. In 1942 he went on tour to California. There, he moved into the Hollywood studio scene as an instrumentalist on soundtracks and as an arranger and composer. He continued to lead a band, which included at various times such rising young players as J. J. Johnson, Miles Davis, Max Roach, and Art Pepper. The fifties and sixties were occupied by arranging and composing assignments in film, TV, and recording studios, interrupted for an occasional playing engagement or record date. In the seventies, Carter has turned his talents in a new direction—education. He has given seminars and workshops at many colleges and spent the fall semester of 1973 as visiting lecturer at Princeton, which awarded him an honorary doctorate in 1974.

During the seventies, he has served the United States Government in two capacities: performing and participating in seminars on a tour of the Middle East under State Department sponsorship and serving on one of the music advisory panels of the National Endowment for the Arts.

His versatility has prevented him from achieving the popular recognition accorded artists whose accomplishments have been more concentrated. As an instrumentalist, Carter, along with Johnny Hodges, was the model for pre-Parker alto saxophonists. He combines flawless technique and fine, pure tone with a rare ability to conceive a solo as a whole (SCCJ-V-5). In addition, he has a distinctive sound on trumpet (the trumpet is his favorite instrument) and has recorded many fine clarinet solos. He has demonstrated his proficiency on other instruments as well.

As an arranger, Carter is credited, along with Don Redman and Fletcher Henderson, with charting the course of the swing-era big band arranging style. His writing for saxophones, in particular, is unexcelled. Carter arrangements have been recorded by Duke Ellington, Count Basie, Benny Goodman, and Glenn Miller, as well as by top jazz and popular vocalists from Billie Holiday and Ray Charles to Lou Rawls and Maria Muldaur.

Under Carter's demanding leadership, his bands were known as proving grounds for musicians of several generations. Among the "graduates" who have acknowledged their debt to Carter as a teacher are J. J. Johnson, Miles Davis, Max Roach, and Art Pepper.

Carter, the composer, is the author of several compositions that have become jazz standards ("When Lights Are Low," SCCJ-V-6), as well as hundreds of works for television and film soundtracks. He has written effectively in all idioms from blues to bossa nova, extended works and dramatic scores. In the mid-seventies Carter, his abilities undiminished, has resumed a more active playing career.

His personal qualities of integrity and modesty, his intellectual interests, and his musical contributions have earned Carter the universal respect of his fellow musicians, who still call him by his short-lived publicity title: "The King."

Further Information

Discography   *The Alto Saxophone and Other Instruments of Benny Carter, 1927–1942.* Compiled by Jan Evensmo. Jazz Solography Series, vol. 11. Hosle, Norway: published privately, 1979.

Carter on LP   *Benny Carter 1933,* Prestige 7643 (earliest recordings of his own orchestra, compositions, and arrangements).
Benny Carter 1940–41, French RCA Black & White 741.073 (Carter big band). Although a foreign issue, this LP is often carried by larger record stores in the United States.
Jazz Giant, Contemporary 7555 (quartet, septet 1957).
Further Definitions, Impulse A12 (arrangements for four saxes, including Coleman Hawkins, 1961).
Carter, Gillespie, Inc., Pablo 2310781 (1976 reunion with Gillespie).
Benny Carter 4, Pablo Live 230824 (live recording at Montreux Festival, 1977).

Coleman Hawkins (Institute of Jazz Studies)

COLEMAN HAWKINS

Even the most original artists in jazz have drawn inspiration (and in many cases received direct instruction) from predecessors on their instrument. Coleman Hawkins had no such models on tenor saxophone, although he cites clarinetist Buster Bailey and several pianists as general musical influences. Hawkins literally carved out alone a place for his horn in jazz.

Born in Saint Joseph, Missouri, in 1904, he studied piano and cello as a youngster, switching to tenor saxophone when he recieved that instrument for his ninth birthday. Shortly thereafter, Hawkins was playing for school dances, and by age sixteen, he was working professionally in Kansas City. In 1921, he joined blues singer Mamie Smith's Jazz Hounds. After touring extensively, Hawkins left this group in New York in 1923. During that year he made his first recordings with the Fletcher Henderson Orchestra. He joined Henderson permanently in 1924 and remained with the band until he decided—almost impulsively—to go to Europe in 1934 (SCCJ-III-6). He worked initially with Jack Hylton's band in England and was later featured with various orchestras on the Continent. He made many recordings during this period, sometimes joined by other American expatriates such as Benny Carter. Hawkins's five-year stay in Europe was influential in the advancement of jazz in Europe. But his greatest fame lay ahead.

In October 1939, only a few months after his return to the United States, he recorded a version of "Body and Soul" that became not only a landmark in jazz, but a popular hit as well (SCCJ-IV-4). Hawkins then formed a big band, which he led for over a year, until early 1941. After 1941, he worked primarily as a leader of smaller groups or as a single (SCCJ-IV-8).* He was a member of the first Jazz at the Philharmonic tour in 1946 and became a JATP regular.

In the forties, when the rift between the traditionalists and the followers of bop was at its height, Hawkins was one of the few musicians of his generation to lend support to the young innovators. Thelonious Monk, for example, made his recording debut with Hawkins in 1944, only a few months after Dizzy Gillespie, Leo Parker, and Max Roach had recorded with Hawkins on what is generally referred to as the first be-bop recording session.

Throughout his career Hawkins continued to listen sympathetically to new developments in music: In the fifties and sixties he recorded with Sonny Rollins and John Coltrane. "Never an imitator, he was a great absorber. He had the rare capacity to transmute and make his own whatever elements struck his fancy in the work of others" (Morgenstern, liner notes to *Bean and the Boys,* Prestige 7824). Hawkins continued to record prolifically and to play club dates and at major festivals until his death in 1969.

Hawkins's hallmark was his powerful, majestic sound, his commanding attack, harmonic sophistication, and his romantic (wide vibrato) treatment of ballads. Although his full tone and extroverted approach were not always in style, Hawkins exerted a vital influence on all saxophonists who followed him. Lester Young said, "He was the first president, right?"

Further Information

Discography *The Tenor Saxophone of Coleman Hawkins, 1929—1942.* Jazz Solography Series, no. 3. Compiled by Jan Evensmo. Hosle, Norway: published privately, 1976.

Hawkins on LP *Fletcher Henderson: Developing an American Orchestra,* Smithsonian P2 13710. (1923—36 recordings, with Hawkins prominently featured until his departure for Europe.)

---

* In addition to the Smithsonian Collection records cited in this section, Hawkins may also be heard on SCCJ-V-6.

Hawk in Holland, GNP 9003 (1935—37 with Dutch group, the Ramb-
    lers).
Coleman Hawkins and the Trumpet Kings, Trip 5515 (1944, small group
    recordings).
The Hawk Flies, Milestone 47015, 2 records, (1944–46 with Monk, Fats,
    Navarro, J. J. Johnson; 1949 Paris session; 1957, sextet, quartet).
Today and Now, Impulse A-34 (1962, quartet).

Roy Eldridge (Frank Driggs Collection)

ROY ELDRIDGE

In the evolution of jazz trumpet styles Roy Eldridge is often described
as the link between Louis Armstrong and Dizzy Gillespie. While Eldridge
was, indeed, influenced by Armstrong and, in turn, inspired Gillespie, his
significance as a musician is far more than transitional.

Eldridge (whose nickname is "Little Jazz") was born in Pittsburgh in
1911. He received musical instruction from his elder brother Joe (who
later played alto in Roy's band in the thirties). After playing drums, Eldridge switched first to the bugle and then to the trumpet. When he was
fifteen, he left home to tour with carnivals. While on the road, he was
often stranded and had to find his own way back to Pittsburgh. By the

age of sixteen, he was already leading his own youth band. From 1928 on, he worked in the bands of Horace Henderson, Zack Whyte, and Speed Webb. Webb's band included Teddy Wilson and Vic Dickenson.

Eldridge moved to New York in 1930 and over the next three years gained experience in some of the top orchestras, including those of Cecil Scott, Elmer Snowden, Charlie Johnson, and Teddy Hill (with whom he made his first recordings in 1935). After a stint with Fletcher Henderson, he formed his own eight-piece band in 1936. In 1938 he briefly left the music business to study audio engineering but soon formed a ten-piece band that was featured for some time at the Arcadia Ballroom in New York. From 1935 on, he recorded prolifically with his own and studio groups.

By the late thirties, Eldridge already exerted a profound influence on his fellow musicians, but, over the next five years, his talents reached a wider audience as featured soloist (and occasional vocalist) with Gene Krupa's orchestra from 1941 to 1943 (SCCJ-V4)* and later with Artie Shaw (1944–45). Eldridge paid a price for this exposure, however; he was deeply affected by the various indignities to which he was subjected in his pioneering role as the only black artist in a white band. Musically, however, it was a highly successful creative period for Eldridge, who provided a needed spark to the two orchestras.

After leading his own big band and small groups in the late forties, Eldridge returned briefly to Krupa's band. He left to join Norman Granz's first Jazz at the Philharmonic tour in 1949. In 1950, he accompanied Benny Goodman to Europe, remaining there to work as a soloist after the Goodman tour. He returned to the United States in 1951 and since that time has led his own small groups, with the exception of several months with Count Basie in 1966. Since 1970, Eldridge has made Jimmy Ryan's club in New York his home base, leading a highly compatible small band.

Eldridge has been a mainstay of producer Granz's musical ventures ever since he first toured with Jazz at the Philharmonic in 1949.

He continues to make frequent tours abroad with Granz and records for his Pablo label.

Eldridge is a competent drummer and pianist, as well as an original and often humorous vocalist. His trumpet style is characterized by his crackling tone, range, and power, unflagging drive, and spontaneous excitement, which often ignites both musicians and audience alike. He never coasts or takes the easy way out. While Roy Eldridge may have

---

* In addition to this recording, Eldridge may be heard on SCCJ-V-5. The Smithsonian is planning to issue a retrospective selection of Eldridge recordings.

reshaped previous styles and heralded new ones, his own manner of playing stands on its own as a unique and vital approach.

Further Information

Discography   Jan Evensmo. *The Trumpet Of Roy Eldridge.* Jazz Solography Series. Hosle, Norway: forthcoming.

Roy Eldridge on LP   *Roy Eldridge at the Arcadia Ballroom 1939,* Jazz Archives 14.
Gene Krupa with Anita O'Day and Roy Eldridge, Columbia PG-32663, 2 records (1945).
Artie Shaw and His Orchestra with Red Allen, Lips Page and Roy Eldridge, vol. 1, French RCA Black & White FXM1-7336 (contains 8 tracks with Eldridge, 1945).
This Is Artie Shaw, vol. 2, RCA VPM6062, 2 records. (contains 6 tracks with Eldridge, 1945).
Sweets, Lips, & Lots of Jazz, Xanadu 123 (small groups, 1941).
Roy Eldridge, GNP 9009 (Paris, 1950).
Diz & Roy, Verve 2524, 2 records. (With Dizzy Gillespie, 1952−54.)
Earl Hines and Roy Eldridge at the Village Vanguard, Xanadu 106 (1965).
What It's All About, Pablo 2310766 (1976).
Roy Eldridge 4, Montreux '77, Pablo Live 2308203.

chapter 6

The Big Apple, Bop, and Modern Jazz

Although a truism, it bears repeating that jazz, an outgrowth of Afro-American music, developed only in places with a substantial, supporting black population. In the post-Civil War period, most black Americans remained in the rural South. There was some culturally and numerically significant migration to cities, but this shift, until World War I, was from rural areas to cities within the South. What population experts now call the "Great Migration" of blacks to the West and North began in 1915 and has continued until recently in various waves, most notably around the time of the two world wars. (Census data indicate some current migration back to the South.) Nearly all the migrants went to the big cities. In 1910 only about 10 percent of the American black population lived in the North and West. By 1940 that figure had jumped to nearly 25 percent. Yet because of large white populations in the North, blacks constituted less than 4 percent of the total northern population in 1940. By 1950 that proportion, especially in the cities, was substantially larger. In 1920 blacks in Boston, Chicago, and New York, for example, made up less than 5 percent of the total populations of those cities. By 1950 the New York City population was 10 percent black. (In 1960 that figure had risen to 14 percent and by 1970 to 21 percent.)

New York City, the Big Apple, is a metropolis that has always been many cities. It epitomizes Weber's notion of the city as marketplace, the theater of opportunity and despair (Weber, 1968). The flamboyant Jimmie Walker, mayor of New York from 1925 to 1932, is reputed to have once said, "This would be a great town—if they ever finish it." New York is process, exchange—a constant becoming. New York is the very center of America's wealth and power, the heart of banking and finance, of communication and advertising. It is the focal point of publishing—words and music. It is the creative hub, the point of convergence for the arts and cultural life. It is also the core of poverty and meanness. New York City is a city of neighborhoods, boroughs, and districts, but also a city of

161

concentrations. More Jews live in New York than in Tel Aviv, more Irish than in Dublin, and so on. And from 1910 on, New York's Harlem became the center of black artistic and cultural life as New York City itself had become white America's lodestar of art and culture since about 1860 (Harris, Neil, 1966).

Around the turn of the century, the area above Central Park in Manhattan became the site of overzealous construction by eager speculators. Apartments and houses stood empty; transportation was not good enough to justify the building craze. Backed by Booker T. Washington and his powerful National Negro Business League, the Afro-American Reality Company bought up houses, apartments, and blocks. In an early example of "economic nationalism," Harlem was systematically "infiltrated" by blacks from a wide socioeconomic range. The transition to a black Harlem was generally peaceful, and a black social world came into being. By 1912, Harold Cruse says, Harlem was "a city within a city" (Cruse, 1967, p. 22).

By the twenties a major cultural and artistic movement was under way in Harlem. Linked with a similar trend among white intellectuals and artists in Greenwich Village, a real flowering of cultural activity occurred. The "Harlem Renaissance" encouraged black artists and intellectuals to express themselves. Eubie Blake, Noble Sissle, Louis Armstrong, Ethel Waters, Langston Hughes, E. Franklin Frazier, and many others found voice and song. Most were not from New York but found in Harlem their spiritual home. Encouraged and supported by the Washington Square group (and the salon of Mabel Dodge, a wealthy patroness of the arts), black Americans had a concentrated and significant impact on cultural "higher circles," on the American artistic and intellectual elite. Acceptance was by no means total, even though Langston Hughes was tolerated when he introduced the life-style cadences of the black underclass into American literature and Blake and Sissle could string together folk-oriented material into their revues. But there was an air of exotica about the racial crossover. Cruse calls it "a tradition of white cultural paternalism [that] swiftly became entrenched in the Harlem movement" (Cruse, 1967, p. 35).

In music there was a New York black establishment just as surely as there was one in Chicago. In New York, however, the establishment was more sure of itself, more entrenched and more sophisticated than the newer and less cosmopolitan Chicago pseudopatricians. Syncopated orchestras and ragtime-influenced show music hinted at the authentic blues of the black underclass only obliquely, if at all. The influx from the West and South of the developing jazz and blues fusion came from the forging of black-oriented music into a "type" by the race-record market and by the development of national black entertainment networks.* Being black meant a double accommodation. Not only did black entertainers have to accept the fact that they were Negroes in a white-controlled market, but they had to renew their art from folk sources in order to keep the essentially segregated society appeased. The art of minstrelsy had not died; it simply took on new aspects. The whole northern racial accommodation was so uneasy that authentic talent from the provinces, such as Louis Armstrong or Bessie Smith, had to be subsumed into the mainstream. The unintended, although largely beneficial, consequence of this was the maintenance of some openness to the infusion of Afro-American authenticity in the popular arts.

The Great Depression hit black people especially hard, particularly in the urban areas where they were the last hired and the first fired. The search for an ideological viewpoint that would offset the desperate economic conditions led some black intellectuals into flirtations with the Communist party and various radical socialist groups. (Perhaps the best known involvement in these organizations was that of Paul Robeson, who later suffered greatly for his beliefs.) All in all, the arts suffered from inattention; bread and butter were more critical. Some famous artists left for Europe, Duke Ellington among them. Others simply failed or slipped into other lines of work.

The thirties became a time of camouflage for much true jazz. The radio and the ballroom demanded swing music, often sweet rather than hot. Ben Sidran argues that during the 1930s a black music underground developed (Sidran, 1971). For the most creative musicians, black and white, the thirties were a time for preservation and experimentation within controlled contexts, during after hours or in very short doses within the big band framework. The drive for musical accomplishment did not die; neither did a sense of the artistry of jazz and the need to extend the form. Jazz became a small island in a huge green sea of commercial music. The bedrock of the jazz island was the blues. The most creative musicians huddled together and carried on the cause, as a group of dedicated monks might have done during Europe's Dark Ages.

ONE MORE TIME: SWING

In the last chapter, swing was discussed as the successor to the music of smaller groups in the Chicago era. Less hot, but more disciplined than

---

* Perhaps the best known of these was the Theater Owners and Bookers Association (TOBA), also known as "Tough on Black Ass." TOBA operated a string of theaters for blacks only in the South and provided a "farm system" for colored acts, especially blues singers and their bands.

the smaller combo, most swing bands found an audience through dance hall circuits and on the radio. Instead of a handful of musicians playing different instruments, the swing band had sections of reeds and brasses and percussion, which yielded a fuller sound. Collective improvisation was out of the question in these larger groups, and the arranger became a key figure. The most important skill of the big band arranger was an understanding of harmonic structure. Taking a horizontal trumpet line, for example, and converting it into a vertical section part for several trumpets, an arranger had to decide whether to score simple unison blocks of sound or create interesting patterns based on a firm knowledge of chordal structure. Bop musicians would later reassert the horizontal dimension of creativity by using underlying chordal harmonics in a linear fashion—creating entirely new melodies as they went along. Bop represented both an evolutionary development in jazz and the cyclical tension between large and small groups of jazz players. Bop had very deep roots.

The large marching bands of New Orleans had given way to smaller combos that converted their ragged call-and-response format into a poly-phonically conceived collective improvisation. In turn, the New Orleans small group grew larger as the demand for dance bands grew. The risks of improvisation were reduced through the precision of tightly structured written-out parts. In many swing bands, especially the more commercial ones, there was an inverse relationship between the importance of the arrangers and the importance of the improvising soloists. Some of the best of the big bands, however, managed to balance tight ensemble passages and sophisticated arrangements with inspired solo efforts. Bands led by Fletcher Henderson, Don Redman, Benny Carter, Benny Goodman, Count Basie, and, of course, Duke Ellington amply demonstrate the potential of swing as a jazz form. Ellington serves as an exemplar of this musical control.

Edward Kennedy Ellington was a unique figure in American music. Without abandoning his jazz roots, he managed to compose wonderful songs that became perfect vehicles for the members of his orchestra. It has been said that he conceptualized his entire band as an instrument (Schuller in Hentoff and McCarthy, 1975, pp. 233–74). Starting in the early 1920s, the Ellington band produced every imaginable musical texture from rough "jungle" sounds to the most delicate impressionistic miniatures. In every case, Ellington remained the mastermind (SCCJ-VI-4 through 8; VII-1 through 3). He controlled the band and bent it to his will, although his arrangers, most notably Billy Strayhorn, served his conceptions well. (A famous jazz trumpet player, who did not play in the Ellington band, though he had been asked to join many times, told me that the Ellington band was a musical monastery and that a vow of

obedience to the musical sense of the abbot was needed.) In his autobiography, *Music Is My Mistress,* Ellington himself hints at the kind of
musical discipline he expected.

> The word "improvisation" has great limitations, because when
> musicians are given solo responsibility they already have a sugges-
> tion of a melody written for them, and so before they begin they al-
> ready know more or less what they are going to play. Anyone who
> plays anything worth hearing knows what he's going to play, no
> matter whether he prepares a day ahead or a beat ahead. It has to
> be with intent (p. 465).

The choice of the words "solo responsibility" in the quotation above
sums up both the strength and the weakness of the powerful com-
poser/bandleader/arranger's control over musical production. The band
was indeed his instrument. In *Jazz Is,* Nat Hentoff quotes Ellington:

> "After a man has been in the band for a while," Ellington once
> told me, "I can hear what his capacities are, and I write to that. And
> I write to each man's sound. A man's sound is his total personality. I
> hear that sound as I prepare to write. I hear all their sounds, and
> that's how I am able to write. Before you can play anything or write
> anything, you have to hear it" (p. 27).

Few swing bands achieved, but many aspired to, the kind of control
that Ellington had. It should also not surprise us that Ellington says in his
autobiography that one of the bandleaders he most admired was Paul
Whiteman.

Another common characteristic of the large swing orchestras* was
the creation of a "band within a band." The "Swing Wing" was such a
group, for example, in the Whiteman band (Tanner and Gerow, 1973, p.
74). Thus small combos persisted throughout the swing era, and much
experimentation occurred within these groups. The band within a band
phenomenon was, in some measure, a formal recognition of the work
being carried out in less formal jam sessions and the growth of individual
artists. These smaller groups also recorded from time to time on their
own and provided the nucleus for the formation of new bands by some
big band personnel. Lionel Hampton and Teddy Wilson were in Goodman's band within a band. Small-group jazz remained very much alive

---

*The word "orchestra" is from the Greek, meaning "a dancing place" and re-
ferred to that portion of the Greek theater reserved for the dancing chorus and
the instrumentalists. Dancing and popular music have a nearly mystical link in
most cultures.

throughout the thirties, both in person and on records. John Kirby's successful little band is one example.

Certain jazz musicians, most notably Coleman Hawkins (with Henderson), Lester Young (with Basie), and Roy Eldridge (with Krupa and Shaw), extended and developed jazz within the context of the big band. Young's genius was his conception of a solo line and his anticipation, by a full decade, of the sense of jazz as cool rather than hot (SCCJ-V-7 and 8; VI-1). His sense of phrasing led Billie Holiday, the greatest jazz singer of all time, to appreciate his vocal conception of jazz (SCCJ-IV-6 and 7). Hawkins, on the other hand, who had remarkable musical sophistication, used a wide vibrato in his playing to the point of wringing a tone poem out of every piece of music he played (SCCJ-III-6; IV-4 and 5; V-6). Eldridge, trumpeter Joe Newman once told me, was the "missing link" between Armstrong and Gillespie, a disciplined musician who could adjust his playing to any context and meet the standard of playing hot with incredible control (SCCJ-V-4 and 5). When he was a young sideman in the Basie band, Newman had a photograph of Eldridge pasted on the bell of his trumpet. That's roots.

BOP

The issue of how to compensate musicians for recorded performances in the mass media has never been resolved. Objecting to the expense of paying nonperforming musicians "standing by" and being paid for recorded music, radio executives balked at this "featherbedding" practice. This issue resulted in a strike called by James Petrillo, president of the American Federation of Musicians, which stopped all union-approved recording on August 1, 1942. A protracted strike followed, and no instrumental recordings were made in the United States until the fall of 1943.* The reasons for the strike were many, but one of the major ones was the growing discontent among most musicians over the use of canned music on the radio or on jukeboxes for which musicians received no compensation. The effect of this strike, which failed to achieve its objective (although a higher union scale was achieved), was a moratorium on mass market recorded music. This meant that the general public had little access to changes occurring in popular music during that period.

World War II contributed to the moratorium. Since so many young

---

* The armed services made recordings in large quantity, however, to send overseas. These recordings provide some continuity for the serious jazz researcher. So do radio transcriptions from this period; they were not considered recorded music.

Americans were overseas, many of them in remote areas, a large number of would-be jazz fans were out of touch with developments in the art form. Travel was restricted by gas and tire rationing; a 20 percent federal cabaret tax darkened many clubs. Private jam sessions grew in popularity, which kept many dedicated jazz fans from finding out what was going on within the music.

After-hours clubs and jam sessions in out-of-the-way places were hard to find and harder still to attend because many of them were restricted to musicians and their friends. They were also usually limited to the larger cities, particularly New York's Harlem. Each of these factors contributed to a respite in the production of commercial music—a deafening silence that fostered experimentation.

By the end of the decade of the forties, the introduction of the LP record meant that musicians were no longer restricted to the two- and three-minute tunes of the 78s. The LP also meant that fewer records might be sold and a profit still be shown by the record companies. As the LP displaced the 78, it gave a wider audience a chance to hear what had happened. That wider audience was bewildered. What had happened to swing? It seemed as though a musical revolution had occurred.

Whether it was a revolution or not, bop had to find a place, a continuity with what had gone before. Ira Gitler said of bop:

> Revolution, it was, to be sure, but significantly, the music was the product of evolution. . . . One of the reasons people looked on the advent of bebop as a revolution was the lack of communication with the public as a crucial time in the development of the music (Gitler, 1966, p. 11).

Dizzy Gillespie is acknowledged as one of the founding fathers of the bop movement in jazz. It is instructive to hear what he has to say about its origins.

> No one man or group of men started modern jazz, but one of the ways it happened was this: Some of us began to jam at Minton's in Harlem in the early forties. But there were always some cats showing up there who couldn't blow at all but would take six or seven choruses to prove it.
>
> So on afternoons before a session, Thelonious Monk and I began to work out some complex variations on chords and the like, and we used them at night to scare away the no talent guys.
>
> After a while, we got more and more interested in what we were doing as music, and, as we began to explore more and more, our music evolved (Hentoff and Shapiro, 1955, pp. 300–01).

The creative-musical part of the bop movement was deeply influenced by alto saxophonist Charlie "Bird" Parker (SCCJ-VII-6 through 9; VIII-1 through 3), from Kansas City and a sideman in Jay McShann's big band. What Parker himself had to say about his "discovery" of bop is interesting.

> Bird had been getting tired of the stereotyped changes in general use. "I kept thinking there's bound to be something else," he said, "I could hear it sometimes, but I couldn't play it." While playing Cherokee with Fleet [guitarist Biddie Fleet], he found that by utilizing the higher intervals of a chord as a melody line and using suitably connected changes with it, he could make the thing he had been hearing an actuality. As Bird put it, "I came alive" (Gitler, 1966, p. 20).

Anyone with a scintilla of musical sense and an open mind will recognize that Charlie Parker was a musical genius. Along with Bach and a few others, Parker shifted the whole direction of Western music and displayed its developmental potentiality. His genius is now widely recognized. But even Parker had to "tough out" the evolution of his own style. He had to make the very large mistakes that contribute to daring innovation. It should be some comfort to every student of any discipline to grasp the pain as well as the triumph of reaching for a new understanding of a specific reality.

> Behind him Charlie had a drummer who would be able to follow anything. He played his line on the first thirty-two bars of *I Got Rhythm*. It was acceptable. He could tell that from the drumming and the audience response. But Charlie wanted to put a "this is mine" stamp on what he was playing. He was afraid to try the double-time stuff. He wasn't that fast yet, or sure. He used one of the passing chords that he had learned from Tommy Douglas. It took him out of the key. He fell back on one of the scales he had mastered at home and the change went off brilliantly. People were startled. There was real suspense now. They were wondering how he was going to come out of it. Charlie was into another key now and beginning to realize that he didn't know the chords. For C-minor seventh you substituted what—? He didn't know. It was part of an art that Tommy Douglas called transposition, that Douglas had learned at the Boston Conservatory. There was a system for it. Tommy Douglas could have called out the proper chords in an instant. Charlie was lost. He didn't know where to go. He missed a phrase. Then he lost his grip on the time, the worst sin of all. The

beat and the line went surging ahead. Jo Jones rode the cymbals like an angry demon. The same terrible thing that had happened at the High Hat was happening all over again, but in worse circumstances. Jo Jones stopped drumming. The smooth, effortless, buoyant song of the drums stopped. Charlie stood there, rigid, frightened, holding the saxophone. The new Selmer. And a cymbal came sailing through the air. Jo Jones had snatched it from the cymbal ring and thrown it at Charlie's feet. The cymbal landed with a shattering crash. In the silence that gripped the crowd at the Reno Club the crash of the cymbal seemed to bounce off every wall and ricochet back to the band shell. Then, as had happened that night a year before at the High Hat Club, came the chorus of laughter, guffaws, and cat-calls. He had flopped in the big time, had been "gonged off" (Russell, 1973, pp. 84–85).

Charlie Parker, of course, went on to master "double-time stuff" and chord-substitution technique. He and the other bop experimenters were anxious to employ their new harmonic discoveries and to extend the rhythmic potential of the jazz form. (The Russell quote is hyperbolic, but it captures the spirit of the moment in poetic terms.)

Thelonious Monk, without training in formal music theory, developed a piano attack that was angular and percussive, and yet explored in a sophisticated way the frontiers of harmonically conceived music structure (SCCJ-IX-4 through 8; X-1). Charlie Christian, out of Oklahoma, played only too briefly in Harlem, although he had wide exposure in the Goodman band. He died very young in 1941 at the age of twenty-three. He extended the possibilities in jazz of single-string improvisation on the amplified guitar (using lines usually played in jazz by Lester Young-like saxophones), liberating that instrument from its traditional jazz function of timekeeping. Kenny Clarke extended the work of Jo Jones and perfected the technique of carrying the beat on the ride cymbal—creating a "sizzle effect" that gave the sensation of acceleration (SCCJ-IX-1 and 2; X-1). In the thirties drummers would "ride" on the beat; bop drummers tended to play slightly ahead of it, maintaining the feeling of effervescence enhanced by the unbelievably fast tempos of players such as Parker.

The whole atmosphere of the early bop period was one of frantic creativity and innovation. The beat, the heartbeat of jazz, was given over to the string bass. After Basie (and Hines, of course), the piano played lines; after Jones, the drum explored rhythmic variation and cross-rhythms. Solo potential was increased manyfold within a small combo. Bop was carried back into the more forward-looking big bands. By the late forties, the spectrum was completed by the fielding of big bands playing in the bop style, most notably the larger groups of Dizzy Gillespie.

An Afro-Cuban infusion also aided and abetted rhythmic variety during the later stages of the bop period. Dizzy Gillespie featured the legendary Cuban percussionist Chano Pozo in his 1947 big band. As far back as the dance craze of the early 1900s, Spanish dances like the tango were popular in the United States. W. C. Handy employed a tango rhythm in "St. Louis Blues." Jelly Roll Morton spoke of "the Spanish tinge." * Willie "The Lion" Smith once told me that all true jazz had a Spanish influence.

Latin music and true jazz have always had an elective affinity. In some ways the simplification of Latin sounds (in the music of Xavier Cugat, Desi Arnez, and others) did for Latin music what Paul Whiteman did for jazz. The connection continued through reggae music to, yes, even current disco.

Because jazz became so closely identified with dance music in the thirties, many music commentators largely ignored developments in the forties. They were as unaware of what was going on as most of the general public. Some jazz critics who were aware of the bop movement were confused by it and, in general, dismissed it as a passing fad that would have little lasting effect on jazz. The music, however, did have some press support, especially in *Metronome,* an influential jazz publication. This cleared the way for the musicians themselves to become labelers and control the definitions of good and bad jazz.

Bop was an "in group" phenomenon and, in large measure, the musicians themselves controlled the contexts in which the new music was developed. This control was exercised, as I have said above, because the contexts in which the music was first heard were not public but took place after-hours or in somebody's apartment. The audience was limited to other musicians and a very few fans. The musicians themselves became self-conscious about their music as art and serious self-expression.

On the other hand, a major reason why bop eventually came to be taken seriously was because the musicians who made the music had the proper jazz credentials and, in retrospect, represented a continuity from the thirties.† Most of the early bop players had jobs in big bands. For ex-

---

* The discussion in chapter 2 concerning the "purer" African influence in the Caribbean should make it clear why Afro-Cuban (and other Latin) influences enhanced rather than conflicted with bop as it evolved. (See also chapter 19 in Stearns, *The Story of Jazz.*)

† I do not hold the thesis, propounded in some quarters, that swing "used up" its jazz potential. New developmental potentialities continually present themselves and are seized upon. Swing is just as viable today as it ever was and just as

ample, Dizzy was with Cab Calloway, Bird with Jay McShann. The critical thing about bop was that jazz became art for its own sake and nonfunctional, that is, nondance music. It is obvious, however, that an audience did develop for the new form of jazz. If it had not, the form would, in all probability, have died. The issue in any analysis of bop becomes: Who made up the bop audience beyond the musicians themselves? Musicians could hardly have sustained the development alone.

It is clear that jazz, up until the advent of bop, had always drawn a major portion of its constituency from dancers and drinkers. After bop this was no longer the case. Bop became a rallying point for many of the alienated and disaffected in American society. In fact, bop became synonymous with rebellion by the late 1940s. Bopsters affected the mannerisms of the bop musicians, especially the free-spirited Dizzy Gillespie— dark glasses, berets, little goatees. Bop removed jazz from the mainstream of commercial popular music. Bop itself never became popular in the sense that the jazz of the 1920s became popular, nor did it lend itself to co-optation in the same sense that jazz in the 1930s had. Bop has had a great influence on American popular music but with a much longer time lag than earlier forms of jazz and with a good deal more indirection. By the time some aspects of bop were incorporated into pop music, jazz had evolved even further. At no time, before or since, did a jazz generation come so close to forming a deviant subculture.

> Among the jazz experiments in the forties was a group in New York which extended the choruses of the swing era into a specialized form of improvisation. Ignoring the original melody (which the initiated knew without reiteration), these musicians improvised their own themes based on their own alteration of the chords of standard tunes. They demanded that audiences listen.
>
> Tempos were set for instrumental performance, not for dancing. This music, called "bop," was a radical protest, not only against a world in war, but against the growing commercialism that threatened the extinction of an American art form.
>
> For its audience bop attracted a comparatively small, but fanatically loyal, group of intellectuals, artists and malcontents, who felt

much fun. Evidence of this is the fine work being done all over the country by various "stage bands," especially on the high school and collegiate level. The success of the Thad Jones/Mel Lewis band and even Sun Ra indicate the interest in big band jazz. Closely arranged ensemble work is still a marvelous way to achieve musical skill and a jazz sense. The work of groups such as the NAJE (the National Association of Jazz Educators) relies heavily on "arranged jazz" as a pedagogical device. The NAJE address is: Box 724, Manhattan, Kansas, 66502.

in the tense new music some of their own revolt from a society that had betrayed them. While the general public sought to escape in popular vocalists, hillbilly tunes, novelty bands and vulgarized interpretations of rhythm and blues, the restless protest fringe was seeking expression of its discontent. Part of that expression was fulfilled in the controlled, masterful, emotional realism of bop.

The continuity of jazz history had been violently disrupted by World War II. Musicians who had served their apprenticeship by playing all kinds of jobs in all styles of jazz and were approaching the age for serious contributions to jazz were in the service. There was a demand for entertainment and a dearth of competent musicians. Crusading bop was the center of creative activity. . . .

Much of the music of the war and postwar years seemed permeated with fear. Its sound and form of presentation reflected a defiance and a distrust, not only of established society, but of the audience, or anyone outside the group (Brubeck and Brubeck in Gleason, 1958, 225–27).

Dave Brubeck saw the bop audience as made up of "intellectuals, artists and malcontents." Others would add the rebellious young and many blacks (Stearns, 1956, chapter 24). One should not characterize the bop audience, however, as simply made up of hipsters and drug users. The disenchanted in America certainly were represented but so were very sober and serious jazz musicians and people who followed musical development for its own sake. Most, however, condemned the form out of hand.

The evil extramusical reputation of bop was a classic case of labeling from the outside. The reasoning followed this line: Hipsters, drug users, and other alienated types were always found listening to bop music; the bop musicians were also drug users; therefore, the whole group was dangerous to American faith and morals. The labeled sometimes accepted the label and lived up to their stereotypes. The esoteric and often bizarre behavior of the boppers fanned the flames.

Only because the number of boppers was so small did they escape society-wide censure. But in the large urban centers, censure did occur, and the cult became a defensive sect. What saved bop as music was the clear recognition by many talented musicians and receptive fans that there was a difference between the music, the sometimes personally disorganized musicians who played it, and the disaffected who were attracted to it.

The bop musician and his audience formed a deviant subculture, if at all, only briefly. This formation was due to the compression of a radical new approach to music into a limited geographic area, mostly in New York, for a relatively short period of time. Protesters saw bop as protest music. The musicians, however, were self-conscious about their work and fully aware that something new was evolving; their "cause" was fundamentally musical. Whatever else the bop musicians were concerned about—for instance, racism and the lack of respect for Afro-American contributions to the arts—they were musical creators first of all.*

This was a group of musicians, moreover, who recognized each other and met on a regular basis. During and just after World War II, their "home" was Fifty-second Street and the uptown clubs in Harlem. By the late forties, Fifty-second Street was lined with nightclubs that featured jazz. Many younger musicians got their chance to play in these clubs because of the shortage of musicians during the war years. Fifty-second Street beckoned the bop players, and the movement from Harlem to "the Street" made the new music more public. Eventually, this shift and the accessibility of midtown Manhattan led to the stylization of bop and, paradoxically, fixed its vocabulary. Sitting-in became more difficult as various experimenters began to understand and extend the pioneering work of Bird, Roach, Dizzy, Monk, and others. Jazzman Billy Taylor explained what it was like:

> The club owners took advantage of the knowledge that a sideman could attract some business on his own if he were publicized. But eventually sitting-in got less and less frequent. For one thing, it got to the place where you had to protect your job. Jobs began to get scarce. Then a second factor is that, as modern jazz evolved, guys would rehearse groups and get things set musically. The patterns within a group got so involved that if you play horn now, you can't sit-in unless you know the men and what they're doing in their writing and arranging. In time, everybody began to work on developing his own lines and everybody began to work on getting something different in group sounds, so it got harder and harder for just anyone to sit-in (Hentoff and Shapiro, 1955, p. 322).

THE MUSIC OF BOP

Bop maximized the ever-present tendency in jazz for improvisation, stifled in heavily arranged swing. With increased musical sophistication and technical knowledge, plus the bold resolve to break with the conven-

---

* An indication of this nonmusical aspect was the adoption of the Muslim religion and new names by many jazz players.

tional music business (and the fact of being frozen out of it), jazz musicians began an extended exploration of harmonic and rhythmic complexities. Of course, such explorations were common in jazz from its beginnings; bop reasserted the fundamental nature of the form itself. Until bop, however, there was never a question about the sovereignty of the melodic element in jazz.* Bop attacked the melodic in a defiant manner. The masters of bop pushed off from the melodic dock into the Sargasso Sea of complex harmony in a manner not unlike that of their blues forebears, but with much less of a sense of compromise.

In early jazz the theme-and-variations format consisted of stating a melody, improvising a solo break with melodic and/or harmonic variations and returning to the melody. Early jazz represented a continuing dialogue with American popular music and a struggle to digest the blues paradigm within the limits set by the dialogue. For the reasons discussed above, bop broke off that dialogue for a time in order to explore musically the jazz paradigm itself.

Every note (tone) implies other secondary tones based on some larger understanding of the nature of music. These higher and lower tones stand in some relation to the single note based on convention. These relationships constitute the "social facts" of music. The most conventional harmonic series of tones in Western music are based on whole note triads such as the familiar C-E-G progression when C, for example, is the tonal center or tonic. (See chapter 1, pp. 17–19.) B may be added (the seventh note up from C on a piano), producing an augmented chord. The ninth note, the eleventh note, or even the thirteenth above the tonal center may also be "piled on," although such usage of the overtone series produces great ambiguities, since these notes are, again by convention, part of other scales in other keys. Most Western composers of serious music approach such stretches with great caution. Bop musicians approached them with great abandon. (To be sure, modern composers were doing the same thing, often losing their audiences in the process.) The conventional triad—C-E-G—can also be tampered with by lowering its upper note, G, to G-flat. This tampering has the effect of defeating expectation without destroying the feeling of a third altogether, which the simple substitution of a fourth or a second might. It also completes a microtonal blues triad around the third, fifth, and seventh intervals.

These alterations create musical surprises, although the addition of the seventh has been common in Western music since the seventeenth and eighteenth centuries, and it is, after all, within the conventional oc-

* See chapter 1 for a full discussion of the critical importance of melody in American music, especially popular music.

tave. The ninth is not and takes us into another key, another chord with another root tone. Thus, "polychords" create ambiguities as movement occurs into the upper reaches of the overtone series. Around the turn of the century, some European composers, most notably Claude Debussy, used the ninth to generate excitement. Bop players used it to the point of cliché.

Bop musicians, as hinted above, also altered the upper note of the expected triad, in the C chord, the note G. Here the blues influence is obvious. The lowered fifth note, G-flat, is the same as the raised fourth, F-sharp. The I-IV-I chord progression offers a sense of expansion and partial relaxation and yet is less "resolved" than the more traditional I-V-I sequence. The I-IV-I progression is often referred to as the "Amen cadence" in contemporary books on music, referring to the use of it in religious music which, in turn, reminds us of the spiritual-blues connection (Daniels and Wagner, 1975, p. 49). The flatted fifth took its place with the other blue notes during the bop era. I would hypothesize that this represented a further exploration of the alterations of American music in favor of its Afro-American element.

Without becoming enmeshed in a discussion of the theory of harmony, I am arguing here that the bop players, especially Charlie Parker, moved jazz harmonically into very sophisticated and difficult territory. The further fact that many jazz and pseudojazz players began "running chords" (arpeggios) instead of creating lines and used ninths and flatted fifths indiscriminately—even mindlessly—should not obscure the puzzling complexities that were introduced (Stearns, 1956; Ostransky, 1977; Tanner and Gerow, 1973). It must be remembered that in any music with a harmonic basis each note implies some chordal structure based upon it according to an informal or implied theory of music. There is, moreover, a feeling of enormous, even dangerous, complexity in superimposing even slight tonal shifts in the selection of notes to be played, if those shifts are purposeful and not simply "mistakes."

The seriousness of the complexities that were being introduced in the jazz music of the forties is indicated by the hostility and consternation expressed by older jazz players more comfortable with the less intricate melodic approach to early jazz. Eddie Condon, a marvelous and straightforward player of the older generation, is reputed to have said of bop: "The boppers flat their fifths, we drink ours!"

The next step the bop players took was to imply rather than to state the melodic reference. (The word "step" is used here only for analytic purposes; these issues were worked out more or less simultaneously.) Instead of stating a melodic theme to be explored, they launched directly into the notes of its implied chordal structure. This created entirely new tunes, which were very often based upon standards but without direct melodic reference. A substantial portion of the bop repertoire came from a few well-known chord progressions: the basic twelve-bar blues progression of I-IV-I-V⁷-I or those of popular and well-known songs such as George Gershwin's "I Got Rhythm." The thirty-two-measure popular-song structure was also widely used, since its A-A-B-A structure permitted extensive modification in the B section while providing an overall framework understood by everyone without extensive rehearsal. These conventions were very important in both jam sessions and on recording dates, which were often hastily put together.

James Patrick refers to the borrowed-harmony technique of jazz composition as "the melodic contrafact," an analogy to text substitution in medieval music.

> In any idiom which relies heavily on improvisation, there must be limits on materials serving as a referential basis. The need for a restricted and commonly-known repertory is especially crucial in the context of the jam session for which there are no rehearsals or regular personnel.
>
> . . . There are economic aspects surrounding the recording of the new and experimental style of the early 1940s. Until the late 1940s, the recording of the new jazz had been the exclusive province of numerous small companies. . . .
>
> Various accounts give a clear picture of the constrained and hectic situation which both producers and performers experienced in the small company recording session. The small companies, with small sales and limited distribution, often operated with narrow profit. Money for composer fees, rehearsals, studio time, and engineering was scarce. Thus the contrafact often provided a cheap and convenient way to record "new" material with a minimum of rehearsals, retakes, and composer fees (Patrick, 1975, pp. 6–11 passim).

Because evolving bop conventions permitted variations on themes never stated, riff support and heavy arrangements were unnecessary, and longer and more inventive solo lines emerged. Changes in rhythm also permitted intense yet relaxed work. It must be reemphasized that all these developments had roots going far back in jazz history; the melodic contrafact was a fact of life for all good jazz. Bop stripped away some of the accretions and compromises that commercial music had brought to jazz. As Martin Williams has rightly pointed out, it will not do to overemphasize the harmonic element in bop. The changes that had been developing in rhythm were also essential, perhaps more essential than harmonic elements. Here again, rhythmic developments had roots far back in jazz history. Citing the pioneering work of Andre Hodeir, Williams put it this way:

> The rhythmic basis of the style [bop] is a subdivision of the quarter-note swing style into an eighth-note pulse. Once grasped, the accentuation of the weak beat, accents between beats, the runs of short notes, the delays—all fall into place as functional, direct, unadorned expression. So do other things: it is provocative to see the history of jazz, granted that it involves simplifications, in terms of a rhythmic evolution: the whole-note rhythmic basis of the cakewalk, subdivided into halves by ragtime, subdivided with syncopated quarters in New Orleans, subdivided fully into quarters by Armstrong, made into even fours by Basie, subdivided into eighths [possibly inspired by the popularity of boogie-woggie, by the way] by a bop style which, partly because of a wartime tax on dancing in clubs, could play for the listener (Williams in Hentoff and McCarthy, 1975, pp. 292–93).

THE 1950S AND THE "BIRTH OF THE COOL"

Bop, as a musical form, laid the foundation that modern jazz would follow for the next two decades. But eventually bop audiences lost interest in bop per se, although they continued to idolize men such as Parker and Monk as much for their *outré* behavior as for their musical creativity. The bopsters became hipsters and later beatniks. Any ties to jazz as music became tenuous. In spite of later attempts to link jazz and social issues, it is clear that music is typically subsequent to, rather than a cause of, social change. While racism and democracy were *the* ideological issue in World War II, the defeat of Nazism in Europe did not lift the stigma of blackness at home. Wagner's music was as much a victim of the Nazi movement in Germany as the music of bop was a victim of the rhetoric of black artistic freedom in America. The flirtation between jazz musicians and American bohemians was rather short-lived, although each group exerted influence and counterinfluence on the other.

By the time the 1950s rolled around, jazz fans had taken off their dark glasses and little berets and gone home to listen to LPs. The jazz audience had shrunk perceptibly; jazz clubs began either to close or to change their music policy. Fifty-second Street died for jazzmen. Jazz had established itself as an art form, but the terms of the new "contract" between the jazz players and their audience changed. Because jazz is serious music and must be taken seriously, the "new" jazz fan prefers the concert hall to the nightclub and the stereo record to both.

Each generation of jazz players generates a parallel generation of jazz fans. There are, in other words, cohorts of jazz fans who develop their taste for jazz at a particular point in time. These fans often develop a loyalty to a jazz style that introduced them to the jazz form in general. There are also revivals of older forms, such as Dixieland, which attract fans through nostalgia or historical interest.

The jazz musician is also influenced by various revivals and fads, since he or she is, after all, part of the cultural milieu. This means that at any given moment in time there is bound to be a mixture of styles mutually affecting each other. Bop musicians grew up in and out of the swing era. Later developments in bop, especially the efforts to orchestrate bop for larger groups, were also results of the swing era.

Two important postwar developments led to profound changes in jazz. One was the growth of the LP record, which catered to specialized markets and led to the possibility of profit from a large markup in the price of LPs. The other was the changes in modes of transportation, for example, the growth of air travel. This second change meant that the big traveling bands no longer had to go on extended road trips but could criss-cross the entire country, and even the world, in a matter of days instead of weeks or months. (Today, Tokyo is a key city on the jazz circuit.) To put the same idea in more general terms: Transportation, communication, and other technological changes have an impact on the production of art in America. Radio, especially FM, television, the modern phonograph, and tape deck have broken down the insulation of various art forms even further. Form itself becomes problematic (Horowitz, 1978).

The postbop era can be characterized as an age of experimentation. As early as 1945, Woody Herman attempted the amalgam of bop and swing. The various "Herman Herds" (bandleader Herman's bands have come to be called "herds") from that time until the present have continued in the same eclectic direction. Many of the finest postbop white players are alumni of the various Herds. Stan Kenton and Boyd Raeburn pioneered a style of jazz that was to become known as progressive jazz, a mixture of swing and classical music with a dash of bop. Out of this progressive jazz tradition developed the popular jazz of the 1950s—the music of Dave Brubeck, Gerry Mulligan, and others. LeRoi Jones (Imamu Amiri Baraka) has characterized Kenton as the Paul Whiteman of the modern jazz era and castigates the developers of this style as too "intellectualized." "Cool jazz" became the vogue, and the coolest was the so-called West Coast jazz, especially the music of Gerry Mulligan and Chet Baker, with its emphasis on "soft, intimate sound and regular rhythms. . . . The innovations that progressive jazz was supposed to have made, contrapuntal jazz and jazz fugue, became standard terms that could be applied to a music whose name had once been a transitive verb unutterable in polite society" (Jones, 1963, p. 212). Cool jazz-black is most closely associated with Miles Davis.

Perhaps the most accurate label for the music of Davis is "detached." Davis, who "paid dues" in bop groups led by Parker and others, extended this detachment beyond a light, pure, middle-register, vibratoless tone into other aspects of his behavior, such a leaving the stage during a performance or turning his back on the audience. Many jazz groups, both black and white, combined jazz and classical forms. The Modern Jazz Quartet, for example (SCCJ-IX-1; X-2; XI-3), under the direction of John Lewis, extended classical forms and tight arranging (SCCJ-IX-1; X-2) in a chamber music format (SCCJ-X-4). Gil Evans, an architectonic arranger, worked with Miles Davis.

John Lewis and Gunther Schuller, pioneered third-stream music. Europe was the first, Africa the second, and Afro-American the third stream of music, Schuller argued. But the connection between the cool school, the third stream, and bop grew more and more tenuous. Even though the bop chordal structure remained, the fire of bop went out. A counterreaction set in, and hard bop was born.

The "funky hard-bop regression" of the fifties was an attempt to put the fire back into overly cool jazz. In order to do this, hard-bop musicians such as Horace Silver and Cannonball Adderley self-consciously sought to return to the "blues roots" of jazz. "Amidst the cellos, flutes, fugues and warmed-over popular ballads of the cool, there was evident, mostly among Negro musicians, a conscious, and many times, affected, 'return to the roots,' as it has been called so often" (Jones, 1963, p. 210).

The hard-bop movement was an important one because it prepared the way for the acceptance of soul music among jazzmen in the 1960s. But, in addition to the musical developments of jazz in the 1950s, something significant was also happening in the attitude of the public toward jazz and jazz musicians. The institutional music critics began to realize the importance of jazz. State Department tours, featuring black and white jazz musicians, were organized. The Voice of America began devoting more of its overseas time to jazz broadcasts. The jazz musician had begun to gain long-sought-after recognition as an artist. College and concert tours by leading jazzmen were successful.

But there was a "cost." Jazz had lost its chance to become America's popular music. The rise of rock 'n' roll to replace the leftover big band vocalists in the popular-music field forced jazz into increased specialization, on the one hand, and increased blending with other forms of music, on the other. Some of the fear of jazz threatening morals was also siphoned off by rock 'n' roll—a vocal music with blues (Afro-American) roots (Kamin, 1975). Cliques within jazz hardened, and the rise to absolute power over popular taste by the disk jockey meant that jazz had no uniform face to present to the rising challenge. The deviance once associated with jazz took hold elsewhere. Narcotics, associated in the popular mind of the 1940s and 1950s with jazz and jazz players, became associated with youth and the rock of the 1960s. The same may be said about the new freedom in dancing. In short, jazz no longer shocks anyone. It is regarded as another art form by most people and certainly no longer a "threat to morals."

Some black jazz musicians, such as Ornette Coleman and Cecil Taylor, have experimented with avant garde forms of jazz (SCCJ-XI-2; XII-1 through 3) and some authors, notably LeRoi Jones, associated this music with black militance. Many avant garde jazz musicians, both black and white, have moved in the same directions as modern chamber musicians, namely, toward atonal free forms with a general concern for sound as sound. For some of these avant garde jazzmen to be made heroes of the Black Nationalist movement has more to do with their outspoken views on racial issues than their music (Horowitz and Nanry, 1975), I do not think anyone today seriously considers the "threat" of black militancy a jazz threat, although younger black jazz players may be caught up in their own sense of jazz as protest music.

ROCK

Some social scientists, most notably Margaret Mead, have argued that the world's history can now be divided into the pre- and post-atomic eras. The threat of push-button global destruction creates a consciousness of the world as a small place, however dangerous. While the first atomic bomb did not explode until 1945, Einstein's theoretical formulation that made it possible was published as early as 1905 and refined in 1915. Moreover, the theoretical roots of relativity physics went back much further than that. So, too, the roots of modern jazz go all the way back to the very origins of the musical form. Parker and his colleagues introduced a theoretical self-consciousness in jazz that went far beyond the craftsmanship emphasized in the music of the thirties.

Bop exploded the jazz atom. Suddenly, the conventional understanding that jazz would forever strive to be popular commercial music disintegrated. With roots in earlier periods, but most clearly in the sixties and seventies, jazz musicians began to reach out self-consciously to European, African, Indian, and other national music for insight and inspiration. Bird's well noted affection for the music of Stravinsky and Hindemith and Coltrane's ofttimes expressed admiration for the music of Ravi Shankar illustrate this tendency. (John Coltrane's equal admiration for Albert Einstein also gives the game away.) In the last two decades, jazz music has become bipolar. On the one hand, many jazz players have moved toward commercial success by emphasizing the blues-oriented, down-home flavor of funky music and, on the other, they have stressed the theoretical potential of jazz fusion with other contemporary art music.

No matter how happy one's own childhood may have been, it can hardly be argued that the 1950s were a good time for American democracy. Americans were caught up in the excesses of making it, free-enterprise style. The rugged illusions of Horatio Alger were replaced by the organization man in his gray flannel suit. The ugly domestic political reality of overconformity led to the excesses of Senator Joseph McCarthy and the dichotomization of the world into monolithic "free" and "Communist" camps. The stalemated Korean War had added to the frustration. Brought partially to our senses by the televised Army-McCarthy hearings, we quickly were caught up in the insanity of the Vietnam war. Between Joe McCarthy and the fall of Saigon in 1975, the War on Poverty was launched. The failure of this "Second Reconstruction" led to the massive urban insurrections in major cities such as Detroit, Los Angeles, and Newark in the late sixties. The war to preserve democracy and forever obliterate the Holocaust that was represented by Auschwitz and Dachau failed to generate an end to racism and disenfranchisement in America. The statistical horror of an infant mortality rate in central Harlem higher than the rate in war-torn Saigon produced a sense of outrage among certain segments of the American populace.

When the Supreme Court spoke in the Brown case in 1954, equality became the law of the land. The path to true equality was, and continues to be, a difficult one. The civil rights movement gathered momentum, and protest was taken into the streets as well as into the courts. The facade of conformity that characterized the fifties was painfully shattered in the sixties. Others found a voice, especially the young and, later, women. Taking their cues from the civil rights strategists, various minority citizens forced America to look at itself. The sight was not a pretty one. The social fabric of America was torn and tattered. Some changes were effected: the war in Vietnam came to a bloody end; formal segregation is being chipped away.

In the late seventies, a sobering and profoundly pessimistic sense of the difficulty of achieving a fair and just social order is with us. Young people, not unlike the silent generation of the fifties, are flocking to vocational and professional schools, especially those for business administration. Colleges are now regarded as places to train for a career, rather than a stage for protest. In the areas of income, housing, and jobs, the poor and minority groups, especially blacks, continue to fall behind. The by-products of industrialization continue to pollute the environment. Older people are beginning to think of themselves as a minority group. The search for alternatives to expensive and dirty fossil fuels has met with little success. Inflation, high unemployment, and the high cost of energy create problems that are at least as ominous as the psychological issues of racism, sexism, and ageism.

Paralleling the social changes of the last two decades, music, especially popular music, has undergone a transformation. Out of the urban blues came rhythm and blues. The term "rhythm and blues" (R&B) was simply the replacement in the late forties for the less sensitive category "race records." R&B did represent a change in presentation from the prewar blues, however. In his excellent history of rock 'n' roll, *The Sound of the City,* Charlie Gillet discusses the origins of R&B.

> Through the first three decades of the twentieth century the blues extended the difference established by black singers and musicians in New Orleans between the bands that played march and dance rhythms with several instruments and the singers who supplied their own accompaniment, usually on guitar. Of these two modes, the band music gradually subdivided into jazz (developed in most regions of the country by bands emphasizing instrumental improvisation and harmony) and band blues (associated from the late twenties mainly with bands in the Southwest—Kansas, Oklahoma, Texas, and parts of Arkansas). At the same time, the self-accompanying blues singers who were first identified with small towns in the rural South began moving into larger towns and cities, and into the North, where they began collecting other musicians to support them, often on piano or harmonica.
>
> Both kinds of bues singing—band- and self-accompanied— were radically affected by the improvements in electrical amplification introduced during the thirties, which enabled singers to be heard without shouting, and guitar-playing techniques to exploit the differences in tone and volume provided by electric amplification. The post-war blues styles of rhythm and blues were different from prewar styles partly because of this difference in equipment; but they were also different because there were new experiences to be accounted for in music, and new moods that the blues had to accommodate. The singer (or musician) who grew up in the farm community life of Mississippi found a different kind of environment when he

moved to Memphis and then to Chicago, different living conditions and different tastes, and his music had to reflect the new conditions. He had moved to the big city. For a time, jazz and band blues had been more or less the same thing, as in the repertoires of Count Basie and Jimmy Lunceford. But once the experiments of the New York "bop" musicians abandoned regular rhythms, jazz and blues became two different kinds of music with different audiences. The most distinctive characteristic of all rhythm and blues styles was the presence of a dance rhythm, and it is primarily this characteristic that distinguished rhythm and blues from post-war jazz, which was rarely recorded as dance music and which could therefore dispense with the convention of maintaining a particular beat throughout a song.

There was a further difference between jazz and the blues in post-war music. In rhythm and blues, the soloists were generally more "selfish," concerned to express their own feelings, depending on the rest of the band to keep the beat going and the volume up while they blew their hearts out and their heads off. In jazz, there was usually more interplay between musicians, more exploration into melody and harmony, less reliance on the emotional force of the musician's tone (pp. 130–31).

Gillet goes on to distinguish different categories of R&B, including Gospel-based styles. Hard bop represented both a "return to the roots" by Horace Silver, Art Blakey, and the Jazz Messengers (important jazz groups in the early sixties) and a recognition of the growing popular appeal of R&B in the race market. Hard bop was a crossover music that linked some of the developments of jazz style in the forties to a broader audience. Later on, Cannonball Adderley (with the late sixties hit, "Mercy, Mercy, Mercy," especially) and currently George Benson and others continue this crossover activity.

Rhythm and blues begat rock 'n' roll; rock 'n' roll begat rock and roll; rock and roll begat rock. The decline of swing and the events surrounding the end of World War II created a vacuum in popular music. Bop, a cult music (Peterson, 1972), moved jazz away from popular music. Into the vacuum rushed a new folk and pop combination. White country music and black blues, America's two folk sources, were drawn upon for the revitalization of popular music. Kamin suggests several factors that opened the way for the new R&B-derived music (Kamin, 1974). Beginning in the early fifties, TV attracted a large portion of the mass audience away from radio, allowing more room for experimentation. During this period teen-agers became a larger proportion of the population than they had ever been before. Many of these young people were affluent, providing a generational tension that would burst into near warfare in the sixties.* The 45-rpm record provided a cheap and durable substitute for the 78 and was better suited to short pop tunes than the more costly and longer playing 33. And, most important, the new music was dance music.

At first rock 'n' roll merely represented some white groups "covering" hits from the R&B market (that is, recording a cleaned-up and softened version of the same songs). The success of some of these cover songs led to the development of vaguely blues-oriented pop music. Rock and roll, like swing a generation earlier, provided a formula pop music and permitted the record companies to reassert control over the product.† Rock emerged in the sixties, as bop had in the forties, as a fine-art branch of a popular musical form. The best rock musicians began to improvise and extend melodic lines. Some crossover with jazz occurred as both jazz and rock musicians played together and listened to each other's work. Experimentation with modal music, especially by the Beatles, also provided a point of contact.

These developments in popular music actually increased the jazz audience. Many young people identified (usually at a safe distance) their status as a minority group with the more authentic civil rights movement. There emerged a genuine interest in black music and musicians. The blues-based character of R&B-derived music conditioned listeners to hear the common chord progressions of rock, which were the twelve-bar blues structure. Blue notes were frequently employed, creating melisma and at least a superficial jazz feeling. Rock, however, never developed the rhythmic sophistication of jazz. The rock beat is steady and square, based on a

---

* The postwar generation was different from any other generation in American history. They were untempered by economic deprivation in the way in which their parents had been tempered by the Great Depression. They had it made since their parents had made it. Unionization and child labor laws meant that children no longer had to work and created a situation of prolonged adolescent dependency. Sociologists have long pointed out that children in agricultural societies and in the early phases of industrialization are an economic asset to their families. In modern urban societies, they are an economic liability and tend to be seen by parents as a source of generative psychological satisfaction. This situation, rather new to the middle classes in America, could result in conflict. Music for the postwar generation became a reasonably safe avenue of protest. Of course, the generational rebellion was not entirely new; the Roaring Twenties had many of the same elements. Massive changes in media technology and the sheer numbers of young people qualitatively altered the impact of the rebellion in the late fifties and on into the sixties.

† This process is discussed at some length in chapter 1, pages 23–24, as the model of monopolistic capitalism. Competitors scramble for market shares and then are either bought out or are squeezed out by an oligopoly as the market becomes viable.

loud succession of equal eighth notes played on the drums not the cymbals (Ostransky, 1977, p. 269). Massive amplification and studio mixing of sounds gave great control to bandleaders and sound engineers who could insure, in a precise technical way, the proper sound.

Although the strong and steady pulse of rock lacked the sophistication of most jazz, it emphasized the supreme importance of rhythm, if only through sheer incessancy. All those young people on Dick Clark's "American Bandstand" who picked new record A over new record B and cited "the beat" as the reason for their selections were not just dumb or inarticulate; they knew what the critical factor in their music was. In a word, this was a dance music. If the decibel level of much of this music was deafening (and it was), it had the virtue of being "up front"; it bespoke the Afro-American origin of popular American vernacular dance in a most unequivocal way (Stearns and Stearns, 1968). Just as Tin Pan Alley had provided the context for jazz in the twenties and thirties, rock was the popular musical environment of jazz in the sixties and seventies.

CONTEMPORARY JAZZ

There have been three major trends in jazz over the last decade and a half. Older jazz styles, such as swing, have gained new fans and a stable audience, especially among the young. Considerable recording activity has been stimulated by the reissuing of out-of-circulation records. Major companies such as RCA and Columbia, as well as small specialized companies such as Biograph, have found it profitable to tap this market. (John Hammond of Columbia told me that another important stimulus to this kind of activity is the low-budget mail order record business, which uses relatively cheap advertising on local television.) *

This trend indicates a significant decline in nonmusical hostility to jazz. Most blacks take a justifiable pride in jazz as a major musical contribution. White Americans, especially on college campuses, are beginning to see jazz as part of their musical heritage as well. The understandable excesses of some Black Nationalists in claiming jazz as the exclusive "property" of black people is now fading. The narrow claims of ethnic exclusivity are giving way to the broader and more humanistic realization of cultural sharing. True jazz, of course, remains peripheral to the popular music industry. This condition is clearly a matter of mass market tastes and, since the ascendance of R&B-based rock, less specifi-

---

* John Hasse has published an excellent review of some of this reissue material. (See Hasse, 1975.)

cally racial. Musicians cross over to pop from jazz more easily now, and many pop musicians, such as Stevie Wonder, employ jazz licks in their music.

A second major trend has been the wider acceptance of black music and musicians in commercial music. It would indeed be foolish to imply that the millennium has arrived and that all the racial barriers have fallen. The fact that the music industry is clique-ridden, that friends hire friends, acts as a drag on color blindness. The market is, however, the controlling mechanism and music that sells—black or white—will get recorded. (What sells is very much a function of "what's out there," of course, and that, too, inhibits the operation of a totally free market.) The breakthrough into popular music of black-based recording companies, such as Motown Records, has lowered the purely racial barriers to musical acceptance.

Much drive and creative vitality have been lost in contemporary popular music. Marshmallow (soft) rock and easy-listening jazz pouring out of Top-40 radio has settled, sweet and sticky, into place. As rock moved into its fine-art phase in the late sixties and early seventies, the field was cleared for a new dance music. Disco has now moved into the breach. Latin-influenced and with a big beat, this form has little to recommend it musically except that it is danceable. The easy affinity of swing hits of the thirties with the disco beat is not hard to discern; pop music is, and always has been, dance music. One fascinating aspect of this new form (and one must keep in mind that the discotheque, with records substituted for live music, has been around for a long time) is the way it has begun to produce "monster" hits with little or no radio air play. Like the race records of an earlier time, disco music simply moved into a vacuum in popular music with something the mass market could understand and dance to with little ideological commitment.*

---

*The Latin connection is a fascinating one. With the disco craze came the Latin hustle. The Latin hustle has about the same organic connection to Latin music as the turkey trot had to authentic jazz in the twenties. Popular Latin music is often called *salsa* (hot sauce) by Latins. The term *"salsa"* has a connotation that parallels the term "soul" among blacks. *Salsa* is an important spice in contemporary jazz and has been a part of jazz as far back as Jelly Roll Morton's acknowledgment of the "Spanish tinge." Joseph Blum has emphasized both the powerful impact of *salsa,* a people's music largely ignored by scholars, and the early connection with jazz.

It was Mario Bauza [a Cuban who came to New York in 1926 and helped to create Machito's famous Latin band; Bauza also worked with many early jazz groups] who got Dizzy Gillespie a trumpet chair with Cab Calloway—Dizzy Gillespie used Chano Pozo to help create his Afro-Cuban sound; Charlie Parker later recorded with Machito—there was an un-

The two trends briefly discussed above describe the external dynamic of jazz. The third has to do with its internal dynamic. That internal dynamic revolves around the further exploration and extension of the bop (fine-art) phase of jazz.

In the midst of major racial tensions in American society in the sixties, many writers and musicians emphasized a "jazz as black music" line. (See especially Jones, *Blues People,* 1963.) In retrospect, that development might have been expected. By now, however, the shrillness has subsided, and jazz remains what it has always been: an American musical form with origins in, and continuing influence from, the Afro-American subculture. Other influences are there as well, especially in complex explorations into melodic, harmonic, and other technical areas. John Coltrane (who died in 1967) and Ornette Coleman clearly represent the jazz continuity of the postbop era in what is now called "free jazz."

Coltrane grew up in, and was an important part of, the bop period. He played with Dizzy Gillespie, Miles Davis (SCCJ-XI-3), and Theolonious Monk. With Davis and with his own groups in the early sixties (SCCJ-XII-4) he pressed the chordal structure of bop to the next logical stage of evolution into a non-key-centered scalar conception. With his phenomenal technical mastery, Trane learned to play two and three notes together through false fingering and lip control. This, in addition to his extraordinary speed, gave his music a great density of texture. Jazz critic Ira Gitler coined the phrase "sheets of sound" to describe this attack. Trane also pushed the idea of very long solo lines much further than the bop players had. He developed a technique and a harmonic approach that, free from the more limiting convention of chordal systems, permitted these extended lines to remain inventive and yet true to the spirit of jazz improvisation.

John Coltrane started out playing clarinet, then switched to alto saxophone and finally to the tenor saxophone. He later also mastered the soprano saxophone and on the instrument performed some of his most lyrical and satisfying work. Since the Charlie Parker days, the field of exploration for saxophone players had been the higher notes in the overtone series. By stretching his tenor's range and shifting upward in tone with the soprano, Trane was able to take this development to the next

> dergound stream of "real" Latin music, alongside the jazz stream, which had little to do with Desi Arnaz, "Babaloo," or Cougie and Abbe. On 52nd Street and Broadway, the jazz corner of the world, Birdland was downstairs and the Palladium was upstairs. Now both are dead, and we have Charo to perpetuate an image of Latins we could very much do without (Blum, p. 145).
>
> I would urge any interested reader to consult the Blum article and the references cited to explore further this fascinating "fourth stream" in jazz.

logical step. While some of his playing, especially on the tenor, moves to such a high and thin pitch that it borders on squeaks and squawks, it is clear that his playing is purposeful and minded. (Some less inventive "new thing" players lost the sense of musical dynamics, so much a part of Trane's playing, and the squeaks and squawks became identified as the style itself—hardly a viable musical position to remain in.) In Coltrane's best work, much credit must be given to his piano player, McCoy Tyner. Tyner's use of the pedal point (a held note usually in the bass sounded against changing harmonies in the upper parts) kept a tonal sense of the music, and his sense of time made a major rhythmic contribution to the group, simultaneously freeing the other members of time-keeping responsibilities.

As Frank Kofsky has pointed out, the major jazz contribution of the Coltrane group was its employment and further exploration of rhythmic displacement. Following a tradition in jazz at its beginnings and consciously highlighted during the bop heyday, this displacement effect must be understood if one is to grasp the essential jazz development in this later period. In each jazz era there has been a "reborn" sense of swing. In the Coltrane era, much credit for a new swinging sense must be given to his drummer Elvin Jones.

> Basically Jones's style involves the superimposition of one or more additional meters, usually involving some ternary division of the beat (i.e., either quarter-note, eighth-note or sixteenth-note triplets), on top of—or rather, to be precise, alongside of—the basic pulse of the piece in question. Yet in itself, this would not be a singularly notable achievement. What gives it such exceptional efficacy in the hands of Jones is his ability to utilize this second meter to deploy a series of accents that create musical tension by suggesting that the beat has been dislodged from its true position (Kofsky, 1977, p. 14).

Now, more than a decade after his death, jazz players continue to find inspiration in the work of John Coltrane and his collaborators. The contrapuntal tension between Jones and Coltrane, the support of Tyner and the inquisitive explorations of Alice Coltrane, John's second wife, all provide enough material for volumes of jazz history. Coltrane is one anchor point of modern jazz; the other is Ornette Coleman.

Ornette Coleman (SCCJ-XII-1, 2, and 3), self-taught and a leading figure in the "free jazz" movement, is regarded by many as the key to understanding future developments in jazz. Coleman is wildly inventive and has experimented with most of the modern musical devices usually thought of as part of the modern chamber ensemble's domain. His free jazz has involved, for example, exploration of the tone row, that is, assembling notes in some ordered fashion from the entire chromatic scale (all the scale notes). His art is perhaps best thought of as musical collage. A Coleman group avoids preset structure, and each instrumentalist is expected to pick up on musical ideas, motifs, and rhythmic organization as they play. He has worked with classical musicians and is respected by them for his work. Ornette Coleman has taken jazz about as far as it can go into atonality and freedom from conventional constraint. At the same time, in spite of great sophistication, there is more than a hint of his raw southwestern origins, the blues, and even rhythm and blues in Coleman's work. The key social element in jazz—the merger of the composer and performer into a single simultaneous entity—has been forcefully reaffirmed by Ornette Coleman.

Coltrane and Coleman represent both continuity and change in jazz. Continuity because one can see how thoroughly they are connected with the jazz of the past. But they also represent change insofar as they both sensed the need for moving jazz innovation away from the conventions of bop. Bop, it turned out, was just as susceptible to cliché and facile recreation as earlier forms, such as swing, had been. Coltrane and Coleman gave impetus to the conscious attempt by a new generation of jazz players to break out of the bop framework.

Exploration jazz was called avant-garde jazz or the "new thing" in the early sixties and finally, by the mid-seventies, free jazz. (*Free Jazz* was the title of a 1960 Coleman recording, and, like the earlier Dizzy Gillespie recording of a tune called "Bebop," the part came to be the label for the whole.) Above all, free jazz represents exploration.

As in all other stylistic areas of jazz, conventions and "rules of the game" established themselves in free jazz—even though the latter's own creation was sparked by a break with most of the norms considered irrevocable before. The conventions of harmonically and metrically confined jazz styles, up to hard bop, could be reduced to a relatively narrow and stable system of agreements; therefore, analysis of a given style could concentrate on detecting and interpreting the congruities present in individual ways of operating within that system of agreements. With the advent of free jazz, however, a large number of divergent personal styles developed. Their only point of agreement lay in a negation of traditional norms; otherwise, they exhibited such heterogeneous formative principles that any reduction to a common denominator was bound to be an oversimplification. The initiators of free jazz drew widely different consequences from the renunciation of harmonic-metrical patterns, of the regulative force of the beat, and of the structural principles of the "jazz piece." As a result, the conventions that arose in free jazz with regard to instrumental technique, ensemble playing, formal organization, etc., were never as universally binding as those in traditional areas of jazz. Variability of formative principles is inherent in free jazz; moreover, specific principles are tied up with specific musicians and groups. In coming to grips with this music, then, it is necessary to adopt a method fundamentally different from the method which still worked for bebop, cool jazz or hard bop. Rudolf Stephan, speaking with reference to avantgarde music in Europe, drew attention to the absorption of the "musically universal" by the "musically particular." This is true of free jazz too; therefore, analysis demands a procedure that allows the particularities in the music of its most important exponents to be brought out, after which we can go on to discover general tendencies and trends (Jost, 1974, pp. 9–10).

Several trends in jazz seem evident. Older styles such as swing, Dixieland, blues, and ragtime are now taken quite seriously by some segments of the public, especially students. After a period of eclipse, which lasted from the forties through the early sixties, "mainstream" musicians and "pioneers" are being rediscovered. Eubie Blake, Roy Eldridge, Benny Carter, Earl Hines, and other "survivors" are now sought out—especially by younger people who realize the value of living history still available to them. Young musicians are also acknowledging their roots and the possibility of peaceful coexistence of a variety of styles within the jazz idiom.

Record companies such as Pablo and Concord successfully devote themselves to mainstream and swing and generate enough interest to survive. The idea of jazz as repertoire music now seems viable with considerable interest in the New York Repertory Company and Chuck Israel's National Jazz Ensemble. Even Sun Ra, long associated with far-out free jazz is playing Fletcher Henderson arrangements. Other gifted younger players, such as Jimmy Owens, Woody Shaw, Scott Hamilton and Warren Vache, Jr., remain close to the jazz mainstream. These younger musicians, however, are not simply re-creators or imitators—they work within the older traditions. Joe Zawinul, Wayne Shorter, Chick Corea, and Herbie Hancock bring electronic music and jazz/rock into a viable fusion that appeals to a wide audience, yet operates pretty much under the bop contract.

Europeans Joe Zawinul, Michael Urbaniak, George Mraz, Jan Hammer, Jean Luc Ponty, and Miroslav Vituous demonstrate the universal appeal of jazz playing. These Europeans (and others) are having a real impact on the development of jazz as a musical genre. Musicians from England, Poland, Czechoslovakia, and Japan play authentic jazz with real authority. This is also true for many of the fine European free-jazz players.

Jazz musicians employ two strategies for dealing with the current music scene. The first is to accommodate the music to suit the market. This strategy is, of course, as old as jazz itself. Jazz is combined with current popular forms in order to produce disco jazz or jazz/rock. Some jazz artists have moved quite far in the direction of producing mass market music. Herbie Hancock, George Benson, Chick Corea, and Freddie Hubbard (among others) are exemplars of this phenomenon. Still others, such as Sonny Rollins and Sonny Stitt, have stayed within the jazz framework while paying lip service to fusion music.

The other strategy is more interesting and represents a partial realization of the dream of many of the early bop players. That dream was to adjust the market to suit the music. One part of the overall strategy has been the creation of small record labels controlled by the musicians themselves. The other part involves finding nontraditional performance space. Loft jazz in New York's Soho area is an example of this movement.

In the seventies a new outlet for jazz performance evolved in New York—the jazz lofts. This movement is not so much an actual style of playing (although most of the musicians involved tend toward free jazz), but an attempt to provide an alternative to the commercial club scene, which has not served the needs of many artists. For example, some have found the traditional jazz nightclub atmosphere creatively stifling. Others, particularly newer artists, have had difficulty obtaining work. Finally, some have been dismayed at the fact that a large segment of the population (including many of the younger blacks they would most like to reach) are denied access to their music because of the prices charged by the clubs. In another sense, the lofts are an attempt to fill the void left by the disappearance of the jam sessions, through which jazz players of earlier eras traded ideas in an informal forum.

The loft movement has been spearheaded by saxophonist Sam Rivers who, with his wife Bea, founded their Studio Rivbea in 1971 in lower Manhattan.

Joseph Papp, an extraordinary presence in the New York theater with his New York Shakespeare Festival and productions of *Hair, A Chorus Line,* and other more serious plays, is now offering loft-type jazz in his experimental Public Theater. One of the best of the free jazz groups—the Art Ensemble of Chicago—has moved to New York and to the Public.

The new jazz represents sophisticated and mature organization by musicians.* The link to theater and the theatricality of some players creates an exciting atmosphere. Sun Ra has always staged jazz performance; the Art Ensemble of Chicago wears costumes, make-up, and employs theatrical devices.

Things are far from perfect. Much prejudice still exists against jazz and jazz musicians. Alienation and despair are still too often the jazz player's lot. At the moment of this writing, there is much jazz playing, but there is also an air of disquiet and even expectancy. Where do we go from here? Has the form been exhausted? Has form itself been exhausted in modern art (Horowitz, 1978)? We shall have to wait for the answer. There is a lot of creative activity, but more perspective is needed to integrate what is happening now with the whole of jazz development.

---

*This process is not limited to free-jazz players either. Veterans such as Eubie Blake (Eubie Blake Music) and Marian McPartland (Halcyon) are also producing and marketing their own records.

JAZZ / The Personal Dimension

John Birks "Dizzy" Gillespie (Raymond Ross Photos)

DIZZY GILLESPIE

In the forties, trumpeter Dizzy Gillespie was the man most able to match the musical flights of Charlie Parker, and, together, they formed the vanguard of bebop.

Dizzy, whose full name is John Birks Gillespie, was born in 1917 in Cheraw, South Carolina, the son of a bricklayer who was also an amateur musician. Although his father died when Dizzy was ten, the youngster was familiar with a variety of instruments by then. He began on trombone but switched to trumpet when he was fourteen. He had no formal training, but he was an impressive enough a musician in his teens to win a scholarship to the Laurinburg Institute, an industrial school for blacks in North Carolina. There he studied harmony and theory, as well as agriculture.

In 1935 the family moved to Philadelphia, and, after graduation, Dizzy joined them. He worked briefly there in a local group led by pianist

Bill Doggett, but soon after joined the Frank Fairfax band, which had some fine musicians, including trumpeter Charlie Shavers. At this time, Gillespie was greatly influenced by trumpeter Roy Eldridge, and his playing was patterned closely after his idol's. Because his style resembled Eldridge's, Gillespie was able to audition successfully in 1937 for Teddy Hill, whose band Eldridge had recently left. While with Hill, the young trumpeter was given the nickname, Dizzy, because of his antics and special sense of humor. Gillespie made his first recordings with Hill and traveled to Europe with the band. By the end of his stay with the Hill orchestra, Dizzy's playing, while still bearing the Eldridge imprint, began to show the earmarks of his own style, as shown in "Hot Mallets," a 1939 Lionel Hampton all-star recording (SCCJ-V-6).

In 1939 Gillespie joined Cab Calloway's band, where he was featured during his two years with the orchestra. At the same time, he became an habitue of Minton's (later to become famous as a bop club), which was managed by his old boss and supporter Teddy Hill. There, he jammed with fellow experimenters such as drummer Kenny Clarke and pianist Thelonious Monk. Gillespie was forced to leave Calloway in 1941 after a misunderstanding over a prank. He worked with Ella Fitzgerald's band for a brief period before joining Benny Carter's sextet at the end of the year. He interrupted his stay with Carter for a tour with Charlie Barnet, and in 1942 worked with the Les Hite and Lucky Millinder orchestras.

In early 1943 he joined the Earl Hines Orchestra. There he began his portentous partnership with Charlie Parker, which was continued a year later in the Billy Eckstine band, as well as informally at Minton's. Between stints with Hines and Eckstine, Gillespie and bassist Oscar Pettiford led a group at the Onyx Club on Fifty-second Street. "The group was the first to offer a regular outlet in downtown New York to the ideas which had been crystallizing since the beginning of the decade in the various big bands and the different Harlem after-hours rendezvous" (James, 1959, p. 12). Although the group did not record at the time, three of its members—Gillespie, Pettiford, and tenor saxophonist Don Byas—did so a year later (SCCJ-VII-5). Gillespie, who had done some arranging while with Calloway, was made musical director of the Eckstine band in spite of his by-now notorious reputation as a practical joker (James, 1959, p. 14).

In May 1945 Gillespie and Parker began an important engagement at the Three Deuces on Fifty-second Street and made historic quintet recordings (SCCJ VII 6 and 7). That same year, Gillespie, who was now beginning to gain a popular following on the strength of his personality as well as his musical ability (Gitler, 1966, p. 78), led his first big band on a brief and rather unsuccessful southern tour. In late 1945, Gillespie went to California, where he and Charlie Parker led a group at Billy Berg's club in Hollywood. But the West Coast was not quite ready for their innovations, and Gillespie soon returned to New York. The trumpeter again tried his hand at leading a big band, and this time was far more successful. Over the next three years, his band, featuring soloists like saxophonists James Moody and Cecil Payne, the conga of Chano Pozo, as well as advanced arrangements by Gil Fuller, Tadd Dameron, and John Lewis, scored a number of triumphs both here and abroad. By 1950, however, the Gillespie group was a victim of the general malaise that befell the big bands around that time.

In 1951 Gillespie, anticipating a trend that was later to become more common, started his own record company, Dee Gee, in order to exert closer control over his recordings. He had, by then, returned to the small-group format, taking a quintet to Europe in 1952 and 1953. In May 1953 he was reunited with Parker for the famous Massey Hall concert in Toronto. That same year, Gillespie was signed by producer Norman Granz, who, over the next few years, recorded him in a variety of settings. (In the seventies, he is again recording for Granz.)

In 1956 Gillespie formed a new big band for a highly successful State Department–sponsored tour of the Middle East, which was soon followed by a Latin American trip. He kept the band together until 1958. Since then, he has worked primarily as leader of his own small groups, although he has led specially assembled big bands on occasion.

Gillespie made a historic visit to Cuba in 1977. He has appeared on many TV programs and his personality has made him a popular entertainer in much the same way that Louis Armstrong was. Although both men had a wide appeal, Gillespie, like Armstrong, has always been totally serious about his music.

Throughout his career, Gillespie's unique vocal style has added a humorous touch to many of his recordings. As a composer, he is reknowned for such bop classics as "Groovin' High," "A Night in Tunisia," and "Woody 'n' You." Recently, he has written in other idioms as well. His electrifying trumpet style remains one of the most exciting sounds in jazz. Gillespie has moved from sideman in the big bands to an *enfant terrible* of bebop and has now gracefully assumed the status of one of jazz's elder statesmen.

Further Information

Biography James, Michael. *Dizzy Gillespie.* Kings of Jazz, 2. London: Cassell, 1959.

Discography   Jepsen, Jorgen Grunnet. *A Discography of Dizzy Gillespie.* 2 vols. Copenhagen: Knudsen, 1969b.

Dizzy Gillespie on LP   *Dizzy Gillespie: The Development of an Amer-
ican Artist, 1940–1946,* Smithsonian P213455, 2 records (with Cab
Calloway, 1940; Les Hite, 1942; Lucky Millinder, 1942; at Minton's,
1941; with Coleman Hawkins, 1944; Billy Eckstine, 1944; Oscar
Pettiford, 1945; various orchestras and small groups, 1945–46).
In the Beginning, Prestige 24030, 2 records (small groups with Charlie
Parker, 1945; big band, 1946; sextet, 1950).
Dizzy Gillespie and His Big Band, GNP-23 (1948).
Dee Gee Days, Savoy 2209, 2 records (recordings for his own com-
pany, 1951–52).
Diz and Getz, Verve 2521, 2 records (1953, 1956, also with Sonny Stitt).
Rollins/Stitt Sessions, Verve 2505, 2 records (1957).
Dizzy Gillespie and the Mitchell/Ruff Duo in Concert, Mainstream MRL-
325 (1971).
The Giant, Prestige 24047, 2 records (Paris, 1973).
Oscar Peterson and Dizzy Gillespie, Pablo 2310740 (trumpet/piano
duets, 1974).
Afro-Cuban Jazz, Pablo 2310771 (with Machito Orchestra, 1975).
Dizzy Gillespie Jam, Montreux '77, Pablo Live 2308211.
See also recordings listed under Charlie Parker (*Verve Years*); Benny
Carter (*Carter, Gillespie, Inc.*); Roy Eldridge (*Diz & Roy*).

Miles Davis (Raymond Ross Photos)

MILES DAVIS

In sharp contrast to the poverty that many of his fellow muscians faced in childhood, Miles Davis came from an affluent family. He was born in 1926 in Alton, Illinois, and shortly afterward moved with his family to East St. Louis. Although his father, a respected dentist, gave Miles his first trumpet when he was thirteen, his parents were not enthusiastic about his becoming a musician—certainly not a jazz musician. Miles took lessons in school as well as with a private teacher, and by the time he was sixteen he had joined a local band, Eddie Randolph's Blue Devils. Clark Terry, another St. Louis trumpeter, who later starred with Duke Ellington and as a soloist, was an early influence.

Miles progressed rapidly and at sixteen received an offer to join the Tiny Bradshaw band, but was refused permission by his mother, who insisted that he finish high school. Two years later, in 1944, the legendary Billy Eckstine band, with Charlie Parker and Dizzy Gillespie, came to town and young Davis, who was acquainted with their innovations (he had, in fact, already met Parker), was able to sit in with the band for two weeks.

His sights now firmly set on New York, Miles persuaded his parents to allow him to enroll at the Juilliard School of Music. Upon his arrival in 1945, he immediately sought out Parker, and soon left school to play with his idol. The young trumpeter was helped musically by Parker and also by Thelonious Monk, Dizzy Gillespie, and others, who recognized his promise. Parker, in particular, tried to instill confidence in his protegé, who no doubt felt awed by the matchless virtuosity of the alto saxophonist.

When Parker left for California later in 1945, Davis returned home to St. Louis, where he joined Benny Carter's band. He went to California with Carter, and while on the West Coast again recorded with Parker. In the summer of 1946, Davis joined the Billy Eckstine band, with which he returned to New York. He remained with Eckstine until the singer disbanded his group in 1947. By this time, Parker had returned from California, and had formed a new quintet, which included Miles, pianist Duke Jordan, bassist Tommy Potter, and drummer Max Roach. Davis's recorded solos with this group, while often hesitant in contrast to the leader's assertiveness, show that the trumpeter was gradually evolving his own style and sound (SCCJ-VIII-1 and 2).

Davis left Parker's group in the summer of 1948 and soon opened at the Royal Roost with a unique nine-piece band. The ensemble had its origins in the Claude Thornhill band, which, while not a modern jazz group, had a number of fine young jazzmen such as altoist Lee Konitz and baritone saxophonist Gerry Mulligan. Thornhill also had a progressive arranger, Gil Evans, who had scored some of Parker's compositions for the band. "There is every reason for believing that Davis found the light textures of the Thornhill band to his taste, for they echoed in an orchestral context the sound for which he himself was evidently striving" (James, 1961, pp. 24–25). Gil Evans, along with John Lewis, Johnny Carisi, and Gerry Mulligan, provided the arrangements for the new band. Although the Royal Roost engagement lasted only two weeks, the band had a great impact through the recordings it made several months later. (SCCJ-IX-1). These sessions are often referred to as the "birth of the cool" movement in jazz. They also marked the first of several successful collaborations between Davis and arranger Gil Evans. In 1949 Miles traveled to Europe with the Tadd Dameron quintet to perform at the Paris Jazz Fair.

During the early fifties, although he continued to record, Davis' career was affected by drug abuse. But by 1954, he had overcome his habit and embarked upon one of his most productive periods. In 1955 he scored a major triumph at the Newport Jazz Festival, and later that year formed his own quintet, whose members eventually included John Coltrane on tenor saxophone, Red Garland on piano, Paul Chambers on bass, and Philly Joe Jones on drums. After disbanding briefly in 1957, Davis re-formed the ensemble and after a period of changes, the group expanded to a sextet with the addition of alto saxophonist Julian "Cannonball" Adderley. The groups led by Miles Davis in the fifties were among the most influential in jazz's history and produced some of its most memorable recordings (SCCJ-XI-3). Miles's own playing reached a new peak; he had by now perfected the pure, vibratoless, almost melancholy sound and studied approach hinted at in his earlier work.

In the late fifties and early sixties, Davis resumed his special relationship with arranger Gil Evans, and their collaborations resulted in such classics as their interpretations of *Porgy and Bess* in 1958 (SCCJ-X-2) and *Sketches of Spain* (1959—60).

By the mid-sixties, Miles Davis had attained a popularity few jazzmen have enjoyed. Among his personnel were new and rising players like pianist Herbie Hancock, reedman Wayne Shorter, bassist Ron Carter, and drummer Tony Williams. These men were profoundly influenced by Davis, and, after leaving him, they became leaders in their own right, shaping the music of the seventies.

Both the repertoire and sound of Miles Davis's groups underwent a change in the late sixties and early seventies. He moved away from the standards with which he had been associated and began to incorporate more electronics and rock rhythms in his performances. To many of those who yearned for the evocative sounds of the Miles Davis of the fifties, this new trend was a sellout, an attempt to cash in on the mass rock market. Although his records were highly successful commercially, his supporters felt that the change was prompted by a sincere desire to reach a new and younger audience. Miles, never content to live off his past successes, was continuing to expand his musical horizons. But controversy and charisma have always surrounded Davis, who in early performances caused a furor by turning his back on audiences and leaving the stage when he wasn't playing (he explained that he felt uncomfortable standing there with nothing to do and did not want to disconcert the soloist).

In 1972, Davis suffered two broken legs in a car accident. These injuries, combined with other ailments, have severely curtailed his musical activities. By mid-1977 he had a new band in rehearsal and had returned to the recording studios in the spring of 1978.

Further Information

Biography/Criticism   Cole, Bill. *Miles Davis: A Musical Biography.* New York: William Morrow, 1974.

James, Michael. *Miles Davis.* Kings of Jazz Series. New York: A. S. Barnes, 1961.

Discography   Jepsen, Jorgen Grunnet. *A Discography of Miles Davis.* Copenhagen: Knudsen, 1969c.

Miles Davis on LP   *Complete Birth of the Cool,* Capitol M-11026 (arranged by Gil Evans, Gerry Mulligan, 1949).

Paris Festival International, Columbia JC-34804 (with Tadd Dameron, 1949).

Collector's Items, Prestige 24022, 2 records (quintets, sextets, including Sonny Rollins, 1951, 1956, Charles Parker, 1953, and Charlie Mingus, 1955).

Walkin', Prestige 7608 (with J. J. Johnson, Horace Silver, 1954).

Tallest Trees, Prestige 24012, 2 records (quartet, 1953, with Charlie Mingus, Percy Heath, Max Roach; quintets, 1954, with Sonny Rollins, Horace Silver, Thelonious Monk, Milt Jackson, and 1956, with John Coltrane).

Miles Davis, Prestige 24001, 2 records (quintet, 1956, with John Coltrane, Red Garland, Paul Chambers, Philly Joe Jones).

Miles Ahead, Columbia PC-8633 (1957, orchestra arranged by Gil Evans).

Milestones, Columbia PC-9428 (1958, sextet with Cannonball Adderley, John Coltrane).

Kind of Blue, Columbia PC-8163 (1959 with John Coltrane, Bill Evans).

Porgy and Bess, Columbia PC-8085 (1959, orchestra arranged by Gil Evans).

Sketches of Spain, Columbia PC-8271 (1959—60, orchestra arranged by Gil Evans).

My Funny Valentine, Columbia PC-9106 (1964, with Herbie Hancock, George Coleman, Ron Carter, and Tony Williams).

Filles de Kilimanjaro, Columbia PC-9750 (1968, with Wayne Shorter, Herbie Hancock, Ron Carter, and Tony Williams).

In a Silent Way, Columbia PC-9875 (1969, with Herbie Hancock, Chick Corea, Wayne Shorter, Joe Zawinul, and John McLaughlin).

Bitches Brew, Columbia PG-26, 2 records (1969, with Wayne Shorter, Chick Corea, and Bennie Maupin).

Get Up With It, Columbia PG-33236, 2 records (1974).

Agarta, Columbia PG-33967, 2 records (1975, live in Japan).

Basic Miles, Columbia C-32025, contains a cross-section of the material recorded by Davis for Columbia, 1955—1962.

See also Charlie Parker (*On Dial* and *Verve Years*).

Thelonious Monk (Raymond Ross Photos)

THELONIOUS MONK

An aura of mystery has always surrounded Thelonious Sphere Monk. One of the most original jazz musicians and composers, he has always lived and worked within his own intensely personal world.

Monk was born in 1917 in Rocky Mount, North Carolina, but the family moved soon after to New York City. Although he began piano lessons at the age of eleven, he was largely self-taught, inspired by the great Harlem stride players and by Duke Ellington. His varied early musical experiences included frequent triumphs at the Apollo Theater amateur nights and touring with a faith healer ("We played and she healed").

In the early forties, Monk was a fixture at Minton's, where many of the innovators of what came to be known as bebop gathered. Although he contributed to this movement, Monk soon evolved a piano style unlike that of any of his contemporaries. In 1942 he worked briefly with Lucky Millinder's band. His only other prolonged experience with a large ensemble was a stint with the Dizzy Gillespie big band in 1946. In 1944 he joined Coleman Hawkins's group and made his recording debut with the veteran tenor saxophonist. For the most part, however, Monk has preferred to work as leader of his own small groups. In 1947 Monk made his first recordings as leader. This was the beginning of a series of recording sessions for Blue Note, which attracted a good deal of attention (SCCJ-IX-4, 5, and 6).

In 1951 Monk was arrested on a narcotics charge, although he was not guilty. The loss of his "cabaret card," which permitted him to work in New York City establishments selling alcohol, followed, and, as a result, he was denied employment in almost all the major clubs. He was sustained during this period by the efforts of his devoted wife, Nellie, as well as his recordings for Prestige (SCCJ-IX-7 and X-1). Monk regained his card in 1957 through the efforts of a longtime supporter, Baroness Nica de Koenigswarter, and soon thereafter led a quartet at the Five Spot Café in New York. The group, which briefly included John Coltrane on tenor saxophone, was highly acclaimed. By this time, Monk had switched to Riverside Records, which released several successful albums, including some solo piano recordings (SCCJ-IX-8). "The man who had threatened to become a dim legend was again on view before the public" (Goldberg, 1965, p. 33).

Through the sixties, Monk continued to lead a quartet. The group, which included tenor saxophonist Charlie Rouse, appeared at major concerts and festivals in the United States, Europe, and Japan, and recorded extensively for Columbia. In 1964 the pianist was the subject of a *Time* magazine cover story. During 1971 and 1972 he joined Dizzy Gillespie, Art Blakey, and Sonny Stitt on a worldwide tour in a group called the Giants of Jazz. By the mid-seventies, his public appearances became extremely rare because of illness. But his appearance at the 1975 Newport Jazz Festival was a high point of that event. And in 1976 Monk gave a memorable concert at Carnegie Hall.

As a pianist, his personal sense of time, touch, and use of dissonance have been misconstrued by some critics as a lack of technique but, as Dan Morgenstern has noted, Monk created his own technique, which serves his unique purposes.

Often overlooked is Monk's role as a teacher. He has left his stamp on all those who worked with him. Among those who have acknowledged his influence are Miles Davis, Sonny Rollins, and John Coltrane.

Many feel that Monk's greatest contribution is his compositions. Unlike Duke Ellington's works, many of which have entered the popular music repertoire, Monk's pieces, with the exception of "'Round Midnight," have become standards only among jazz players. Among the best-known are "Straight, No Chaser," "Ruby, My Dear," "Blue Monk," "Epistrophy," and "Well, You Needn't." His music is unpredictable, often humorous, and always accessible, featuring unexpected but somehow logical twists.

Further Information

Discography   Jepsen, Jorgen Grunnet. *A Discography of Thelonious Monk and Bud Powell.* Copenhagen: Knudson, 1969d.

Thelonious Monk on LP   *Charlie Christian,* Archive of Folk Music FS-219 (at Minton's, 1941).

Complete Genius, Blue Note LA579-H2, 2 records (1947−52).

Monk, Prestige 24006, 2 records (1952−54).

Pure Monk, Milestone 47004, 2 records (solo, 1955−59).

Brilliance, Milestone 47023, 2 records (with Sonny Rollins, 1957−58).

Thelonious Monk and John Coltrane, Milestone 47011, 2 records (1957−58).

Monk's Dream, Columbia Special Products JCS-8765 (1962).

Straight, No Chaser, Columbia CS-9451 (1966).

Something in Blue, Black Lion BL-152 (solo and trio, 1971, with Art Blakey). Although issued in England, this record is often available in the United States and is one of the few recorded examples of Monk's playing in the seventies. See also Miles Davis (*Tallest Trees*).

Charlie "Bird" Parker (Institute of Jazz Studies)

CHARLIE PARKER

No single artist, with the possible exception of Louis Armstrong, has had so profound an effect on the course of jazz as alto saxophonist Charlie Parker. With the concepts he brought to jazz in the mid-forties, he influenced a generation of musicians and determined the path the music was to follow for decades to come.

Charles Parker, Jr. (later nicknamed "Bird" or "Yardbird") was born in Kansas City, Kansas, in 1920. His father, a part-time singer and dancer who worked as a railroad chef, spent little time at home and soon abandoned the family completely. Charlie, who was nine at the time, was brought up by his devoted mother, Addie, who bought him his first alto saxophone. In Lincoln High School, which had a solid musical tradition, Parker played baritone horn in the band, but at first showed no great musical ability. He also began to play saxophone in a group organized by some older students called the Deans of Swing. At that time (the mid-thirties), Kansas City was a center of musical activity, and the young Parker was drawn to its musical life. Unfortunately, at the same time, he was also exposed to some of the vices of the wide-open city; by the age of fifteen he was addicted to narcotics, a habit that was to plague him for the rest of his life.

After several humiliating rejections by established older musicians in jam sessions, Parker, at the age of seventeen, left town to work in a band at a summer resort. There, he devoted himself totally to his instrument. Between 1937 and 1939, much improved as a musician, he played in top local bands, including one led by alto saxophonist Buster Smith, an early influence, and the up-and-coming, blues-based band of pianist Jay McShann. During this period, Parker made his first trip to New York City, where he worked for a short time as a dishwasher, as well as playing in local nightclubs. Rejoining McShann, Parker made his first recordings in 1940. These transcriptions, made for a Wichita radio station, show the twenty-year-old Parker to be an accomplished musician already showing signs of his mature style. By the time Parker left McShann in 1942, he was beginning to attract attention. He soon joined Earl Hines's band, where he played with trumpeter Dizzy Gillespie. The two found they had much in common musically, and both joined Billy Eckstine's band in 1944, where they came in contact with new ideas. Parker also frequented Minton's playhouse, one of the spots where musicians, especially the younger ones, gathered to jam.

After leaving Eckstine, Parker briefly led his own trio and worked with Noble Sissle's band before joining forces with Gillespie in May 1945 at the Three Deuces on Fifty-second Street. That same year, he and Gillespie made a series of recordings that became the first definitive statements of the new music on record (SCCJ-VII-6 and 7). Later in 1945, Parker and Gillespie went to California, where they led a group at Billy Berg's club in Hollywood. Their music was rather coldly received, and the band decided to return to New York. Parker, however, remained on the coast, where he recorded for the Dial label (with the young Miles Davis) and appeared with Jazz at the Philharmonic. His mental and physical condition was deteriorating, however, and in May 1946 he suffered a nervous breakdown. Parker was commited to Camarillo State Hospital, where he spent six months under psychiatric care. Upon his return to the East, he worked primarily as leader of his own quintets which included, over the next few years, trumpeters Miles Davis, Red Rodney, and Kenny Dorham, pianists Bud Powell, Duke Jordan and Al Haig, bassist Tommy Potter, and drummers Max Roach and Roy Haynes. The 1947—48 period is regarded by many as the zenith of his career (SCCJ-VII-8 and 9; VIII-1, 2, and 3).

In 1949 Parker made his first trip to Europe, playing at the Paris Jazz Festival. He followed this with a trip to Scandinavia the next year. And in

1950 a club named for Parker—Birdland—opened in New York.

In the fifties, Parker toured with a string ensemble, a collaboration he found commercially successful as well as artistically satisfying. By the early fifties, however, Parker's narcotics habit, drinking, frantic pace, and emotional problems began to take their toll. Although he was still capable of brilliant playing, there were periods during which he was unable to work at all. He died on March 12, 1955. Although the cause of death was technically a heart seizure, Parker had, in fact, burned himself out. On the death certificate the coroner estimated Parker's age at fifty-three; he was thirty-four.

Parker was not only a remarkable instrumentalist, but a prolific composer as well, a master at creating daring new melodies based on the chord progressions of standard tunes and the blues.

The innovations of Parker, Gillespie, and others created a rift among jazz followers; many traditionalists considered the new music (later known as bebop) nothing short of heresy. In retrospect, however, Parker's playing was solidly within the jazz tradition, and today his music seems far closer to the styles that preceded it than to some of those that followed. For example, Parker was a consummate blues player and drew extensively from this most basic of jazz sources for much of his music.

Further Information

Biography   Harrison, Max. *Charlie Parker*. Kings of Jazz, 6. London: Cassell, 1960 (also in American paperback).

Reisner, Robert George. *Bird: The Legend of Charlie Parker*. New York: Citadel, 1962. (While not strictly a biography, this fascinating collection of reminiscences of those who knew Parker is a most valuable source in gaining insight into the man.)

Russell, Ross. *Bird Lives! The High Life and Hard Times of Charlie (Yardbird) Parker*. New York: Charterhouse, 1973. (In attempting to give a vivid portrait of the subject, the author re-creates scenes and discussions that are not always in accordance with factual evidence.)

Discography   Jepsen, Jorgen Grunnet. *A Discography of Charlie Parker*. Copenhagen: Knudsen, 1968.

Koster, Piet, and Bakker, Dick M. *Charlie Parker*. 4 vols. (Vol. 1: 1940–1947; vol. 2: 1948–1950; vol. 3: 1951–1954; vol. 4: additions and indexes.) Alphen aan den Rijn, Holland: Micrography, n.d. (This is part of Bakker's *On Microgroove* series and lists LP issues of Parker's recordings.)

Charlie Parker on LP   *First Recordings,* Onyx 221 (Wichita transcriptions, 1940, with Jay McShann, various dates, 1942−45).

Bird/Savoy Recordings (Master Takes), Savoy 2201, 2 records (1944−48).

Encores, Savoy 1107 (alternate takes of Savoy material, 1944−48).

Charlie Parker on Dial, vols. 1−6, Spotlite 101−106 (1946−47).

One Night in Birdland, Columbia JG-34808, 2 records (1950, live at Birdland).

Verve Years (three 2-record sets):

1948−50, Verve 2501 (with strings, 1948−49; with Dizzy Gillespie and Thelonious Monk, 1950); *1950−51,* Verve 2512 (with strings, 1950; quintet with Miles Davis, 1951); *1952−54,* Verve 2523 (with strings, 1952; Latin date, 1952; with singers, 1953; quartet/quintet, 1953−54).

See also Dizzy Gillespie, *In the Beginning.*

John Coltrane (Frank Driggs Collection)

JOHN COLTRANE

John William Coltrane was born in 1926 in Hamlet, North Carolina, and spent his early childhood in High Point, North Carolina. His father, a tailor, was an amateur musician, and his mother played the piano and sang in the church choir. In school, Coltrane first played the clarinet, later switching to alto saxophone. His father died when John was thirteen, and his family moved soon after to Philadelphia. Coltrane remained in North Carolina until graduation from high school, joining them in 1944.

In Philadelphia, the talented young musician furthered his formal training at the Ornstein School of Music and the Granoff Studios, where he won a scholarship. After playing in cocktail lounges in 1945, he was drafted into the navy, where he played in a service band for two years. After being discharged, Coltrane's early band experience included stints with the blues-based groups of Joe Webb, King Kolax, and Eddie Clean-head Vinson. At this time, he switched from alto to tenor saxophone. In 1947 he played briefly with Miles Davis and Sonny Rollins in New York before joining Dizzy Gillespie's big band. Coltrane also worked briefly in Dizzy's small group.

By 1951 he was increasingly troubled by drug problems and also began to question his own musical direction. Like many saxophonists, he strove to discover his own musical persona in the face of the all-encompassing influence of Charlie Parker. He returned to Philadelphia and, after working intermittently in local rhythm and blues bands, he played with groups led by two alto saxophonists—first Earl Bostic's and later Johnny Hodges's band—from 1952 to 1954. From Bostic, a masterly technician, he learned some of the finer points of playing his instrument. During his tenure with Hodges, he acquired a new lyricism and a feeling for the music of an earlier era.

After a brief return to Philadelphia, again working with a variety of bands and studying on his own, Coltrane was recruited by Miles Davis in 1955. The classic ensembles led by Davis in the fifties provided Coltrane with the perfect atmosphere in which to develop his own style (SCCJ-XI-3), which soon was referred to as "sheets of sound." Coltrane played in Davis's groups from 1955 to 1960, with a break in 1957 when he worked with Thelonious Monk, from whom he learned much. When he returned to Miles's ensemble in 1958, his playing took on a new sense of purpose and he began to emerge as a stylistic force in jazz. His recordings as a group leader attracted notice; in 1959 he signed a contract with Atlantic Records (he had been recording for Prestige).

In 1957 Coltrane underwent a period of intensive spiritual activity, prompted to some extent by his wife Naima's devotion to Islam. His deepening introspection and spiritualism were to affect his playing profoundly.

By 1960 Coltrane was more than ready to lead his own group. The men who eventually joined him—pianist McCoy Tyner, bassist Jimmy Garrison, and drummer Elvin Jones—each played an essential role in one of the most cohesive units in the modern jazz era (SCCJ-XII-4). Coltrane's own playing during the early sixties was shaped by a variety of influences. He studied Indian music and incorporated some of the advances of free jazz experimenters Ornette Coleman and Sun Ra. Eric Dolphy, who worked with the group from time to time, also had an effect on him.

In 1960 Coltrane began playing soprano saxophone in addition to tenor and was responsible for the recent renewal of interest in that instrument. His recording of "My Favorite Things" on soprano sax was his first really popular hit. In 1961 he began to record for Impulse Records.

Coltrane was by no means universally accepted; in fact, one critic (John Tynan) called his playing antijazz. His music evolved so rapidly that it allowed little time for the assimilation by his followers of one innovation before moving on to another. By the mid-sixties, the sound of Coltrane's group grew more complex. His own playing was intense, which is evident in recordings such as *A Love Supreme* (1964) and *Ascension* (1965).

In 1965 Elvin Jones and McCoy Tyner left the group and were replaced by drummer Rashied Ali and pianist/harpist Alice McLeod (who soon became the second Mrs. Coltrane). When saxophonist Pharaoh Sanders joined the group, the music became even less conventional. Coltrane's solos became more impassioned musical self-revelations.

Toward the end of his life, Coltrane became fascinated with percussion, particularly African rhythm, and studied with Nigerian drummer Olatunji to further his knowledge.

In 1967 a liver ailment that had flared up the year before worsened, and on July 17 Coltrane died at the age of forty from cancer of the liver.

John Coltrane's influence was comparable to that of Armstrong and Parker. His life was spent in a musical and spiritual search, and the recordings that document his journey are among the most profound and lasting statements in contemporary music.

Further Information:

Biography/Criticism   Cole, Bill. *John Coltrane.* New York: Schirmer, 1976.

Simpkins, Cuthbert Ormond. *Coltrane: A Biography.* New York: Herndon House, 1975.

Thomas, J. C. *Chasin' The Trane: The Music and Mystique of John Coltrane.* New York: Doubleday, 1975.

Discography   Davis, Brian. *John Coltrane: Discography.* London, England: privately published, 1976.

Jepsen, Jorgen Grunnet. *A Discography of John Coltrane.* Copenhagen: Knudsen, 1969e.

Wild, David. *The Recordings of John Coltrane: A Discography.* Ann Arbor: Wildmusic, 1977.*

Williams, Martin. "Coltrane: Man in the Middle," in *The Jazz Tradition.* New York: Oxford University Press, 1970.

John Coltrane on LP   *Wheelin',* Prestige 24069, 2 records (1957, sextets).

Coltrane, Prestige 24003, 2 records (1957–58, quartet with Red Garland, Paul Chambers, Art Taylor).

Blue Train, Blue Note 81577 (1957, with Lee Morgan).

Giant Steps, Atlantic 1311 (1959, quartet with Tommy Flanagan).

*Available from Wildmusic, P.O. Box 2138, Ann Arbor, Michigan 48106.

My Favorite Things, Atlantic 1361 (1960, quartet, with McCoy Tyner, Elvin Jones).

Live at the Village Vanguard, Impulse 10 (1961, with Eric Dolphy).

Impressions, Impulse 42 (1961−63, with Eric Dolphy).

Ballads, Impulse 32 (1962−63).

Crescent, Impulse 66 (1964, quartet).

A Love Supreme, Impulse 77 (1964).

Ascension, Impulse 95 (1965, with Pharaoh Sanders, Archie Shepp, Freddie Hubbard).

Interstellar Space, Impulse 9277 (1967, duets with drummer Rashied Ali).

See also Dizzy Gillespie (*Dee Gee Days* contains one Coltrane solo); Thelonious Monk (*Thelonious Monk and John Coltrane*); Miles Davis (various LPs from the fifties).

Ornette Coleman (Raymond Ross Photos)

ORNETTE COLEMAN

The earliest musical experiences of the man who was to take jazz in a new direction in the late fifties were far removed from any avant-garde milieu. Ornette Coleman was born in 1930 in Forth Worth, Texas. The son of a seamstress (his father died when Ornette was seven), Coleman was quickly drawn to the active music scene in Fort Worth, which was steeped in the rhythm-and-blues tradition. His mother bought him an alto saxophone when he was fourteen, and, although he played in a school band, he was largely self-taught. Ornette was soon playing tenor saxophone in local bands, copying the rhythm-and-blues styles of Big Jay McNeely, Louis Jordan, Arnett Cobb, and Gene Ammons, to which he soon added some of Charlie Parker's techniques. "By 1949, nineteen-year-old Ornette Coleman had come to some kind of an impasse in Fort Worth which he did not understand. Bebop and rhythm-and-blues seemed intransigent musics to him now, although he recognized them as head and feet of the same body" (Spellman, 1966, p. 96).*

Coleman's playing, even at that early stage in his career, was considered weird by his fellow musicians and, consequently, he was unable to

---

*Much of the information for this summary of Coleman's career comes from Spellman's work.

find work in a standard touring big band. Anxious to leave Forth Worth, he joined a minstrel show named Silas Green from New Orleans. Coleman found the musical environment stifling and was fired for allegedly trying to convert the band's other tenor saxophonist to bebop. He joined a rhythm-and-blues band led by Clarence Samuels, which stranded him in New Orleans. Staying with a friend, clarinetist Melvin Lassiter, and working at various day jobs, Coleman, who had now switched to alto sax, managed to work out some of his musical ideas. In 1949 he traveled with the Pee Wee Crayton band and by 1950 had settled in Los Angeles, where, except for a brief return to Fort Worth, he remained for nine years.

This Los Angeles period was one of frustration for Coleman. He encountered not only scarcity of work (to which he was accustomed) and rejection by the public but also the scorn of supposedly open-minded musicians. Again he was forced to work at nonmusical jobs and again he used this time to study on his own.

On the other hand, in Los Angeles Coleman began to meet some like-minded musicians, including drummer Ed Blackwell, trumpeter Bobby Bradford, pianist Paul Bley, tenor saxophonist James Clay, and the man with whom he was to form a long-lasting partnership, trumpeter Don Cherry. Through Red Mitchell, an established bassist who saw some promise in Coleman (though mostly as a composer), Ornette and his group made their first record (for Contemporary in 1958) of what came to be called "the new thing."

Coleman's music began to find some influential supporters, among them Gunther Schuller and pianist John Lewis, of the Modern Jazz Quartet, who helped him obtain a recording contract with Atlantic and a scholarship to the Lenox School of Jazz in Massachusetts.

In the fall of 1959, Coleman's group, which now consisted of himself, Don Cherry, bassist Charlie Haden, and drummer Billy Higgins, opened at the Five Spot Café in New York City. The alto saxophonist soon became the center of great controversy, hailed as the herald of the future of jazz by some, denounced as a musical fraud by others. Although he made a number of records over the next three years (SCCJ-XII-1, 2 and 3), appeared at major festivals, and presented his music at Town Hall (which he rented for the purpose), by 1962 Coleman had become disillusioned in his business dealings with club owners, believing he was not being offered what he was worth. He made no public appearances for two years (1963 and 1964), during which time he learned to play trumpet and violin (he has since performed in public on bassoon as well). He returned to public performance at the Village Vanguard in 1965 and shortly thereafter left on a European tour with drummer Charles Moffett and bassist David Izenzon. In the late sixties he found another compatible horn partner, saxophonist Dewey Redman.

For the past decade, Coleman has been active mainly as a composer. In 1972 he recorded his most ambitious work, *Skies of America,* with the London Symphony. He opened his own club—Artist House—in New York, and has made occasional concert appearances both in the United States and abroad.

The controversy that Ornette Coleman has generated has made an objective assessment of his contributions difficult. He is perhaps most universally acclaimed as a composer, one who can evoke a variety of moods.

As an alto saxophonist, he has retained many of the traces of his rhythm and blues background. Many consider his playing—harmonic and rhythmic innovations aside—to be an extension of the blues tradition. "He is concerned with duplicating the sounds and emotions of the human voice on his instrument, a goal that is present in the trumpet growls and trombone moans of the oldest jazz, as well as in the raucous harmonicas and twanging guitars of the most primitive bluesmen" (Goldberg, 1965, p. 237). To express these sounds more accurately, Coleman has effectively incorporated the technique of pitch variation into his alto playing.

On trumpet and violin, Coleman has often been accused of lack of technique, but the highly personal purposes to which he applies these instruments in his music make standard measures of technique somewhat irrelevant.

In the final analysis, Coleman's greatest contribution may lie in the conceptions of musical freedom—freedom from standard harmonic progressions and regulated rhythmic pulse—that he has imparted, and in the ideals of collective improvisation that he and his musicians represent. His concepts have not only laid the groundwork for the free-jazz movement but affected musicians in other genres as well.

Further Information

Biography   Spellman, A. B. *Four Lives in the Bebop Business.* New York: Pantheon, 1966. Reprinted in paperback as *Black Music: Four Lives in the Bebop Business.* New York: Schocken, 1970.

Ornette Coleman on LP   *Coleman Classics,* Improvising Artists L611 (1957).
Something Else, Contemporary 7551 (1958).
Tomorrow Is the Question, Contemporary 7569 (1959).

The Shape of Jazz to Come, Atlantic 1317 (1959).

Change of the Century, Atlantic 1327 (1960).

Free Jazz, Atlantic 1364 (double quartets with Eric Dolphy, Don Cherry, Freddie Hubbard, 1960).

This Is Our Music, Atlantic 1353 (1961).

At the Golden Circle, 2 vols., Blue Note 84224/5 (trio, 1965).

Science Fiction/Skies of America, Columbia CG-33669, 2 records. (1972, *Science Fiction,* current group and reunion, includes Don Cherry, Bobby Bradford, Ed Blackwell; *Skies of America,* extended work recorded with London Symphony.)

Charlie Haden, *Golden Number,* Horizon 727 (duets, 1976).

PART 3
Jazz

Research

chapter 7

A Student's Guide to Jazz Research

In recent years dedicated amateurs in the field of jazz research have been joined by professional researchers with expertise in various disciplines—musicology, sociology, Afro-American studies, history, popular culture, and library science. Jazz literature of all types—reference works, histories, surveys, essays, biographies, and autobiographies—is constantly expanding. Some of these sources are easily located in standard reference works (*Readers' Guide to Periodical Literature, Books in Print*) that are readily available in public and college libraries. Others are of a more specialized nature and may not be found so easily. These sources include the many esoteric and often short-lived jazz periodicals and privately produced reference works that may not be documented in commonly used indexes. This chapter offers a guide to the various types of information sources currently available to the student of jazz, as well as a selected listing of the major works under each category.

Some of these information sources should be available in a good college or public library. If they are not, many librarians would welcome the suggestion that some of these works be purchased. Most libraries also belong to the intercollege library loan system, and reading material may be borrowed through that service.

GENERAL HISTORIES, INTRODUCTIONS, AND SURVEYS

Berendt, Joachim. *The Jazz Book, From New Orleans to Rock and Free Jazz.* New York: Lawrence Hill, 1975 (paperback.) A comprehensive survey covering developments into the seventies.
Brask, Ole, and Morgenstern, Dan. *Jazz People.* New York: Abrams, 1976. (Also in paperback.) A collaboration between a photographer

218

and a jazz historian presenting the story of jazz through visual and verbal portraits of its major contributors. The majority of photographs are originals; some historical reproductions.

Hodeir, André. *Jazz: Its Evolution and Essence.* New York: Grove Press, 1956 (also in paperback). A general discussion and survey with musical analysis. More opinionated than Stearns's *The Story of Jazz* (see below).

Jost, Ekkehard. *Free Jazz.* Studies in Jazz Research, 4. Graz: Universal Edition, 1974. A discussion and musical analysis of the work of the major contributors to the "free jazz" movement, including John Coltrane, Charlie Mingus, Ornette Coleman, Cecil Taylor, Archie Shepp, Albert Tyler, Don Cherry, the Association for the Advancement of Creative Musicians, and Sun Ra.

McCarthy, Albert. *Big Band Jazz.* New York: Putnam's Sons, 1974. General history of the development of the big band style and the musicians, both famous and obscure, who helped shape it.

Schuller, Gunther. *Early Jazz, Its Roots and Musical Development.* New York: Oxford University Press, 1968. An exhaustive musical analysis of musicians and stylistic developments until approximately 1932.

Simon, George T. *The Big Bands.* New York: Macmillan, 1974. Background material on the era and brief descriptions of major and minor bands as well as some interviews with leading figures.

Stearns, Marshall W. *The Story of Jazz.* New York: Oxford University Press, 1956 (also in paperback). The basic jazz history. Covers periods to the mid-fifties. Particularly strong on African origins and jazz prehistory.

Tirro, Frank. *Jazz: A History.* New York: Norton, 1977. A general history of jazz with some musical analysis.

Williams, Martin. *Where's the Melody? A Listener's Introduction to Jazz.* New York: Pantheon Books, 1967. A general introduction to jazz and how to approach a jazz performance. The book focuses on several figures and specific performances.

Wilson, John S. *Jazz: The Transition Years 1940–60.* New York: Appleton-Century-Crofts, 1966. Discusses various aspects of the period, including changes in the music and the reactions they triggered.

ESSAYS

Balliett, Whitney. *Dinosaurs in the Morning.* Philadelphia and New York: Lippincott, 1962.

Balliett, Whitney. *Ecstasy at the Onion*. Indianapolis: Bobbs-Merrill, 1971.

――――. *Improvising: Sixteen Jazz Musicians and Their Art*. New York: Oxford University Press, 1977.

――――. *New York Notes, A Journal of Jazz 1972–75*. Boston: Houghton Mifflin, 1976 (also in paperback).

――――. *The Sound of Surprise*. New York: Dutton, 1959.

――――. *Such Sweet Thunder*. Indianapolis: Bobbs-Merrill, 1966.

Whitney Balliett has been jazz critic for *The New Yorker* since 1957, and these works are periodic compilations of his writings for that magazine, as well as some additional pieces. Included are all types of material—from brief notes, concert and record reviews, to extensive profiles of musicians. All volumes except *New York Notes* are indexed.

Williams, Martin. *The Art of Jazz: Essays on the Nature and Development of Jazz*. New York: Oxford University Press, 1959. Essays on a variety of figures from many sources.

Williams, Martin, ed. *Jazz Panorama*. Crowell Collier, 1962 (also in paperback). A collection of essays, reviews, and interviews that originally appeared in *The Jazz Review*. Covers a wide range of artists.

Williams, Martin. *The Jazz Tradition*. New York: Oxford University Press, 1970. Chapters on major figures from Jelly Roll Morton to Ornette Coleman, some of which appeared elsewhere. Brief discographical notes on each artist.

MACMILLAN JAZZ MASTERS SERIES

A useful set of works devoted to the basic periods of jazz history.

Gitler, Ira. *Jazz Masters of the Forties*. New York: Macmillan, 1966 (also in paperback). Traces the history of the period by individual instruments, concentrating on Charlie Parker, Dizzy Gillespie, Bud Powell, J. J. Johnson, Oscar Pettiford, Kenny Clarke, Max Roach, Dexter Gordon, Lennie Tristano, Lee Konitz, and arranger Tadd Dameron. Selective discographies and bibliographies.

Goldberg, Joe. *Jazz Masters of the 50's*. New York: Macmillan, 1965. Figures discussed are Gerry Mulligan, Thelonious Monk, Art Blakey, Miles Davis, Sonny Rollins, Modern Jazz Quartet, Charlie Mingus, Paul Desmond, Ray Charles, John Coltrane, Cecil Taylor, and Ornette Coleman. Selected discographies.

Hadlock, Richard. *Jazz Masters of the Twenties*. New York: Macmillan, 1965 (also in paperback). Chapters on Louis Armstrong (from 1924 to 1931), Earl "Fatha" Hines, Bix Beiderbecke, Fats Waller, James P. Johnson, and Bessie Smith. Selected discographies and bibliographies.

Stewart, Rex. *Jazz Masters of the Thirties.* New York: Macmillan, 1972. A collection of essays, many of which appeared in *Down Beat,* written by the late trumpeter. Revealing portraits of many of his contemporaries and descriptions of the general scene of the period.

Williams, Martin. *Jazz Masters in Transition, 1957–1969.* New York: Macmillan, 1970. A collection of short essays by Williams that originally appeared in various publications.

Williams, Martin. *Jazz Masters of New Orleans.* New York: Macmillan, 1967. Chapters covering major figures of the New Orleans period, including Jelly Roll Morton, Joe Oliver, Sidney Bechet, Louis Armstrong, and others. Selected discographies and bibliographies.

ENCYCLOPEDIAS

This type of source is useful for basic biographical data on musicians. The information usually includes the musician's early training, bands played with, basic chronology, and, sometimes, influences. Some of the works include brief stylistic judgments and appraisals. There is often a listing of recordings for each artist.

Chilton, John. *Who's Who of Jazz: Storyville to Swing.* London: Bloomsbury Book Shop, 1972. Biographies of American musicians born before 1920. Includes many not covered by Feather's encyclopedia (see below).

Feather, Leonard. *Encyclopedia of Jazz* series. 3 vols. *The New Edition of the Encyclopedia of Jazz,* New York: Horizon Press, 1962; *The Encyclopedia of Jazz in the Sixties,* New York: Horizon Press, 1966; *The Encyclopedia of Jazz in the Seventies,* New York: Horizon Press, 1976. Major portion consists of biographical entries for musicians of all eras. Volumes are not cumulative; only the basic facts are repeated. Earlier editions must be consulted for fullest details of all periods of an artist's career. The latest volume brings biographies current to 1975. Also contains bibliographies, selected discographies, features on jazz education, jazz films, and jazz poll tabulations.

Kinkle, Roger D. *The Complete Encyclopedia of Popular Music and Jazz, 1900–1950.* New Rochelle, N.Y.: Arlington House, 1974. Biographies of contributors to American music from 1900 to 1950, including popular music and jazz. Careers are covered to 1974, with selected discography for each artist. The discographies are useful for locating material on reissue LPs, as well as recent recordings that may not be covered in the major discographies. Also contains year-by-year listing of musicals and popular songs with composers. Appendixes include jazz poll winners, a time chart of release dates for the major record companies from 1924 to 1945, and a numerical listing of the major labels. Thoroughly indexed by artist and title.

Rose, Al, and Souchon, Edmond. *New Orleans Jazz: A Family Album,* rev. ed. Baton Rouge: Louisiana State University Press, 1978. Biographies of New Orleans jazzmen, including many obscure figures. Also contains historical listings of New Orleans bands and clubs.

BIBLIOGRAPHIES

Jazz bibliographies are helpful starting points for research, although most have faults that limit their usefulness. One problem is a certain arbitrariness in the inclusion of items from periodicals. Neither Merriam nor Reisner claim to have systematically indexed all the periodicals included. The fact that there is no article listed on a particular subject or figure does not mean that one doesn't exist. Another drawback to most of these works is the broad subject headings used in the indexes. The large number of citations under these headings makes these sources somewhat unwieldy. On the other hand, these works are valuable efforts at bibliographic control of a widely dispersed literature.

Gregor, Carl, Duke of Mecklenburg. *International Jazz Bibliography.* Graz, Austria: Universal Edition, 1969. A 1970 supplement was published: Graz, Austria: Universal Edition, 1971 (part of the series, Studies in Jazz Research, 3). 1971, 1972, and 1973 supplements were also published: Graz, Austria: Universal Edition, 1975 (part of the series, Studies in Jazz Research, 6). The 1969 Bibliography lists jazz books from 1919 through 1968 and is arranged by author with subject and artist indexes. The supplements, unlike the original work, are arranged within broad subject categories. Gregor is in the process of preparing *Chronological International Bibliography of Jazz Books,* which will eventually replace this series.

Kennington, Donald. *The Literature of Jazz.* London: The Library Association, 1970. Basic, selective, critical guide to all types of literature.

Merriam, Alan P. *A Bibliography of Jazz.* Philadelphia: The American Folklore Society, 1954. (Reprinted by DaCapo Press, 1976.) Selective books and periodical articles to 1950, listed by author with subject and artist indexes.

Reisner, Robert George. *The Literature of Jazz: A Preliminary Bibliography.* New York: The New York Public Library, 1954. A highly selective checklist of books and periodical articles by author; no index.

PERIODICALS AND PERIODICAL INDEXES

Considering the relatively short span of jazz's history, an extraordinary number of periodicals about jazz have been published. They range from the general-interest, wide-circulation magazines, such as *Down Beat,* to the narrowly focused specialty publications. In addition, valuable information on jazz and jazz-related subjects may be found in the more general periodicals, either in the form of regular columns or special features. An example is jazz writer Whitney Balliett's work in *The New Yorker.* These general-interest publications are indexed in basic library sources such as *Readers' Guide to Periodical Literature.* Material on jazz topics in the New York *Times* may be located through the New York *Times Index.* Another source for biographical information on deceased jazz figures is obituaries, easily located through the New York *Times Obituary Index.*

Of the periodicals devoted specifically to jazz, the major English-language magazines published currently are:

The Black Perspective in Music, semiannual, began 1973, $5. Foundation for Research in the Afro-American Creative Arts, Inc., P.O. Drawer 1, Cambria Heights, NY 11411.

Cadence: The American Review of Jazz and Blues (U.S.), monthly, began 1976, $8. Route 1, Box 345, Redwood, NY 13679.

Coda (Canada), 10 issues per year, began 1958, $8.50. P.O. Box 87, Postal Station J, Toronto, Ontario, Canada, M4J 4X8.

Down Beat (U.S.), biweekly, began 1934, $11. 222 West Adams Street, Chicago, IL 60606.

Jazz Journal (England), monthly, began 1948, $14. 7 Carnaby Street, London, W1V 1PG, England.

Jazz Magazine (U.S.), quarterly, began 1976, $10. P.O. Box 212, Northport, NY 11768.

In addition, there are a large number of defunct jazz periodicals that contain a wealth of information. One of the most comprehensive of these was *Metronome,* which was published from 1884 to 1961, although it became jazz-oriented only after 1935. Although short-lived (1958–1960), the *Jazz Review* was a milestone in jazz journalism as a pioneer of scholarly publication. The *Journal of Jazz Studies,* published by the Institute of Jazz Studies at Rutgers University, is the only current English language scholarly jazz periodical.

Many specialized periodicals answer the needs of jazz readers interested in a particular aspect or style of the music. These include works aimed at the discographer, record collector, and jazz educator, as well as newsletters covering activities in a certain city or state.

For a basic listing of English-language jazz periodicals, see Thomas G. Everett's "An Annotated List of English-Language Jazz Periodicals," *Journal of Jazz Studies,* Vol. 3, No. 2 (Spring, 1976).

Europe has always been interested in jazz, and this is reflected in the large numbers of periodicals published there. Several of these date back to the early thirties and contain some of the most complete coverage of the music during that era. The major current European periodicals are:

Jazz Forum—The Magazine of the International Jazz Federation (Poland)
Jazz Hot (France), monthly
Jazz Magazine (France), monthly
Musica Jazz (Italy), monthly
Orkester Journalen (Sweden), monthly

In addition to Europe and the United States, Latin America publishes several jazz magazines. Mention must also be made of the Japanese *Swing Journal,* a lavishly illustrated, 400-page monthly, which is the most ambitious of all the current publications. Although it is almost entirely in Japanese, some of its features, such as the excellent individual artist discographies, contain enough English data (as well as album-cover reproductions) to make them useful sources.

Several indexes have been compiled to attempt to provide access to the burgeoning jazz periodical literature. These include:

Down Beat annuals, beginning with the 1960 edition, include indexes to the issues of the magazine published during the previous year.
Jazz Index. Published quarterly (began in 1977). Covers all major American and foreign jazz periodicals. Single alphabetical listing of subjects and artists. Yearly author index to be published. Contains a "list of unconventional literature," that is, publications available only from private or specialized sources. Plans include bimonthly publication and expansion of scope to include blues.
The Music Index. Published monthly (1949–   ). Over the years, it has expanded jazz coverage to include both American and foreign major jazz periodicals as well as publications devoted to all other types of music. One alphabetical listing containing authors, subjects, and

names. Has included *Down Beat* and *Metronome* from its inception. Latest annual cumulation: 1972 (published in 1976).

Tudor, Dean, and Armitage, Andrew D. *Popular Music Periodicals Index.* Metuchen, N.J.: The Scarecrow Press, 1973–   . Published yearly. Indexes cover approximately fifty-five English-language periodicals, including *Coda, Down Beat, Jazz Journal, Journal of Jazz Studies,* and *Storyville.* Arranged by subjects and artists, with author index.

DISSERTATIONS

With the great increase in academic interest in jazz in recent years and the proliferation of formal degree programs, the dissertation is becoming a valuable source for scholarly information on many aspects of jazz, its practitioners, and the social climate and historical forces that shaped it. *Dissertation Abstracts International* provides access to these sources through a "key word" index, a general subject classification, and an author index. The dissertations can usually be obtained from University Microfilms, Ann Arbor, Michigan, either in microfilm or Xerox form.

DICTIONARIES

Gold, Robert. *Jazz Talk.* Indianapolis: Bobbs-Merrill, 1975. Definitions and examples of the usage of hundreds of jazz slang words and phrases.

Major, Clarence. *Dictionary of Afro-American Slang.* New York: International Publishers, 1970. Largely, although not exclusively, jazz-oriented.

Townley, Eric. *Tell Your Story.* Chigwell, Essex, England: Storyville Publications, 1976. Explains the significance of many jazz song titles, including the people, places, and ideas from which they originate.

PHOTOGRAPHS

Photography has always been part of the jazz literature in varying degrees, and almost all the general histories, encyclopedias, and biographical works have photo sections. The following are works devoted primarily to photographs of jazz artists:

Brask, Ole, and Morgenstern, Dan. *Jazz People.* New York: Abrams, 1976.

Condon, Eddie, and O'Neal, Hank. *Eddie Condon's Scrapbook of Jazz.* New York: Galahad Books, 1973. An informal look at an important circle of jazz players.

Esquire's World of Jazz. New York: T. Y. Crowell, 1975. A collection of essays with many photos and other artwork.

Fox, Charles. *The Jazz Scene.* (Special photography by Valerie Wilmer.) London: Hamlyn, 1972. A collection of recent photos of musicians from several schools, including mainstream, blues, and "free jazz," with brief descriptions of each style.

Keepnews, Orrin, and Grauer, Bill Jr. *A Pictorial History of Jazz.* 2d ed., rev. New York: Crown Publishers, 1966. Photos from many sources depicting New Orleans from the origins of jazz to the early sixties.

Rose, Al, and Souchon, Edmond. *New Orleans Jazz: A Family Album.* Baton Rouge: Louisiana State University Press, 1967. Photos of New Orleans jazzmen and landmarks integrated within an encyclopedia format.

JAZZ ON FILM

Two works are devoted to this valuable source, and more are sure to come with recent renewed interest and discoveries.

Hippenmeyer, Jean-Roland. *Jazz Sur Films.* Yverdon (Sw.): Editions de la Thiele, 1972. Entries for 800 films made between 1917 and 1972, arranged alphabetically by title within each year, with artist and title index. Some commentary (in French).

Meeker, David. *Jazz in the Movies: A Guide to Jazz Musicians, 1917–1977.* New Rochelle, N.Y.: Arlington House, 1977. There are 2,239 feature films, shorts, cartoons listed by title, with an artist index. Critical commentary on each.

Also, Feathers' *Encyclopedia of Jazz in the Seventies* includes "Guide to Available Jazz Films."

LINER NOTES

Liner notes are descriptive material accompanying a record. They are an often overlooked source of critical, biographical, and dis- cographical information for the jazz researcher. Liner notes vary in quality from inaccurate and misleading advertisements for the record to detailed, analytical essays going far beyond the scope of the records they describe. The latter group include some of the booklets accompanying major reissue projects, such as those undertaken by RCA, Columbia, and the Smithsonian. Notes of this type may contain historical data, interviews with musicians, and even musicological analysis unavailable elsewhere in print.

AUTOBIOGRAPHY

As useful as the other types of jazz writing are, the words of the musicians themselves are often the most effective means of capturing the spirit of the jazz experience. The following autobiographies are prime sources:

Bechet, Sidney. *Treat It Gentle.* New York: Hill & Wang, 1960.
Broonzy, William, as told to Yannick Bruynoghe. *Big Bill Blues.* London: Cassell, 1955.
Calloway, Cab, and Rollins, Bryant. *Of Minnie the Moocher and Me.* New York: Thomas Y. Crowell, 1976.
Condon, Eddie. *We Called It Music: A Generation of Jazz.* New York: Henry Holt and Co., 1947.
Foster, Pops, as told to Tom Stoddard. *Pops Foster: The Autobiography of a New Orleans Jazzman.* Berkeley: University of California Press, 1971.
Hawes, Hampton, with Don Asher. *Raise Up Off Me.* New York: Coward, McCann and Geoghegan, 1972.
Holiday, Billie, with William Dufty. *Lady Sings the Blues.* New York: Doubleday, 1956.
Kaminsky, Max, with V. E. Hughes. *My Life in Jazz.* New York: Harper and Row, 1963.
Lyttelton, Humphrey. *I Play as I Please: The Memories of an Old Etonian Trumpeter.* London: MacGibbon and Kee, 1954.
———. *Second Chorus.* London: MacGibbon and Kee, 1958.
Manone, Wingy, and Vandervoort, Paul, II. *Trumpet on the Wing.* New York: Doubleday, 1948.
Mezzrow, Mezz, and Wolfe, Bernard. *Really the Blues.* New York: Random House, 1946.
Mingus, Charles. *Beneath the Underdog.* New York: Alfred A. Knopf, 1971.
Shaw, Artie. *The Trouble with Cinderella.* New York: Farrar, Straus and Young, 1952.

Smith, Willie "The Lion," with George Hoefer. *Music on My Mind: The Memoirs of an American Pianist.* New York: Doubleday, 1964.

Waters, Ethel, with Charles Samuels. *His Eye Is on the Sparrow.* New York: Doubleday, 1950.

Wells, Dicky, as told to Stanley Dance. *The Night People: Reminiscences of a Jazzman.* Boston: Crescendo, 1971.

Hentoff, Nat, and Shapiro, Nat. *Hear Me Talkin' to Ya.* New York: Rinehart, 1955. A compilation of quotes from jazz people of different eras.

SOURCES OF INFORMATION ON JAZZ RECORDINGS

As we have seen in other chapters, the essence of jazz, more than in most other types of music, lies in its actual performance. Musical notation has always been of secondary importance. Because of the role of improvisation and individual interpretation in jazz, recordings—and not written scores—are the primary source for the preservation and study of the music. We are fortunate that the technology of sound recording appeared early enough in the development of jazz history to provide at least a representation of all but its earliest manifestations.

We shall first review the forms in which these recordings appear and then the reference sources that provide access to them.

78 rpm Phonorecords

From the beginning of jazz recording in 1917 until the late forties, the 78 disk was the primary vehicle for the dissemination of recorded jazz. In some ways, the 78 is inherently simpler to deal with than other forms. Most 78s have approximately three minutes of recorded material on each side. Although this limit must have often been creatively stifling for musicians, it did result in a uniform pattern of one complete performance on each side. Thus the practice of including many unrelated items on the same disk (as is often the case with long-playing records) was virtually nonexistent. At most, two separate items could be issued on one disk (one on each side), and these two items were usually performed by one artist. Furthermore, each side of the 78 was embossed with a number identifying the material on that side. Ths number, called the matrix or master number, is located between the last groove and the label and is usually repeated on the label, as shown in Figure 7.1.

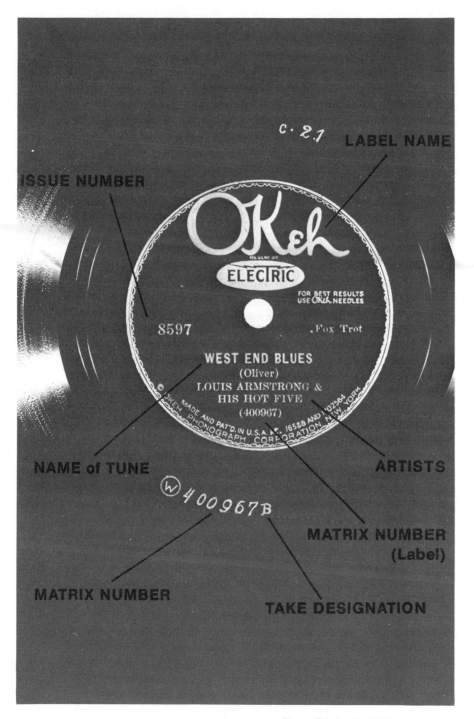

Figure 7.1 An Okeh 78 phonorecord.

The matrix number was assigned by the record company and generally consisted of two parts. The first was a unique number (or combination of letters and numbers) assigned to a performance. It was often followed by a dash and a second number (or letter) called the "take" number. The same tune was often recorded more than once at a recording session, and the take considered best at the time was selected for issue. But judgments of what was best changed from time to time, and it was not unusual for more than one take of a tune from the same session to find their way onto a record. In jazz, which relies so heavily on improvisation, two versions of the same tune, recorded only minutes apart, can be radically different, thus making the identification of these takes essential. The importance of these alternate takes is illustrated by the recent issue of LPs consisting entirely of previously unissued takes of performances by several major jazz figures.

In addition to the matrix number, each 78 had an "issue" number. This was simply a catalogue number under which that disk was marketed. This number served for both sides of the 78. A single take of one tune (with its unique matrix number) could, and often did, appear on several different issues under different issue numbers (and often on 78s manufactured by different companies).

33⅓ rpm LPs

In the late forties, 33⅓ rpm jazz microgroove records (LPs) first appeared. With their infinitely more faithful reproduction characteristics and their longer playing times, they caused a revolution not only in jazz but in all recordings. (To a lesser extent the same point applies to 45 rpm records.) Artistically, they broke through the artificial three-minute limit imposed on the performer and enabled recorded jazz to move closer to the live version that was not subject to such constraints.

With the advent of LPs, many of the discographical conventions that identified material on the 78s were lost. First, much more material can be included on an LP. Whereas a 78 could contain, at most, two unrelated items, it is not uncommon for anthological LPs to contain sixteen tunes played by totally different groups. Second, and even more important, is the absence on LPs of the main identifying feature of a particular recording, the matrix number. (New recording techniques and the large amount of material on each disk has made the inclusion of matrix numbers impractical.)

These two problems could be offset by the record companies' inclusion of full discographical information on the jacket, but many companies neglect this essential service, some by oversight and some by design.

Such negligence may disguise the fact that the material offered is not new and has already been issued several times. This can result in the purchaser buying recordings which he or she already owns but cannot recognize from the scanty data. Or the company may attempt to capitalize on a musician's name by selling a record on which he plays a minor role and on some tracks may not play at all. There are even cases where a musician's name and photograph are prominently displayed, although he or she does not play a single note on any track of the record. In all fairness, it must be said that some record companies do provide full discographic data.

Several types of recordings may be contained on LPs. They may may be categorized as follows:

1. Material not previously issued in any form
    a. recorded for microgroove (LP)
    b. recorded for 78
    c. noncommercial recordings such as air checks and private recordings
2. Material previously issued
    a. on LPs
    b. on 78s
    c. on both

Category 1a (material recorded for LP but not previously issued); may include both relatively new material and older recordings, which, for various reasons, the company chose not to issue at the time they were made.

A common example of 1b (material recorded for 78s but not issued) would be an alternative take of a tune that is issued for comparison with the take originally selected.

LPs can include recordings from 2a (material previously issued on LPs) either by duplicating exactly the contents of an entire LP or by including items from various LPs.

It should be mentioned that a single LP can include material from all the categories described above.

DISCOGRAPHY

The term "discography" is often used to convey different ideas. It may mean anything from a list of five records following an article about an artist in a popular magazine to a 400-page documentation of a musician's recording career, complete with biographical and musicological notes—the product of twenty years' research by an individual or a group of researchers. This problem of usage is analogous to that of the term "bibliography." As is the case with "bibliography," "discography" can have two main meanings: a general one that refers to the science of the description of recordings and a specific one denoting a listing of recordings.

The field of jazz discography had its beginnings in the early thirties. It arose in response to the basic question posed by fans and record collectors: Who's playing? As the number of serious listeners and students of jazz increased, they sought additional information, with the result that more specialized sources have been developed. In addition to the identification of personnel, discographies can aid in establishing what has been recorded, the location of the work of one artist, and the study of musical influences and "networks" (who recorded with whom). They serve a wide range of researchers, including critics, historians, musicologists, and social scientists.

As in other types of research, the methods of discography have become more and more sophisticated. In many ways, the discographical documentation of jazz recording is more advanced than that of other types of music. Although the early jazz discographies may seem primitive today, each new work often incorporates those preceding it. Pioneer efforts such as Hilton Schleman's *Rhythm on Record* and Charles Delaunay's *Hot Discography,* both published in 1936 (see Figures 7.2a and 7.2b) provided the essential foundations for later research. Delaunay, in particular, had great influence in this area and is credited with being the first to understand the value of the matrix number for identification of jazz recordings.

Types of Discographies and How to Use Them

General Discographies   Bruyninckx, Walter. *50 Years of Recorded Jazz, 1917–1967.* Mechelen, Belgium: published privately, n.d. Largely duplicates Rust and Jepsen (see below) but occasionally contains data not found in the others, and 1967 termination date is later than most of Jepsen. Difficult to use because of looseleaf format. No index.

Jepsen, Jorgen Grunnet. *Jazz Records 1942–.* Copenhagen, Denmark: Knudsen, 1963–1970. The basic source for the period. In eleven volumes. Termination date for coverage varies between 1962 and 1969 depending upon volume. No index.

Rust, Brian. *Jazz Records 1897–1942.* 4th revised and enlarged edition, 2 vols. New Rochelle, N.Y.: Arlington House, 1978. The basic source for the period. Lists 78 issues only, except when recording appeared first on LP. Artist and title indexes.

CHARLES   DELAUNAY

FOREWORDS   BY

HUGUES & LUCIENNE PANASSIÉ

AND

HENRI   BERNARD

Translated into English
by **IAN MUNRO SMYTH**

1 9 3 6

Edited by

15, Rue du Conservatoire, 15
PARIS-9ᵉ

Figure 7.2 Title pages (a) Delaunay's Hot Discography and (b) Schleman's Rhythm on Record (p. 234).

RHYTHM

ON

RECORD

BY

HILTON R. SCHLEMAN

A complete survey and register
of all the principal recorded
dance music from 1906 to
1936, and a who's who of the
artists concerned in the making

LONDON

MELODY MAKER LTD.

93 Long Acre - W.C.2

Telephone - - Temple Bar 2468
(50 lines)
Telegraphic Address - Southernwood, Rand,
London

Figure 7.2 Title page (b) Schleman's Rhythm on Record.

The general jazz discographies attempt to cover all jazz recordings made within a certain period. The most common arrangement is alphabetical listing by the artist under whose name the recordings were originally issued. Within each artist's listings, the arrangement is chronological, by recording session. Basic information found in the general discographies includes: the *date of recording,* the *place of recording,* the *titles of the tunes,* the *personnel,* the *matrix and take numbers,* and the *issue (or catalogue) number. Figure 7.3 is a sample page from Rust's Jazz Records.* The entry is for a 1939 Lionel Hampton session at which "When Lights Are Low" (a selection included in the Smithsonian Collection) was recorded.

The problem of indexing is a crucial one in these works. Because they are arranged under the name of the performing group's leader, an index is needed to locate a particular artist's recordings as a sideman, that is, when he is not the leader. For many artists, such recordings constitute the bulk of their recorded work or an important segment of their careers. Such an example is Harry Carney, the most influential baritone saxophonist in jazz. Under his own name, in the general discographies, a total of six recording sessions are listed. Yet he is present on virtually all the records made by the Duke Ellington Orchestra from 1927 until Carney's death in 1974. In addition, he recorded occasional sessions under other leaders. Unfortunately, only Rust's *Jazz Records,* of the major general discographies, currently has an index that facilitates the location of such material.

One way to compensate in part for the lack of indexing for the period after 1942 is to establish the biographical details of a musician's career—for example, what bands he played in—and then to use this information as the starting point for a search for his recorded work.

Specialized Discographies These works can cover a particular aspect of jazz with more accuracy and in greater detail than the comprehensive general discographies. Specialized discographies focus on an individual musician, band, era, style, country, or recording company. The *individual artist discography* is the most common. These works are generally arranged in chronological order, listing all recordings by the artist, regardless of the person under whose name they were originally issued. (For example, a Louis Armstrong discography would include his work while a member of the Fletcher Henderson Orchestra.)

In addition to supplying detailed information about a musician's recording activity (such as solos), the specialized discography affords a convenient overview of an artist's total recording career. The sample page in Figure 7.4 is from Walter Allen's *Hendersonia,* a biodis-

Rex Stewart-c/Lawrence Brown-tb/Harry Carney-bar/Clyde Hart-p unless otherwise stated/Billy
Taylor-sb/Sonny Greer-d/Lionel Hampton-vib; p-v where shown.
                                New York, June 13, 1939.

037630-1	Memories Of You	Vic 26304, HMV B-9475,HN-2167,JK-2188
037631-1	The Jumpin' Jive - vLH	- - - -
037632-1	12th Street Rag - pLH	Vic 26362, 420-0014, HMV B-9088,
		JO-23, K-8465, X-6907, El EG-7716

Dizzy Gillespie-t/Benny Carter-as-a/Coleman Hawkins-Ben Webster-Chu Berry-ts/Clyde Hart-p/
Charlie Christian-g/Milt Hinton-sb/Cozy Cole-d/Lionel Hampton-vib-v.
                                New York, September 11, 1939.

041406-1	When Lights Are Low	Vic 26371, HMV B-9750, EA-2644,
		JK-2172, SG-288, X-6572, BA 234
041407-1	One Sweet Letter From You - vLH	Vic 26393, HMV B-9027, JK-2240,
		K-8432, V-Disc 360
041408-1	Hot Mallets	Vic 26371, HMV EA-2612, JK-2172,
		JO-18, K-8733, X-6572, BA 234
041409-1	Early Session Hop	Vic 26393, HMV B-9027,JK-2240,K-8432

Henry Allen-t/J. C. Higginbotham-tb/Earl Bostic-as/Clyde Hart-p/Charlie Christian-elg/Art-
ie Bernstein-sb/Sidney Catlett-d/Lionel Hampton-vib-v.
                                New York, October 12, 1939.

042941-1	I'm On My Way From You - vLH	Vic 26476, HMV JK-2227, X-6573
042942-1	Haven't Named It Yet	- - -
042943-1-2	The Heebie Jeebies Are Rockin' The Town -	Vic 26423, HMV JK-2243, X-6591
	vLH	

Ziggy Elman-t/Toots Mondello-cl-as/Ben Webster-Jerry Jerome-ts/Clyde Hart-p unless otherwise stated/Albert Casey-g/Artie Bernstein-sb/Slick Jones-d unless otherwise stated/Lionel
Hampton-vib; or p-d-v as noted.   New York, October 30, 1939.

043246-1	The Munson Street Breakdown - pLH	Vic 26453, HMV B-9137, JK-2235, BA 233
043247-1	I've Found A New Baby - pLH	Vic 26447, A-1083, HMV B-9130, JK-2161
043248-1	I Can't Get Started	Vic 26453, HMV B-9152, JK-2235
043249-1	Four Or Five Times - vLH	Vic 26447, A-1083, HMV B-9130,
		JK-2161, N-4452
043250-1	Gin For Christmas - dLH	Vic 26423, HMV EA-2565,JK-2243,X-6591

Benny Carter-t/Edmond Hall-cl/Coleman Hawkins-ts/Joe Sullivan-p/Freddy Greene-g/Artie Bern-
stein-sb/Zutty Singleton-d/Lionel Hampton-vib.
                                New York, December 21, 1939.

046024-1	Dinah	Vic 26557, 68-0848, HMV B-9063,
		EA-3550, JK-2264
046024-2	Dinah	Vic EPV-501
046025-1	My Buddy	Vic 26608, HMV EA-2753
046026-1	Singin' The Blues	Vic 26557, 68-0848, HMV B-9063,
		EA-2710, JK-2264

Ziggy Elman-t/Toots Mondello-Buff Estes-as/Jerry Jerome-Budd Johnson-ts/Spencer Odun-p/Er-
nest Ashley-g/Artie Bernstein-sb/Nick Fatool-d/Lionel Hampton-vib.
                                Chicago, February 26, 1940.

044724-1	Shades Of Jade	Vic 26604, HMV EA-3550, JK-2085
044725-1	Till Tom Special	- HMV EA-2710 -
044726-1	Flying Home	Vic 26595, 68-0873, HMV B-9334,
		JK-2120, El EG-7763
044727-1	Save It, Pretty Mama	As above
044728-1	Tempo And Swing	Vic 26608, HMV EA-2753

Figure 7.3 Page from Rust's Jazz Records, 1897–1942, *giving data on Lionel Hampton
recordings*

236

FLETCHER HENDERSON AND HIS ORCHESTRA   (E)   New York, Friday, May 14, 1926.

(2)   FLETCHER HENDERSON & HIS ORCH.

Russell Smith, Joe Smith, Rex Stewart, trumpets; Benny Morton, trombone; Buster Bailey, Don Redman, clarinets and alto saxes; Coleman Hawkins, clarinet and tenor sax; Fletcher Henderson, piano; Charlie Dixon, banjo; Ralph Escudero, tuba; Kaiser Marshall, drums.

Rex Stewart and Benny Morton have confirmed their presence on these sides, being their first solos with Henderson. Matrices 142205 2 and 142206-3 were 2nd Choice. Matrices 142202-03-04 are by Earl Gresh and his Orchestra; 142207 by Arthur Fields.

w142205 -1-2-3   THE STAMPEDE   (1)   Columbia 654-D
                  (Henderson) Fox Trot   (1) * Columbia 35669, Columbia (F) DF 3466
                  (* : as STAMPEDE)   (2) * Columbia (Au) DO-2272
                  (# : as Fletcher 'Smack' Henderson) (1) # Columbia (Sw) MZ 336 (dub, 3-142205)
                                                   LP   Columbia (F) FP 1021, Columbia (Sd) 33 FP 1021
                                                   LP   Columbia (It) 33 QS 6027
                                                   LP   Columbia (US & C) CL 1682, CBS (E)
                                                             BPG 62001, Columbia (J) PMS 104
                                                   LP   Philips (N) A-13654 JL

                  (Piano and saxes intro, 4 b; Stewart trumpet, 4 b; piano and saxes, 4 b; Stewart
                  trumpet, 4 b; Henderson piano, 2 brks; Hawkins tenor sax, 24 + 4 b + brks; Joe
                  Smith trumpet, 30 b; Henderson piano brk; clarinet trio, 30 b; Stewart trumpet,
                  2 + 12 b.) Arr : Don Redman.

w142206 -1-2-3   JACKASS BLUES   (1)   Columbia 654-D
                  (Stitzel and Kassel) Fox Trot   (1) * Columbia (Sw) MZ 336 (dub, 3-142206, = -2)
                  (* : as Mel Stitzel)   LP   Folkways FP 69 and FJ 2808 (= 142206-2)
                                                   LP   Columbia (US & C) CL 1682, CBS (E)
                                                             BPG 62001, Columbia (J) PMS 104 (=-2)
                                                   LP   Philips (N) A-13654 JL

                  (Joe Smith trumpet lead, 12 b; Morton trombone, 12 b; Bailey clarinet, 12 b;
                  Stewart trumpet, 12 b.) Arr : Don Redman.

*   *   *   *   *   *   *

CLARA SMITH. Vocal - Piano Accomp. by   (E)   New York, Wednesday, May 26, 1926.
Fletcher Henderson.

Personnel is on the label and in the Columbia files. Matrices 142252-4 and 142253-1 were 2nd Choice.
Matrices 142250-51 are by Clara Smith, acc. Lem Fowler, piano; 142254-55 by Franklyn Baur.

w142252 -1-2-3-4   SALTY DOG (Jackson)   (1)   Columbia 14143-D
                                                   EP   Philips (N) 436003 A-JE, Philips (E) BBE 12491

                  (Piano intro, 4 b, and coda only.)

w142253 -1-2-3-4   MY BRAND NEW PAPA   (1)   Columbia 14143-D (-2; -3, unconfirmed)
                   (Roth and Roth)   EP   Philips (N) 436003 A-JE & (E) BBE 12491 (= -2)

                  (Piano intro, 4 b + bridge, only.)

*   *   *   *   *   *   *

Harrison Smith states that the Fletcher Henderson orchestra recorded a test of I FOUND A NEW
BABY for the Gold Seal label, of St. Paul, in "1926".   Gold Seal's material was derived from the
Gennett company exclusively, as far as we know now.   The only Gennett masters of this title were
X 179A, recorded (in New York) by Ben Finger's Parady Club Orchestra, v. c. Bob Blake, rec'd
June 19, 1926 and never issued; and X 513, by Andy Preer, which was issued on Gennett 6056-B.

*   *   *   *   *   *   *

THE DIXIE STOMPERS   (A)   New York, Wednesday, October 20, 1926.

Joe Smith, Rex Stewart, trumpets; Benny Morton ?, trombone; Buster Bailey, clarinet and alto sax;
Don Redman, clarinet, alto and soprano saxes; Coleman Hawkins, clarinet and tenor sax; Fletcher
Henderson, piano; Charlie Dixon, banjo; Kaiser Marshall, drums.

The identity of the trombone soloist remains in doubt for the present; although Morton says he remained with Henderson for some time until he left to join Chick Webb in 1928, he may have been
joined periodically by Charlie Green as section mate, or have had to have a substitute on some particular record date such as this. The soloist here sounds somewhat like Green, without the growl.

Matrices 142845-1, 142846-3 and 142847-2 were all 2nd Choice. Matrices 142839-44 inclusive are by
pianist Art Gillham; 142848-49 by the Columbia Concert Orchestra.

142845 -1-2-3   OFF TO BUFFALO   (1)   Harmony 299-H, Velvet Tone 1299-V
                 (Candullo and Carroll) Fox Trot   LP   Only For Collectors OFC-39, Par (E) PMC 7109

                  (Saxes intro, 4 b; saxes lead, 16 b; trumpets lead, 8 b; saxes lead, 8 b; Hawkins
                  tenor sax, 8 b; Stewart trumpet, 16 b; saxes, 8 b; Stewart trumpet, 8 b; Bailey
                  clarinet obligato, 16 b; Bailey clarinet, 8 b.)

142846 -1-2-3   BROTHERLY LOVE   (1)   Harmony 299-H, Velvet Tone 1299-V
                 (Meyers and Schoebel) Fox Trot   LP   Parlophone (E) PMC 7109

                  (Clarinet/sax trio, 16 b; saxes, 32 b; Stewart trumpet, 16 b; brass trio, 16 b;
                  clarinet trio, 8 b; brass trio, 8 b; Morton ? trombone, 8 b; clarinet/sax trio, 8 + 6 b.)

142847 -1-2-3   ALABAMA STOMP (from "Earl   (1)   Harmony 283-H, Velvet Tone 1283-V
                 Carroll's Vanities") (Johnson and LP   Only For Collectors OFC-39, Par (E) PMC 7109
                 Creamer) Fox Trot

                  (Henderson piano brk in intro; saxes, 32 b; brass + clarinet/soprano sax trio, 16 b;
                  brass trio, 8 b; brass + clarinet/soprano sax trio, 8 + 32 b; Stewart trumpet, 30 b;
                  Bailey clarinet, 2 + 24 b.)

Figure 7.4 Page from Allen's Hendersonia, *giving data on Fletcher Henderson's recordings.*

237

cography (integrating biographical and discographical data) of bandleader-pianist Fletcher Henderson. (The session documented here is the one that produced the 1926 recording of "The Stampede" included in the Smithsonian Collection.) In addition to standard data, such as personnel, matrix numbers, date, titles, and issue numbers, this monumental work includes the complete solo routine for each recording, composer, and arranger credits, as well as other details such as alternate take information. Two other types of individual artist discographies have been developed recently. One is the "solography." This format, pioneered by Jan Evensmo, focuses on all the recorded solos of a particular artist during a given period and offers critical commentary (see Figure 7.5). Another is the "On Microgroove" series, published by Dick Bakker of *Micrography,* a magazine devoted to discographical research. This series concentrates on locating and identifying an artist's earlier recordings that have been issued on LPs.

Discographies of Related Music   As we have seen, the history of jazz is closely connected with the development of other types of music, such as the blues, gospel, ragtime, and popular music. For this reason, and because the term "jazz" obviously means different things to different people, the following discographies contain valuable data for the jazz researcher.

Godrich and Dixon, *Blues and Gospel Records, 1902–1942*
Jasen, *Recorded Ragtime, 1897–1958*
Leadbitter and Slaven, *Blues Records, 1943–1966*
Rust, *The American Dance Band Discography, 1917–1942*
Rust, *The Complete Entertainment Discography,* (mid-1890s–1942)

Discographical Periodicals and Bibliography

In addition to *Micrography,* mentioned above, the following periodicals regularly publish discographical research and/or articles on discographical methods: *Jazz Forschung/Jazz Research* (Austria), *Jazz Journal* (England), *Journal of Jazz Discography* (Wales), *Journal of Jazz Studies* (U.S.), *Matrix* (England), *Record Research* (U.S.), *Storyville* (England), and *Swing Journal* (Japan).

The following bibliographies are useful in locating jazz discographies:

A Bibliography of Jazz Discographies Published Since 1960. 2nd ed. Compiled by Peter Moon. Middlesex, England: The British Institute of Jazz Studies, 1972.

worthy representations of Hawkins' music and remind of "My Buddy", the first solo of this new style. They are no sensations but attractive, no quality differences of importance, but a little plus to "... Ball".

LIONEL HAMPTON AND HIS ORCHESTRA   NYC. Sept. 11, 1939

D. Gillespie (tp), B. Carter (as), C. Berry, B. Webster (ts), C. Hart (p), C. Christian (g), M. Hinton (b), C. Cole (dm), L. Hampton (vib, vo-041407).

041406-1	When Lights Are Low Vi 26371	Solo 20 bars. (FM)
041407-1	One Sweet Letter From You Vi 26393	Solo 16+8 bars, vib on bridge. (SM)
041408-1	Hot Mallets Vi 26371	No solo.
041409-1	Early Session Hop Vi 26393	No solo.

Hawkins' first session after his return to the U.S. contains two fine soli. A nice, restrained, relatively straight "... Sweet Letter ...", and a driving and inspired "... Lights ...", supported by a quite extraordinary rhythm section. There are certain objections which must be made, though. Even in the slowest tune, certain lesser defects are present. For instance the sound is not quite patent and in "... Lights ..." it is really too rough. The atmosphere has a touch of vulgarity and his playing lacks elegance. Possibly some lack of concentration is the reason for this, but his style has certainly changed to the rougher.

COLEMAN HAWKINS AND HIS ORCHESTRA   NYC. Oct. 11, 1939

J. Guy, T. Lindsay (tp), E. Hardy (tb), J. Fields, E. Moore (as), G. Rodgers (p), W.O. Smith (b), A. Herbert (dm), T. Carpenter (vo-042935).

042933-8	Meet Doctor Foo BB B-10477	Solo with orchestra 8 bars. Solo 16+8 bars, tp on bridge. Solo 8 bars. (FM)
042934-12	Fine Dinner BB B-10523	Soli 4, 16 and 4 bars. (FM)
042935-1	She's Funny That Way BB Rejected, but test exists.	Intro with tp 4 bars. Solo 32 bars. Coda. (SM)
042935-2	She's Funny That Way BB B-10477	Soloing as take 1. (SM)
042936-1	Body And Soul BB B-10523	Solo 64 bars. (SM)

Here, now, we encounter Hawkins' great and immortal record. The one that suddenly brought him forth to the renewed attention of the jazz world after his long self-chosen exile, and which gave him the nickname "Body and Soul of the Saxophone". It is in fact, superfluous to try to add any further praise to all that has been said about it during the last 30 years. But if I did, it would be deserving. The solo which fills the record is an unusual perfect construction, without defects of any sort, technically or musically. No other tenor saxophonist can show a corresponding success, and the success will last as long as a single jazzfan is still alive. "... Funny ..." is far behind in musical quality, even if it is emotional and contains many fine details, it is a little restless compared to "Body ...", as if the soloist does not quite manage to relax. This is

Figure 7.5 Page from Evensmo's Solography of Coleman Hawkins *with information about solos, including critical commentary.*

Cooper, David Edwin. *International Bibliography of Discographies.* Keys
to Music Bibliography Series, 2. Littleton, Col.: Libraries Unlimited,
1975. Useful source for location of discographies. Separate jazz,
blues, and classical sections. Concentrates on the period between
1962 and 1972 but contains some earlier works. Includes mono-
graphs as well as discographies contained in perioridals. Includes listings by individual artists, record labels, periods, and countries as well
as selective buying guides. Fully indexed.

OTHER SOURCES OF INFORMA-
TION ON RECORDS

Phonolog.   Available in most record stores, this useful source has a
song-title index that refers the reader to specific recordings of a particular title, as well as the standard artist index. Furthermore, there is
an index of LP titles, listing the contents of each LP. Because it is in
a looseleaf format and is intended to be kept up-to-date, one would
have to locate older, unrevised copies for use in retrospective coverage.

Record company catalogues.   These sources serve as a valuable
supplement to discographies, especially in the popular field where
discographical coverage is weak. They are also interesting historical
documents in their own right.

Schwann Long Playing Record Catalog.   Apart from its intended
use as a listing of current LPs, older issues of the catalogue can answer varied discographical needs. For example, it can help in locating pop music that may be of some jazz interest but is not in the
standard discographies. It may also be used as a rough guide in
dating a recording (by establishing its first date of entry into the
catalog).

Also see description of Kinkle's *Complete Encyclopedia of Popular
Music and Jazz,* p. 221.

CRITICAL RECORD GUIDES

Harrison, Max, et. al. *Modern Jazz, 1945–1970: The Essential Records.*
London: Aquarine Books, 1975. Not as complete or as well organized as *Jazz on Record* (see below).
McCarthy, Albert, et al. *Jazz on Record: A Critical Guide to the First 50
Years, 1917–1967.* New York: Oak Publications, 1968. A well-
organized, basic introduction to the important recorded work of a
wide range of artists.

RECORD REVIEW INDEXES

Armitage, Andrew D., and Tudor, Dean. *Annual Index to Popular Music Record Reviews*. Metuchen, N.J.: The Scarecrow Press, 1972—
Companion volume to *Popular Music Periodicals Index*. Covers major English-language jazz publications, general music periodicals, as well as those devoted to other music such as folk, blues, bluegrass. Arranged by artist within general music categories; numerical rating summary of each review.

Down Beat Record Reviews. From 1956 to 1963, reviews were cumulated in annual volumes. Since 1967, reviews have been indexed in the *Down Beat Annuals*.

The Music Index. (See description under Periodicals and Periodical indexes, p. 224.)

OBTAINING RECORDS

Although a wide selection of major-label jazz LPs is available in most large record stores, some of the smaller companies' releases, as well as foreign issues, may require more specialized sources. The last page of the booklet accompanying the Smithsonian Collection (see p. 27) lists some of these sources. They include jazz specialty stores and mail order dealers.

Recent reissue projects have put a wide range of recorded jazz of all eras on the market. Yet, at any given time, a large percentage of recordings remain out of print. A network of dealers and collectors who specialize in buying and selling this material, exists, but the recordings can be prohibitively expensive. Dealers' and collectors' sales and auction lists can be obtained by consulting the classified advertisement sections of the major jazz periodicals. The Smithsonian Collection booklet also has a list of some of the stores carrying out-of-print material.

Finally, less systematic, but far cheaper, sources for older records include antique and junk shops, garage sales, and flea markets.

OBTAINING BOOKS AND PERIODICALS

Early issues of even the major jazz periodicals may be difficult to find, and complete runs of some of the more esoteric publications are all but nonexistent. Standard library sources such as the *Union List of Serials* and *New Serial Titles* can help in the identification of United States library holdings of specific titles.

A project completed recently by the Greenwood press (51 Riverside Avenue, Westport, CN 06880) has made twenty-two varied jazz periodicals available on microfilm in more or less complete runs.

Reprint series for jazz books have been undertaken by Greenwood and also by Da Capo Press (227 West 17th St., New York, NY 10011).

Oak Lawn Books (Box 2663, Providence, R.I., 02907) is the largest jazz specialty book dealer in the United States and periodically publishes a comprehensive catalogue.

ARCHIVES

The two archives devoted specifically to jazz and the more general collections with jazz components are primary sources for hard-to-obtain material, as well as general research assistance. Although most of these collections are noncirculating, they generally have some provision for taping or duplicating.

The *Institute of Jazz Studies* of Rutgers University, Newark, New Jersey, houses the largest collection of jazz research materials in an academic institution. Holdings include 50,000 recordings, 2,000 books, clipping files, periodicals, and memorabilia covering all eras of jazz. The staff will provide reference assistance, including the taping of recordings not commercially available, to scholars, students, and others engaged in jazz-related research.

The *William Ransom Hogan Jazz Archive,* Tulane University, New Orleans, contains over 20,000 recordings and 1,000 books, as well as periodicals, photographs, and various special collections. Specializing in the music of New Orleans, the archive has an extensive series of taped interviews with musicians of that city.

The *Smithsonian Institution,* Washington, D.C., through its jazz program has been actively engaged in an oral-history project, which involves interviewing many of the figures who helped shape jazz. The material is being edited, and transcripts are available.

chapter 8

Jazz and All That Sociology

For someone trained in music and primarily interested in musical form, jazz presents a straightforward, though special, set of problems. The musical analysis of jazz calls for the development of special notation.* Jazz, a performer's music, is typically embedded in the grooves of records rather than in music scores. Those who would study jazz music must learn discography in order to carry out musical analyses.†

Historians and critics use aesthetic criteria in selecting jazz players who are artistically and stylistically important. Psychologists select those who provide important clinical case-study material for analysis. The impulse of such discussants is elitist insofar as it tends to disregard the ordinary jazz player. Sociologists, on the other hand, tend to be less interested in individual artistry than in the discovery of structural patterns that lie behind and control individual artistic expression. In his brilliant discussion of this issue, "Jazz Appreciation and the Sociology of Jazz," Phillip S. Hughes suggests that those trained in sociology have criteria of relevance such as representative sampling procedures, the elicitation of confidential information, and a lack of concern for jazz stars unless they are discussed as role models. This approach is unappealing to jazz fans and jazz critics. "Thus, where jazz critics and historians take 'public' data and apply aesthetic judgments to them, sociologists work with confidential data provided by jazzmen selected for study without regard to their artistic merit" (Hughes, 1974, p. 80).

My intent in this chapter is to present in some detail a theoretical model that emerged out of my own research on New York jazz musicians. The focus of that research was occupational success. What I found was that aspiring jazz musicians were more likely to "make it" if they con-

---

*See, for example, Eli Newberger, "The Transition From Ragtime to Improvised Piano Style," *Journal of Jazz Studies,* vol. 3, no. 2 (Spring 1976), pp. 3–6.

†See, for example, Walter C. Allen, "Discographical Musicology," *Journal of Jazz Studies,* vol. 1, no. 2 (June 1974), pp. 27–37.

formed to conventional middle-class work norms rather than to the unconventional and disorganized life style often conventionally attributed to artists. But much jazz literature and folklore have emphasized unconventionality and disorganization in the lives of jazz players. Young musicians who failed to perceive the lack of balance in jazz lore and literature courted failure since they had little insight into the real workaday world of most jazz players. They were caught up in what I termed the "jazz myth."

THE JAZZ MYTH

The jazz myth is a constellation of attitudes and behaviors on the part of jazz musicians. It has resulted in part from overly romantic and celebrationist notions about jazz and jazz musicians. The jazz myth to some degree stems from a lack of critical and academic concern with jazz. Some jazz writers, sympathetic to black culture and/or deviance, have understandably failed to be analytical and critical about jazz. Many writers with critical and analytic ability have opted for more prestigious art forms. It has taken jazz a long time to be recognized as a legitimate art form. Part of the reaction to jazz can be attributed to racism, part to its origins as black American folk music. But whatever the reasons, many jazz writers have had limited knowledge about jazz as music. Many have been rank amateurs in music, writing, and/or critical ability.

Jazz musicians themeloves have also contributed to the myth. An example of the myth in action among jazzmen is the "beautiful syndrome." The beautiful syndrome represents a penchant on the part of many jazz musicians to be uncritical of one another. If you ask one jazz musician about another's playing, the most likely response is, "Man, he's beautiful." In the beginning of my research, I assumed that this response was reserved for outsiders. It is not. Jazzmen also "jive" each other because they do not want to risk alienating anyone, including fellow musicians, who might control employment.

JAZZ AND THE SCHOOLS OF SOCIOLOGY

Sociological types can be as valid and as useful in understanding jazz as the historical (the Swing Period, the Bop Period) or the chronological (the twenties, the thirties) approaches. The discipline of sociology is not better than the discipline of history or music theory in jazz research. But it is different and may illuminate facets of jazz not amenable to other approaches. Sociology represents the search for structure, the uncovering of patterns of behavior, which can add to the comprehension of the jazz phenomenon. In the paragraphs that follow, I shall present some conclusions from my work on occupational aspects of jazz in the hope that it illustrates this point (Nanry, 1970). It may also illustrate, incidentally, why this book has taken the shape it has with less emphasis on stars and styles than is typically found in more historically oriented jazz writing.

As jazz writers, sociologists may be conveniently divided into two schools or styles. The first is the "subculture school" exemplified by the jazz writings of Carlo Lastrucci (1941), Becker in Nanry (1972), William Bruce Cameron (1954), Alan Merriam and Raymond Mack (1960) and Robert Stebbins (1964). This school views jazz musicians as part of deviant subcultures. Their major emphasis is on those characteristics that set jazzmen apart from others.

The second style of jazz and sociology writing, what I call the "assimilationist school," is more historically oriented. In general, authors who belong to this school tend to see jazz as part of cultural history. Their emphasis is typically on the place of jazz in the larger context of American society. These authors are usually concerned with the impact of social change on jazz and, in general, they paint on a larger canvas than the subculturists. Social change is typically critical in their work. Sociologists such as Morroe Berger (1947), Neil Leonard (1962), Edward Harvey (1967), and Richard A. Peterson (n.d.) exemplify this tradition.

Members of the two schools usually analyze different issues. Little is to be gained from simply disputing what they have said. The central problem for all sociologists who write about jazz is the same: representative sampling. The sampling framework in much jazz sociology is often unspecified or simply assumed.

Part of the problem is that no one has yet come up with a satisfactory definition of jazz. Without that definition, it is difficult to type jazz musicians. One person's jazz may be another's commercial pap. Self-definition is one way out of this dilemma, namely, those who call themselves jazz musicians *are* jazz musicians. The assumption here is that a self-definition will be impossible to maintain over time if others do not agree. But this solution does not fully solve the critical sampling problem either. We need a typology of jazz musicians and reliable techniques for selecting representative samples. My own research indicates that relatively few musicians call themselves jazz musicians. Most prefer to be labeled as musicians who play jazz. Some black musicians find they cannot shake the jazz label; some whites cannot earn it. Miles Davis and Duke Ellington rejected the jazz label, for example, but listeners refuse to follow suit. Other criteria as well as self-definition are obviously involved. Below is a modest sampling proposal. It is based on the assumption that

jazz researchers have identified types of jazz musicians but that the existing literature must be reorganized. The two schools of jazz and sociology,
the subculture school and the assimilationist school, typically discuss different types of musicians. By way of example and in order to clarify the
orientation of these schools, I shall briefly discuss the work of Howard
Becker, representing the subculturists, and Morroe Berger, representing
the assimilationists.

Becker's major theoretical concern, as expressed in *Outsiders,* is with
deviance:

> Social groups create deviance by making the rules whose infrac-
> tion constitutes deviance. . . . [Deviance is] . . . a consequence of
> the application by others of rules and sanctions to an "offender"
> (p. 25).

Jazz values are opposed to commercial values by Becker in order to
illustrate the labeling process. Becker talks about dance musicians who
have either artistic values (which he equates with jazz) or commercial values. His study is not, nor does it pretend to be, a comprehensive study of
jazz musicians. Jazz for Becker is free self-expression, artistry; commercial
music is music susceptible to outside pressure and compromise. The true
jazzman is presumed to be an artist; the commercial musician a craftsman.

Although Becker does not give us data on the race and age of the
musicians he discusses, I think it is reasonable to assume that he is talking
about frustrated dance-band players who hold the artistic value of freedom of expression in a restrictive musical context. These deviants are
dance musicians, not jazz musicians, who perceive a hypothetical reference group of idealized jazzmen. They are musicians caught up in the jazz
myth.

The subculturists in general talk about scattered coteries of musicians
caught up in the lonely value of artistic self-expression. The assimilationists, on the other hand, are more concerned with the historical contexts of black jazz. In "Jazz: Resistance to the Diffusion of a Culture-Pat-
tern," Morroe Berger states the theme most clearly:

> The purpose of this paper is to examine the implications, for the
> diffusion of jazz, of the fact that the Negroes, with whom jazz is cor-
> rectly associated, are a low-status group in the United States. The
> evidence to be presented will confirm the hypothesis that in the dif-
> fusion process the prestige of the donors has considerable bearing
> on the way in which a borrowing group reacts to cultural traits of
> other groups (p. 461).

It serves no useful purpose to fault the assimilationists because of historical bias, that is, their nonsystematic selection of data. It is sufficient to say that, like the subculturists, they have not solved the sampling problem.

THE SAMPLING PROBLEM

A new synthesis is needed to properly "place" the existing literature as well as extend it. Critics of jazz-and-sociology literature are often uneasy because what they read fails to describe jazz as they know it. In order for that criticism to be constructive, however, they must reanalyze what others have done rather than cast it aside. The sampling problem may never adequately be solved in any case, for the jazz label is "unprotected" by licensing procedures. But we must be able to categorize those about whom we speak.

Certain values long associated in the minds of jazz insiders with the art form—the jazz myth—are, in reality, values that belong only to a segment of those who have traditionally been labeled as jazz musicians. Frustrated dance-band musicians do not, and have not, fairly represented jazz. Except as role models, men such as Louis Armstrong, Duke Ellington, Miles Davis, and John Coltrane do not fairly represent jazz either. The many kinds of music we think of as jazz must be analytically distinguished before they can be linked together, a task undertaken in the earlier pages of this book. The same is true for types of jazz players. If we fail in either effort, arbitrary and sterile generalization may result. A typology of jazz musicians must reflect the complexity of jazz and its historical development.

Jazz does not exist in a social and cultural vacuum. The assimilationist school has given us ample evidence of the impact of social and technological change on jazz. The subculture school has documented the dynamic tension between the role of performer and the role of creator. But confusion has resulted from accepting either as typical of all jazz. The tension between the internal and external dynamics of jazz must be distinguished.

The first distinction I would propose is that jazz as a musical category be separated from notions about particular jazz players constituting social groups. Jazz as a musical category is an art form, distinguishable from other music; normative and learned, jazz represents values that must be transmitted. As a category it has the characteristics of Durkheim's social facts: it is outside of any single individual and constrains behavior (see chapter 1, pp. 12–13). The consideration of jazz as a musical category leads ultimately to a musicological problem; consideration of it, on the other hand, as a group phenomenon leads to a sociological one.

Jazz performers in social groups interact. One thing that presumably brings them together is their relation to the category of music called jazz. But other nonmusical characteristics such as race and age also have an impact on group behavior and attitudes. Jazz is but one of many social facts that concern jazz musicians. Any group of jazz players will, therefore, be affected by one or more overlapping sets of interactive social facts. It is possible to study jazz musicians and the effect of their jazz identification only if some of the major influences are untangled. In considering them, we ought to keep in mind that we are dealing with people who are musicians *and* who play jazz. Every school child who learns music is a potential jazz musician. Most kids who play music, however, do not become jazz musicians. Black kids, for example, are more likely than white kids to be exposed to jazz. With little opportunity to move into other musical careers, many blacks, until recently, were limited to jazz. Jazz selects blacks; whites select jazz.

But these facts must be linked to a theoretical perspective that can explain their interrelationships. In my own research, reference group theory has served that purpose.

REFERENCE GROUPS

I see nothing mysterious about the notion of reference groups. From one point of view, the notion is simply an extension of the idea of group culture. In industrial societies there are competing ways of doing things; hence alternative models of behavior are, at least potentially, available. Reference group theory is an attempt to discover the process whereby one group's values are adopted rather than another's. Manford Kuhn, in *The Dictionary of the Social Sciences,* defines a reference group this way:

> The term denotes a social group with which an individual feels identified and to which he aspires to relate his identity. A person derives from his reference groups his norms, attitudes and values and the social objects these create. He also derives significant social categories, both the ones to which he is assigned and the ones with which he is, in one way or another, contrasted (p. 581).

Subcultures may develop based on actual membership in a particular reference group. One may also refer to deceased or even imagined reference others—to a "mystical body" that overreaches time. Jazz musicians may think of Jelly Roll Morton as an "other" in the same way that a poet may see his work in relation to Homer's.

Jazz players may see themselves in relation to other jazz players, living and dead. But when they do, they will not, in all likelihood, relate to all jazz (past and present) or emulate all those who call themselves jazz musicians. The question is how any jazz musician relates to jazz as a category or art form *and* how he relates to existing groups of jazz players and audiences. Of course there is a synergistic effect on the individual adjusting both to the form and to others. Jazz worlds, therefore, have their own internal dynamics, which we may call the "within jazz" structure, the internal dynamic idea used throughout this book.

But jazz musicians have always had to articulate their expression with the larger world of entertainment. This articulation has created modes of accommodation to, for example, the music industry. This adds a "between jazz and nonjazz structures" dimension to our analysis, the external dynamic.

Jazz worlds with their own internal dynamics may be distinguished from and related to other "worlds" that the musician's activities carry him through. The relationships are far from simple. The history of jazz confronts us with many puzzling facts. Most jazz musicians have been part of the larger world of entertainment in America. Under the impact of industrialization in America, the professionalization of the entertainment sector and of jazz, grew apace. With the growth of the mass media, the demand for skill, for example, the ability to read music well, increased. At the same time, jazz performers have continued to make innovations within jazz and to change and revitalize the art form. Jazz, in other words, has never been simply swallowed up by mass entertainment in America.

A partial explanation of this phenomenon comes from an understanding of the impact of racism in the United States. Black musicians were usually not allowed to become too prominent within the overall structure of mass entertainment. They had to be creative in order to survive, of course, since mere competence was not enough. But the relatively small number of black musicians who did achieve noticeable success—Louis Armstrong is the best example—won their triumphs by a strategy of accommodation, striking their bargains with the devil of mass appeal.

BUREAUCRACY AND CHARISMA

In addition to reference group theory, another theoretical perspective I have considered is Max Weber's theory of bureaucracy. Weber's general thesis is that there is a "strain for rationality" in the West that constantly pressures institutions toward bureaucratic organization. Yet pure bureaucracy, by definition, is unable to cope adequately with major social changes. Changing technology, industrialization, and urbanization demand innovation in social structure. One way out of the dilemma of bureaucratic "rationality" is through the development of charisma. In the aesthetic area, as in others, pure bureaucracy, by itself, would eventually bring everything to a halt.

In his masterly analysis of music in the West, *Rational and Social Foundations of Music,* Weber puts his notion of alternating rationality and irrationality in music to the test. Weber analyzes the development of Western music and attempts to demonstrate that, in spite of increasing rationalization (for example, the development of the well-tempered scale), certain elements kept escaping the process (for example, the "irrational" properties of the dominant seventh chord). Some "irrationalities" have social origins. The difficulties incurred in attempting to coordinate male and female voices or the need to tune instruments for ensemble playing are but two examples cited by Weber (Weber, 1958b).

The application of Weber's theory of bureaucracy (Weber, 1947, pp. 358–63) to jazz is delightfully straightforward. The career structure faced by those labeled as jazz musicians at any given moment reflects the way music production is organized in their society at that moment. Any variation from that organization of work and the ground rules of jazz playing represents a charismatic challenge. The charismatic challenge, that is, innovation, however, will not be felt unless that innovation is routinized.*

The routinization of charisma or innovation in jazz involves the founding of schools of jazz through mechanisms such as playing together (interaction). It also affects jazz as a musical category through the establishment of self-conscious styles.

It may also be that certain individual musicians or groups of musicians can build a power base outside of jazz itself by parlaying "audience rewards" to the point where jazz itself is forced into accommodation. This clearly is what happened in the case of swing. Jazz, which has freely used folk, popular, or classical music elements as source material, may be particularly vulnerable to this kind of development.

It is not my intention to claim isomorphism between Weber's analysis of the ideal typical bureaucracy and the threats to it from charisma, on the one hand, and jazz, on the other. But the jazz mainstream or "es-

* Musical organization may also be altered accidentally through lack of formal training. The possibility of innovation through accident introduces an element of irrationality that is nonetheless important. Some early jazz players may indeed have made a contribution through "faking it," or making do with limited resources.

tablishment" continues to be threatened by the avant garde. The Weberian perspective offers an opening gambit. Its application suggests the eventual need for serious *audience* research. We must know what segments of the jazz and/or other audiences tend to support what types of bureaucratic or charismatic jazz players. For example, in my research in the late sixties, I found evidence to indicate that a radical polarization occurred within jazz. Young black players perceived their music as black music, while young whites were more likely to value "artistic" or "jazz myth" orientations. Both perceptions of what is true jazz represent clearly differentiated charismatic challenges to the jazz establishment. Rock and jazz/rock enhanced the challenge.

Bop, for example, was partially a reaction against the bureaucratization of swing. Bop represented both musical and social protest. Bop musicians reacted against all too predictable and heavily ritualized swing arrangements, as well as Uncle Tom expectations on the part of audiences for black musicians.* Bopsters, musicians, and nonmusicians alike, saw themselves as the antithesis of a complacent, racist, and desiccated society and its popular art. The dialectic continues, alternating between establishment jazz and charismatic challenge based on nonmusical as well as musical developments. The early rejection of Ornette Coleman's music by many jazz insiders is another example (Spellman, 1970).

THE LOCAL-COSMOPOLITAN CONTINUUM

An important development within reference group theory has been the elaboration of the "local-cosmopolitan" continuum. The dimension along which this continuum is organized represents one's general occupational orientation. A local is one who is oriented toward those around him, a cosmopolitan to a larger grouping usually based on specialized interests. The popular metaphor of the big frog in the little pond (presumably a successful local) and the little frog in the big pond (presumably a less than successful cosmopolitan) captures the spirit of the typology.

Alvin Gouldner (1957, 1958) has explicitly included a reference group aspect in his empirically operationalized definition of this continuum. The issue for him pivots upon what social identities are called upon in the occupational reference group process. He defines the poles of the continuum as follows:

---

*Louis Armstrong rejected bop as nonmusic, and bopsters sniped at Armstrong's Tomism in a classic example of this antipathy.

1. Cosmopolitan: those low on loyalty to the employing organization, high on commitment to specialized role skills, and likely to use an outer reference group.
2. Locals: those high on loyalty to the employing organization, low on commitment to specialized role skills, and likely to use an inner reference group orientation.

By "inner reference group" Gouldner means face-to-face or membership groups, while "outer reference groups" are those that are broader and less personal.

Table 8.1 illustrates in a graphic way the cross-classification of these two dimensions, that is, the bureaucratic-charismatic and the local-cosmopolitan. This cross-classification creates a new typology that permits us to name types of musicians who might be found where these dimensions intersect. The bureaucratic-charismatic dimension refers to the internal structure of jazz. The local-cosmopolitan dimension refers to the relationship of jazz to other structures. The former dimension is internal; the latter external. Both have self-other and social organization implications.

CROSS-CLASSIFICATION OF VARIABLES

The cross-classification of the two variables outlined above is grounded in my own empirical investigations. It developed out of thinking about the contradictory material in the sociological and psychological literature on jazz. Rather than presumptuously characterizing that literature as "wrong," the better strategy became one of placing or specifying

Table 8.1
A TYPOLOGY OF JAZZ MUSICIANS

Within Jazz	Between Jazz and Other Musicians	
	Local	**Cosmopolitan**
Bureaucratic	Dance Band Musicians and Other "Club Date" Musicians	The "Studio" Jazzmen/ Craftsmen
Charismatic	"Real Jazz" Players in Nonjazz Bands	The Jazz "Innovator"

the generalizations within a theoretical framework that reduced the apparent contradictions.

Becker, Stebbins, Merriam and Mack, and the other members of what I have labeled the subculture school write mostly about the potential frustrations of local-bureaucratic musicians. In terms of the above typology, the musicians who attempt to break away and are uncontrolled are the local charismatics who see themselves as true believers and are likely to be staunch defenders of the jazz myth. They wish to improvise in contexts not amenable to "real" jazz, for example, at dances. Players from Beiderbecke to Ornette Coleman, in his early career, exemplify the difficulties of being local-charismatics.

The assimilationist school of Berger and Leonard is more concerned with the dynamics between cosmopolitan-bureaucratic and cosmopolitan-charismatic types. With the above typology, their arguments make more analytic sense, that is, we have a better idea about what "slice of reality" they are discussing. They are more likely to focus on the jazz elite than on local players.

Table 8.1 refers to jazz as a group phenomenon. Each cell in the cross-classification involves types of musicians. It is also possible to extend the same heuristic technique to jazz as a musical form. Table 8.2 refers to the same dimensions applied to jazz as a category of music.

The difference between local- and cosmopolitan-charismatic jazz revolves around whether or not it extends the art form into some new dimension. The best of jazz-rock evolved from building a new sound on jazz roots. Bureaucratic-cosmopolitan jazz would be, for example, a TV commercial that employs the skills of studio musicians trained in the jazz tradition.

By maintaining the group-category distinction, it is possible to type musicians on several dimensions at once. Becker's frustrated dance

---

Table 8.2
A TYPOLOGY OF JAZZ-RELATED MUSICS

Within Jazz	Between Jazz and Other Musicians	
	Local	**Cosmopolitan**
Bureaucratic	"Standard" Charts Out of the Swing Era	Jazz-Influenced "Universal" Music and "Pop" Jazz
Charismatic	Music Improvised *Within* a Jazz Style	Music Improvised *From* a Jazz Style

bandsmen are in a local-bureaucratic group but attempt to play in a cosmopolitan style. The conditions under which conflict may be generated flow from the playing of an inappropriate style for the particular membership group to which a musician belongs.

Jazz innovators who are cosmopolitan-charismatic are often forced to play bureaucratic music in order to make a living. The general problem of the creative artist who is hard pressed to develop a large audience emerges for them. It is not a problem unique to jazz but rather one occurring in the arts.

I do not wish to imply that any musician, however, is necessarily confined to any one space in the typology. If that happens, it is a matter for empirical determination. In fact, one major use of these typologies may be to think of the points in them as stages through which musicians may move. It might be possible to construct "paths" through these typologies as "typical" for some musicians. Linked with other data characteristics, this strategy may help us to further untangle some "knots" in the music world.

An example may best illustrate the foregoing. It may be appropriate for someone to be a local-bureaucratic musician when he is in his teens and discover the charismatic-local style, shifting his reference group as he shifts his reference others to other local charismatics. The Austin High Gang in Chicago (see chapter 4) serves as an illustration. If he or she waits until twenty to do this, it may preclude a certain type of career pattern. In other words, there are timing norms in the music business just as there are in other fields. You are an old ball player at thirty-five but a young philosopher.

The generation of typologies out of existing literature, however, leads to other problems. The typology generated in this way has been imposed, even if it is empirically derived. The four sections in either of my cross-classifications have a kind of artificiality about them. I propose that they represent "theoretical subcultures" and demand further investigation.

In my own research, successful young musicians moved from a local-bureaucratic position to the cosmopolitan-bureaucratic stage, pausing at the local-charismatic stage only long enough to acquire improvisational techniques. Young black musicians seemed to do this more easily than young whites. Many young white musicians caught up in the jazz myth are represented here as local charismatics. Hiring practices in jazz tend to be informal and clique-ridden. It is easy to get "bum steers" in jazz because communication is often nonverbal and, presuming competence, who you know is more than what you know.

Most successful jazz professionals are bureaucratic-cosmopolitans, with a few influential inside stars becoming charismatic-cosmopolitans, that is, having purely artistic values and reference others. Their innovations tend to be absorbed slowly, however, like those of other creative artists.

A CONCLUDING NOTE

Chapter 8 illustrates the potential benefits of combining various academic disciplines and their techniques in order to better understand the jazz phenomenon (Nanry, 1971). The endeavor represents intellectual variation on the theme of jazz as part of American social structure. The classification introduced in this chapter* only hints at the potential of such an inquiry. "There still remains the problem of how to incorporate those overlapping bases of differentiation such as age, race, and geographical location, without whose incorporation no picture of the jazz world as a whole will be even minimally satisfying" (Hughes, 1974, p. 81). The economics of jazz, the psychology of jazz, and the political economy of the jazz life should provide the serious student with enough interest to last a lifetime without compromising either jazz or scholarly pursuit.

---

* I have not presented the actual data upon which my reasoning is based since that would tax the patience of even sympathetic readers. The data are available to the interested reader (Nanry, 1970).

BIBLIOGRAPHY

Aasland, Benny H. *The "Wax Works" of Duke Ellington.* Stockholm: Published privately, 1954.

Allen, Walter C. *Hendersonia: The Music of Fletcher Henderson.* Highland Park, N.J.: Published privately, 1973.

———. "Discographical Musicology," *Journal of Jazz Studies,* 1 (1974): 27–37.

Allen, Walter C., and Rust, Brian. *King Joe Oliver.* London and New York: Sidgwick and Jackson, 1958.

Apel, 'Willi, and Daniel, Ralph T. *The Harvard Brief Dictionary of Music.* New York: Pocket Books, 1961.

Armitage, Andrew D., and Tudor, Dean. *Annual Index to Popular Music Record Reviews.* Metuchen, N.J.: Scarecrow Press, 1972–.

Armstrong, Louis. *Swing That Music.* London and New York: Longmans, Green, 1936.

———. *Satchmo: My Life in New Orleans.* New York: Prentice-Hall, 1954.

———. *Louis Armstrong—A Self Portrait. The Interview by Richard Meryman.* New York: Eakins Press, 1971.

Bakker, Dick M. *Duke Ellington on Microgroove, 1923–1936,* vol. 1. Alphen aan den Rijn, Holland: Micrography, 1977.

Balliett, Whitney. *The Sound of Surprise.* New York: Dutton, 1959.

———. *Dinosaurs in the Morning.* Philadelphia: Lippincott, 1962.

———. *Such Sweet Thunder.* Indianapolis: Bobbs-Merrill, 1966.

———. *Ecstasy at the Onion.* Indianapolis: Bobbs-Merrill, 1971.

———. *New York Notes: A Journal of Jazz 1972–75.* Boston: Houghton Mifflin, 1976. New York: DaCapo, 1977, paper.

———. *Improvising. Sixteen Jazz Musicians and Their Art.* New York: Oxford University Press, 1977.

Bechet, Sidney. *Treat It Gentle.* New York: Hill & Wang, 1960.

Becker, Howard S. "The Professional Dance Musician and His Audience," *American Journal of Sociology,* 57 (1951): 136–44.

———. "Some Contingencies of the Professional Dance Musician's Career," *Human Organization,* 12 (1953): 22–26.

———. "The Culture and Career of the Dance Musician," *Social Problems,* 3 (1955): 18–24.

———. *Outsiders: Studies in the Sociology of Deviance.* New York: Free Press, 1963.

Bell, Daniel. *The End of Ideology.* New York: Collier, 1961.

Berendt, Joachim. *The Jazz Book, From New Orleans to Rock and Free Jazz.* New York: Lawrence Hill, 1975.

Berger, Edward. "Benny Carter—Part I: A Discographical Approach," *Journal of Jazz Studies,* 4 (1976): 47–74.

Berger, Morroe. "Jazz: Resistance to the Diffusion of a Culture Pattern," *Journal of Negro History,* 32 (1947): 461–94.

Berton, Ralph. *Remembering Bix: A Memoir of the Jazz Age.* New York: Harper and Row, 1974.

Blesh, Rudi, and Janis, Harriet. *They All Played Ragtime.* New York: Oak, 1966.

Blum, Joseph. "Problems of *Salsa* Research," *Ethnomusicology,* 22 (1978): 137–49.

Brask, Ole, and Morgenstern, Dan. *Jazz People.* New York: Abrams, 1976.

Broonzy, William, and Bruynoghe, Yannick. *Big Bill Blues.* London: Cassell, 1955.

Brubeck, Iola, and Brubeck, Dave. "Jazz Perspective." In *Jam Session: An Anthology of Jazz.* Edited by Ralph Gleason, pp. 222–33. New York: Putnam, 1958.

Bruyninckx, Walter. *50 Years of Recorded Jazz, 1917—1967.* Mechelen, Belgium: Published privately, n.d.

Buerkle, Jack V., and Barker, Danny. *Bourbon Street Black: The New Orleans Black Jazzman.* New York: Oxford University Press, 1973.

Burnett, James. *Bix Beiderbecke.* London: Cassell, 1959. New York: A. S. Barnes, 1961.

Butcher, Margaret Just. *The Negro in American Culture.* New York: New American Library, 1956.

Calloway, Cab, and Rollins, Bryant. *Of Minnie the Moocher and Me.* New York: Crowell, 1976.

Cameron, William Bruce. "Sociological Notes on the Jam Session," *Social Forces,* 33 (1954): 177–82.

Castelli, Vittorio; Kaleveld, Evert; and Pusateri, Liborio. *The Bix Bands: A Bix Beiderbecke Disco-biography.* Milan, Italy: Raretone, 1972.

Cayer, David A. "Black and Blue and Black Again: Three Stages of Racial Imagery in Jazz Lyrics," *Journal of Jazz Studies,* 1 (1974): 38:–71.

Charters, Samuel B. *The Country Blues,* rev. ed. New York: DaCapo, 1975.

Chase, Gilbert. *America's Music.* New York: McGraw-Hill, 1966.

Chilton, John. *Who's Who of Jazz: Storyville to Swing.* London: Bloomsbury Book Shop, 1972.

Chomsky, Noam. *Language and Mind.* New York: Harcourt, Brace & World, 1968.

Cole, Bill. *Miles Davis: A Musical Biography.* New York: William Morrow, 1974.

Condon, Eddie. *We Called It Music: A Generation of Jazz.* New York: Henry Holt, 1947.

————, and O'Neal, Hank. *Eddie Condon's Scrapbook of Jazz.* New York: Galahad, 1973.

Connor, D. Russell, and Hicks, Warren W. *B. G. on the Record: A Biodiscography of Benny Goodman.* New Rochelle, N.Y.: Arlington House, 1969.

Couch, Stephen R. "Class, Politics, and Symphony Orchestras," *Society,* 14 (1976): 24–29.

Cruse, Harold. *The Crisis of the Negro Intellectual: From Its Origins to the Present.* New York: William Morrow, 1967.

Dance, Stanley. *The World of Duke Ellington.* New York: Scribner's, 1970.

Daniels, Arthur, and Wagner, Lavern. *Listening to Music.* New York: Holt, Rinehart and Winston, 1975.

Davies, John R. T., and Wright, Laurie. *Morton's Music.* Essex, England: Storyville Publications, 1968.

Delaunay, Charles. *Hot Discography.* Translated by Ian Munro Smyth. Paris: Hot Jazz, 1936.

Denisoff, R. Serge. *Solid Gold: The Popular Record Industry.* New Brunswick, N.J.: Transaction, 1975.

Dollard, John. *Caste and Class in a Southern Town.* New Haven: Yale University Press, 1937.

Drake, St. Clair, and Cayton, Horace. *Black Metropolis.* New York: Harcourt, Brace & World, 1945.

Durkheim, Emile. *Division of Labor in Society.* New York: Free Press, 1947.

————. *The Rules of Sociological Method.* New York: Free Press, 1950.

————. *The Elementary Forms of Religious Life.* New York: Free Press, 1954.

Elkins, Stanley M. *Slavery: A Problem in American Institutional and Intellectual Life.* New York: Grosset & Dunlap, 1963.

Ellington, Duke. *Music Is My Mistress.* New York: Doubleday, 1973.

Ellington, Mercer, and Dance, Stanley. *Duke Ellington in Person: An Intimate Memoir.* New York: Houghton Mifflin, 1978.

Erikson, Kai T. *Wayward Puritans: A Study in the Sociology of Deviance.* New York: Wiley, 1966.

Esquire's World of Jazz. New York: Crowell, 1975.

Evans, Philip R., and Dean-Myatt, William. "Bix Beiderbecke on Record:

A Comprehensive Discography." In *Bix: Man and Legend,* by Richard M. Sudhalter and Philip R. Evans, pp. 401–72. New Rochelle, N.Y.: Arlington House, 1974.

Evensmo, Jan. *The Tenor Saxophone of Coleman Hawkins, 1929–1942.* Hosle, Norway: Published privately, 1976.

———. *The Alto Saxophone and Other Instruments of Benny Carter, 1927–1942.* Hosle, Norway: Published privately, 1978.

Everett, Thomas G. "An Annotated List of English-Language Jazz Periodicals," *Journal of Jazz Studies,* 3 (1976): 47—57.

Ewen, David. *The Life and Death of Tin Pan Alley.* New York: Funk & Wagnalls, 1964.

Feather, Leonard. *Encyclopedia of Jazz. The New Edition of the Encyclopedia of Jazz,* vol. 1. New York: Horizon Press, 1962.

———. *Encyclopedia of Jazz. The Encyclopedia of Jazz in the Sixties,* vol. 2. New York: Horizon Press, 1966.

———. *Encyclopedia of Jazz. The Encyclopedia of Jazz in the Seventies,* vol. 3. New York: Horizon Press, 1976.

Foster, Pops, and Stoddard, Tom. *Pops Foster: The Autobiography of a New Orleans Jazzman.* Berkeley: University of California Press, 1971.

Fox, Charles. *The Jazz Scene.* London: Hamlyn, 1972.

Frazier, E. Franklin. *The Black Bourgeoisie.* New York: Free Press, 1957.

Gammond, Peter, ed. *Duke Ellington. His Life and Music.* New York: Roy, 1958.

Gillet, Charlie. *The Sound of the City: The Rise of Rock and Roll.* New York: Sunrise Books, 1970.

Gilmore, H. W. "The Old New Orleans and the New: A Case for Ecology." In *American Sociological Review,* 9 (1944): 385–94.

Gitler, Ira. *Jazz Masters of the Forties.* New York: Macmillan, 1966.

Gleason, Ralph, ed. *Jam Session: An Anthology of Jazz.* New York: Putnam, 1958.

Godrich, John, and Dixon, Robert M. W. *Blues and Gospel Records, 190221942.* London: Storyville, 1969.

Goffin, Robert. *Horn of Plenty. The Story of Louis Armstrong.* New York: Allen, Towne and Heath, 1947.

Gold, Robert. *Jazz Talk: A Dictionary of the Colorful Language that Has Emerged from America's Own Music.* Indianapolis: Bobbs-Merrill, 1975.

Goldberg, Joe. *Jazz Masters of the 50's.* New York: Macmillan, 1965.

Goodman, Benny, and Kolodin, Irving. *The Kingdom of Swing.* New York: Stackpole Sons, 1939.

Gregor, Carl. *International Jazz Bibliography.* Graz, Austria: Universal Edition, 1969. 1970 supplement. Graz, Austria: Universal Edition, 1971. 1971–72–73 supplement. Graz, Austria: Universal Edition, 1975.

Hadlock, Richard. *Jazz Masters of the Twenties.* New York: Macmillan, 1965.

Handy, W. C. *Father of the Blues.* New York: Collier, 1970.

Harris, Neil. *The Artist in American Society.* New York: Braziller, 1966.

Harrison, Max. *Charlie Parker.* London: Cassell, 1960. New York: A. S. Barnes, 1961.

———, and others. *Modern Jazz, 1945–1970: the Essential Records.* London: Aquarine Books, 1975.

Harvey, Edward. "Social Change and the Jazz Musician," *Social Forces,* 46 (1967): 34–42.

Hasse, John. "The Smithsonian Collection of Classic Jazz: A Review Essay," *Journal of Jazz Studies,* 3 (1975): 66–71.

Hawes, Hampton, and Asher, Don. *Raise Up Off Me.* New York: Coward, McCann and Geoghegan, 1972.

Hawley, Amos. *Human Ecology.* New York: Ronald Press, 1950.

Hennessey, Thomas J. "From Jazz to Swing." Unpublished Ph.D. dissertation, Northwestern University, 1973.

———. "The Black Chicago Establishment, 1919–1930," *Journal of Jazz Studies,* 2 (1974): 15–45.

Hentoff, Nat. *The Jazz Life.* New York: Dial Press, 1961.

———, and Shapiro, Nat. *Hear Me Talkin' to Ya.* New York: Rinehart, 1955.

———. *Jazz Makers.* New York: Rinehart, 1957.

———. *Jazz Is.* New York: Random House, 1976.

———, and McCarthy, Albert J., eds. *Jazz: New Perspectives on the History of Jazz by Twelve of the World's Foremost Jazz Critics and Scholars.* New York: DaCapo, 1975.

Herskovits, Melville J. *The Myth of the Negro Past.* New York: Harper & Row, 1941.

Hippenmeyer, Jean-Roland. *Jazz sur Films.* Yverdon, Switzerland: Editions de la Thiele, 1972.

Hirsch, Paul. *The Structure of the Popular Music Industry.* Ann Arbor, Mich.: The Institute for Social Research, 1964.

Hodeir, André. *Jazz: Its Evolution and Essence.* New York: Grove Press, 1956.

Hodes, Art. "Chicago." In *Jam Session: An Anthology of Jazz.* Edited by Ralph Gleason, pp. 41–43. New York: Putnam, 1958.

Holiday, Billie, and Dufty, William. *Lady Sings the Blues.* New York: Doubleday, 1956.

Horowitz, Irving Louis. "Authenticity and Originality in Jazz: A Paradigm in the Sociology of Music," *Journal of Jazz Studies,* 1 (1973): 57–64.

———. "Style and Stewardship: Sociological Considerations on the Professionalization of Music," *Journal of Jazz Studies,* 5 (1978): 3–20.

———, and Nanry, Charles. "Ideologies and Theories About American Jazz," *Journal of Jazz Studies,* 2 (1975): 24–41.

Horricks, Raymond. *Count Basie and His Orchestra. Its Music and Musicians.* London: Victor Gollancz, 1957.

Hughes, Phillip S. "Jazz Appreciation and the Sociology of Jazz," *Journal of Jazz Studies,* 1 (1974): 79–96.

James, Michael. *Dizzy Gillespie.* London: Cassell, 1959.

———. *Miles Davis.* New York: A. S. Barnes, 1961.

Jasen, David A. *Recorded Ragtime, 1897–1958.* Hamden, Conn.: Archon, 1973.

Jepsen, Jorgen Grunnet. *A Discography of Duke Ellington.* 3 vols. Copenhagen, Denmark: Debut Records, 1959.

———. *Discography of Louis Armstrong.* 3 vols. Copenhagen, Denmark: Debut Records, 1960.

———. *Jazz Records 1942–.* 11 vols. Copenhagen, Denmark: Knudsen, 1963–1970.

———. *A Discography of Charlie Parker.* Copenhagen, Denmark: Knudsen, 1968a.

———. *A Discography of Lester Young.* Copenhagen, Denmark: Knudsen, 1968b.

———. *A Discography of Count Basie, 1951–1968.* Copenhagen, Denmark: Knudsen, 1969a.

———. *A Discography of Dizzy Gillespie.* 2 vols. Copenhagen, Denmark: Knudsen, 1969b.

———. *A Discography of Miles Davis.* Copenhagen, Denmark: Knudsen, 1969c.

———. *A Discography of Thelonious Monk and Bud Powell.* Copenhagen, Denmark: Knudsen, 1969d.

———. *A Discography of John Coltrane.* Copenhagen: Knudsen, 1969e.

Jewell, Derek. *Duke: A Portrait of Duke Ellington.* New York: Norton, 1977.

Jones, LeRoi. *Blues People.* New York: William Morrow, 1963.

Jones, Max, and Chilton, John. *Louis: The Louis Armstrong Story.* New York: Little, Brown, 1972.

Jost, Ekkehard. *Free Jazz.* Graz, Austria: Universal Edition, 1974.

Kamin, Jonathan. "Parallels in the Social Reactions to Jazz and Rock," *Journal of Jazz Studies,* 2 (1974): 95–125.

———. "Musical Culture and Perceptual Learning in the Popularization of Black Music," *Journal of Jazz Studies,* 3 (1975): 54–65.

Kaminsky, Max, and Hughes, V. E. *My Life in Jazz.* New York: Harper and Row, 1963.

Keepnews, Orrin, and Grauer, Bill Jr. *A Pictorial History of Jazz.* 2d ed., rev. New York: Crown, 1966.

Keil, Charles. *Urban Blues.* Chicago: University of Chicago Press, 1966.

Kennington, Donald. *The Literature of Jazz.* London: Library Association, 1970.

Kinkle, Roger D. *The Complete Encyclopedia of Popular Music and Jazz, 1900–1950.* New Rochelle, N.Y.: Arlington House, 1974.

Kofsky, Frank. "Elvin Jones—Part II: Rhythmic Displacement in the Art of Elvin Jones," *Journal of Jazz Studies,* 4 (1977): 11–32.

Koster, Piet, and Bakker, Dick M. *Charlie Parker.* 4 vols. Alphen aan den Rijn, Holland: Micrography, n.d.

Kuhn, Manford. "Reference Groups." In *The Dictionary of the Social Sciences.* Edited by Gould and Kolb, pp. 580–81. Glencoe, Ill.: Free Press, 1964.

Kuhn, Thomas S. *The Structure of Scientific Revolutions.* Chicago: University of Chicago Press, 1970.

Lambert, G. E. *Duke Ellington.* London: Cassell, 1959. Reprint. New York: A. S. Barnes, 1961.

Lastrucci, Carlo. "The Professional Dance Musician," *Journal of Musicology,* 3 (1941): 168–72.

Leadbitter, Mike, and Slaven, Neil. *Blues Records, 1943–1966.* New York: Oak, 1968.

Leonard, Neil. *Jazz and the White Americans: The Acceptance of a New Art Form.* Chicago: University of Chicago Press, 1962.

Lomax, Alan. *Mister Jelly Roll: The Fortunes of Jelly Roll Morton, New Orleans Creole and "Inventor of Jazz."* New York: Duell, Sloane and Pearce, 1950.

———. "Song Structure and Social Structure." In *The Sociology of Art and Literature: A Reader.* Edited by Milton C. Albrecht, James H. Barnett, and Mason Griff, pp. 55–71. New York: Praeger, 1970.

Lovell, John, Jr. "The Social Implications of the Negro Spiritual," *The Journal of Negro Education,* October, 1939: 634–43.

Lyttleton, Humphrey. *I Play as I Please: The Memories of an Old Etonian Trumpeter.* London: MacGibbon and Kee, 1954.

———. *Second Chorus.* London: MacGibbon and Kee, 1958.

Major, Clarence. *Dictionary of Afro-American Slang.* New York: International, 1970.

Manone, Wingy, and Vandervoort, Paul II. *Trumpet on the Wing.* New York: Doubleday, 1948.

Marden, Charles F., and Meyer, Gladys. *Minorities in American Society.* 5th ed. New York: D. Van Nostrand, 1978.

McCarthy, Albert J. *Louis Armstrong.* New York: A. S. Barnes, 1961.

————. "Jimmie Lunceford: A Reply." In *Jazz Panorama.* Edited by Martin Williams, pp. 136–38. New York: Crowell-Collier, 1962.

————. *Big Band Jazz.* New York: Putnam, 1974.

————; Morgan, Alun; Oliver, Paul; and Harrison, Max. *Jazz on Record: A Critical Guide to the First 50 Years, 1917–1967.* New York: Oak, 1968.

McLuhan, Marshall. *Understanding Media: The Extension of Man.* New York: McGraw-Hill, 1964.

Meeker, David. *Jazz in the Movies: A Guide to Jazz Musicians, 1917–1977.* New Rochelle, N.Y.: Arlington House, 1977.

Mellers, Wilfrid. *Music in a New Found Land.* New York: Knopf, 1967.

Merriam, Alan P. *A Bibliography of Jazz.* Philadelphia: American Folklore Society, 1954.

————, and Mack, Raymond W. "The Jazz Community," *Social Forces,* 38 (1960): 211–22.

Merton, Robert K. *Social Theory and Social Structure.* New York: Free Press, 1957.

Mezzrow, Milton, and Wolfe, Bernard. *Really the Blues.* New York: Random House, 1946.

Mills, C. Wright. *White Collar.* New York: Oxford University Press, 1953.

Mingus, Charles. *Beneath the Underdog.* New York: Knopf, 1971.

Moon, Peter. *A Bibliography of Jazz Discographies.* 2nd ed. Middlesex, England: British Institute of Jazz Studies, 1972.

Morgenstern, Dan. "Jazz as an Urban Music." In *Music in American Society 1776–1976: From Puritan Hymn to Synthesizer.* Edited by George McCue, pp. 133–43. New Brunswick, N. J.: Transaction Press, 1977.

Music Index Publishers. Detroit, Michigan: Information Coordinators.

Nanry, Charles. "The Occupational Subculture of the Jazz Musician: Myth and Reality." University Microfilms, No. 71-3087. Unpublished Ph.D. dissertation, Rutgers University, 1970.

————. "Jazz and Social Science." In *Studies in Jazz Discography,* Institute of Jazz Studies, pp. 25–30. New Brunswick, N.J.: Transaction, 1971.

————. *American Music—From Storyville to Woodstock.* New Brunswick, N.J.: Transaction, 1972.

Newberger, Eli. "The Transition from Ragtime to Improvised Piano Style," *Journal of Jazz Studies,* 3 (1976): 3–18.

Oliver, Paul. *Blues Fell This Morning: The Meaning of the Blues.* London: Cassell, 1960.

————. *Screening the Blues.* London: Cassell, 1968.

Ostransky, Leroy. *Understanding Jazz.* Englewood Cliffs, N.J.: Prentice-Hall, Spectrum Books, 1977.

Panassie, Hugues. *The Real Jazz.* London: Smith and Durrell, 1942.

————. *Louis Armstrong.* New York: Scribner's, 1971.

Patrick, James. "Charlie Parker and Harmonic Sources of Bebop Composition: thoughts on the Repertory of New Jazz in the 1940s," Journal of Jazz Studies, 2 (1975): 3–23.

Peterson, Richard A. *The Industrial Order and Social Policy.* Englewood Cliffs, N.J.: Prentice-Hall, 1972.

————. "Critics and Promoters, The Moralizers of Art: Their Impact on Jazz." Mimeographed. Vanderbilt University, n.d.

————, and Berger, David G. "Cycles in Symbol Production: the Case of Popular Music," *American Sociological Review,* 40 (1975): 158–73.

Pleasants, Henry. *The Agony of Modern Music.* New York: Simon and Schuster, 1955.

Ramsey, Frederic, Jr., and Smith, Charles Edward. *Jazzmen.* New York: Harcourt, Brace, Harvest Book, 1939.

Reisner, Robert George. *The Literature of Jazz, A Preliminary Bibliography.* New York: New York Public Library, 1954.

————. *Bird: The Legend of Charlie Parker.* New York: Citadel, 1962.

Rose, Al, and Souchon, Edmond. *New Orleans Jazz: A Family Album.* rev. ed. Baton Rouge: Louisiana State University Press, 1968.

Rostow, W. W. "The Takeoff into Self-Sustained Growth," *The Economic Journal,* 66 (1956): 25–48.

Russell, Ross. *Jazz Style in Kansas City and the Southwest.* Berkeley and Los Angeles: University of California Press, 1971.

————. *Bird Lives! The High Life and Hard Times of Charlie (Yardbird) Parker.* New York: Charterhouse, 1973.

Rust, Brian. *The American Dance Band Discography, 1917–1942.* 2 vols. New Rochelle, N.Y.: Arlington House, 1975.

————. *Jazz Records 1897–1942.* 4th ed. 2 vols. New Rochelle, N.Y.: Arlington House, 1978.

————, and Debus, Allen G. *The Complete Entertainment Discography.* New Rochelle, N.Y.: Arlington House, 1973.

Schafer, William J. "Thoughts on Jazz Historiography: 'Buddy Bolden's Blues' vs. 'Buddy Bottley's Balloon,'" *Journal of Jazz Studies,* 2 (1974): 3–14.

————, and Riedel, Johannes. *The Art of Ragtime.* Baton Rouge: Louisiana State University Press, 1973.

Scherman, Bo, and Hallstrom, Carl A. *A Discography of Count Basie, 1929–1950.* Copenhagen, Denmark: Knudsen, n.d.

Schleman, Hilton R. *Rhythm on Record.* London: Melody Maker, 1936.

Schuller, Gunther. "The Ellington Style: Its Origins and Early Development." In *Jazz,* by Nat Hentoff and Albert J. McCarthy, pp. 231–74. New York: Rinehart, 1959.

———. *Early Jazz: Its Roots and Musical Development.* New York: Oxford University Press, 1968.

Scott, Allen. *Jazz Educated, Man.* Washington, D.C.: American International, 1973.

Shaw, Artie. *The Trouble with Cinderella.* New York: Farrar, Straus and Young, 1952.

Shibutani, Tamotsu. *Improvised News: A Sociological Study of Rumor.* New York: Bobbs-Merrill, 1966.

Shih, Hsio Wen. "The Spread of Jazz and the Big Bands." In *Jazz,* by Nat Hentoff and Albert J. McCarthy, pp. 171–87. New York: Rinehart, 1959.

———. "Count Basie." In *Jazz Masters of the Thirties,* by Rex Stewart, pp. 195–206. New York: Macmillan, 1972.

Sidran, Ben. *Black Talk.* New York: Holt, Rinehart and Winston, 1971.

Simmel, Georg. *The Sociology of Georg Simmel.* Translated by Kurt H. Wolff. New York: Free Press, 1950.

Simon, George T. *The Big Bands.* rev. ed. New York: Collier, 1974.

Skinner, B. F. *Verbal Behavior.* New York: Appleton-Century-Crofts, 1957.

Smith, Willie "The Lion," and Hoefer, George. *Music on My Mind: The Memoirs of an American Pianist.* New York: Doubleday, 1964. London: MacGibbon and Kee, 1965.

Southern, Eileen. *The Music of Black Americans: A History.* New York: Norton, 1971.

Spellman, A. B. *Four Lives in the Bebop Business.* New York: Pantheon, 1966. Reprinted as *Black Music: Four Lives in the Bebop Business.* New York: Schocken, 1970.

Stearns, Marshall W. *The Story of Jazz.* New York: Oxford University Press, 1956.

———, and Stearns, Jean. *Jazz Dance: The Story of American Vernacular Dance.* New York: Macmillan, 1968.

Stebbins, Robert. "The Jazz Community; The Sociology of a Musical Subculture." Unpublished Ph.D. dissertation, University of Minnesota, 1964.

Stewart, Rex. *Jazz Masters of the Thirties.* New York: Macmillan, 1972.

Stone, Gregory P., and Farberman, Harvey A. *Social Psychology*

Through Symbolic Interaction. Waltham, Mass.: Ginn-Blaisdell, 1970.

Sudhalter, Richard M., and Evans, Philip R. *Bix: Man and Legend.* New Rochelle, N.Y.: Arlington House, 1974.

Tanner, Paul O. W., and Gerow, Maurice. *A Study of Jazz.* Dubuque, Iowa: William C. Brown, 1973.

Thomas, William I. *The Unadjusted Girl.* Boston: Little, Brown, 1923.

Timner, W. E. *Ellingtonia: The Recorded Music of Duke Ellington. A Collectors' Manual.* Montreal: 1976.

Townley, Eric. *Tell Your Story.* Chigwell, Essex, England: Storyville Publications, 1976.

Truzzi, Marcello. "The Decline of the American Circus: The Shrinkage of an Institution." In *Sociology and Everyday Life,* by Marcello Truzzi, pp. 314–22. Englewood Cliffs, N.J.: Prentice-Hall, 1968.

Ulanov, Barry. *Duke Ellington.* New York: Creative Age Press, 1946.

Van den Berghe, Pierre L. *Race and Racism.* New York: Wiley, 1967.

Wareing, Charles H., and Garlick, George. *Bugles for Beiderbecke.* London: Sidgewick and Jackson, 1958.

Waterman, Richard A. " 'Hot' Rhythm in Negro Music," *Journal of the American Musicological Society,* 1 (1948): 24–37.

Waters, Ethel, and Samuels, Charles. *His Eye Is on the Sparrow.* New York: Doubleday, 1950.

Weber, Max. *From Max Weber: Essays in Sociology.* Translated by Hans H. Gerth and C. Wright Mills. New York: Oxford University Press, 1946.

―――. *The Theory of Social and Economic Organization.* New York: Free Press, 1947.

―――. *The Protestant Ethic and the Spirit of Capitalism.* New York: Scribner's, 1958a.

―――. *The Rational and Social Foundations of Music.* Translated by Martindale, Riedel and Neuwirth. Carbondale, Ill.: Southern Illinois University Press, 1958b.

―――. *The City.* New York: Free Press, 1968.

Wells, Dicky, and Dance, Stanley. *The Night People: Reminiscences of a Jazzman.* Boston: Crescendo, 1971.

Whitcomb, Ian. *After the Ball: Pop Music from Rag to Rock.* New York: Simon and Schuster, 1973.

Wilensky, Harold L., and Lebeaux, Charles N. *Industrial Society and Social Welfare.* New York: Russell Sage, 1958.

Williams, Martin *The Art of Jazz. Essays on the Nature and Development of Jazz.* New York: Oxford University Press, 1959a.

————. "Bebop and After: A Report." In *Jazz*, by Nat Hentoff and Albert J. McCarthy, pp. 287–301. New York: Rinehart, 1959b.

————. *King Oliver.* New York: A. S. Barnes, 1961.

————. *Jelly Roll Morton.* New York: A. S. Barnes, 1963.

————. *Jazz Masters of New Orleans.* New York: Macmillan, 1967a.

————. *Where's the Melody?* New York: Funk & Wagnalls, 1967b.

————. *The Jazz Tradition.* New York: Oxford University Press, 1970a.

————. *Jazz Masters in Transition, 1957–1969.* New York: Macmillan, 1970b.

———— ed. *Jazz Panorama: From the Pages of Jazz Review.* New York: Crowell-Collier, 1962.

Wilson, John S. *Jazz: The Transition Years 1940–60.* New York: Appleton-Century-Crofts, 1966.

INDEX

269